D1624423

VICKSBURG

47 DAYS OF SIEGE

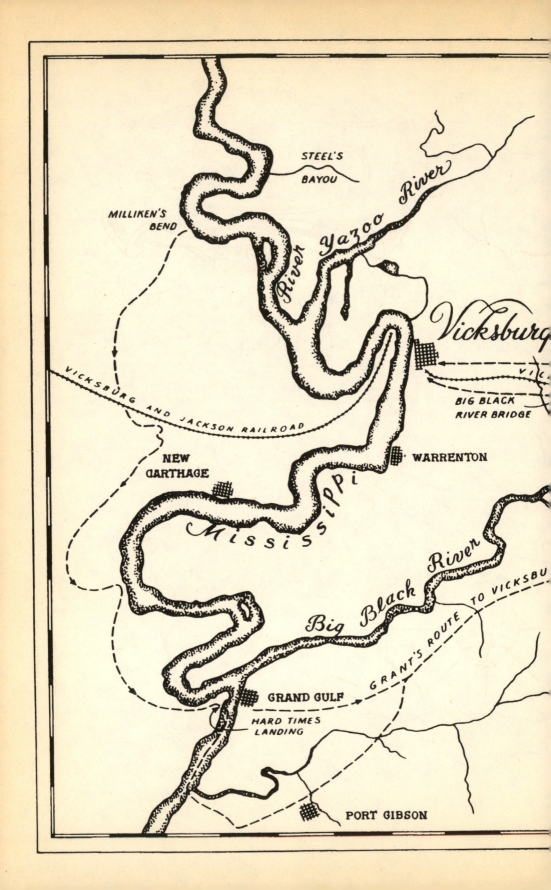

STEEL'S
BAYOU

MILLIKEN'S
BEND

River Yazoo River

Vicksburg

VICKSBURG AND JACKSON RAILROAD

VIC

BIG BLACK
RIVER BRIDGE

NEW
CARTHAGE

WARRENTON

Mississippi

Big Black River

GRAND GULF

GRANT'S ROUTE TO VICKSBU

HARD TIMES
LANDING

PORT GIBSON

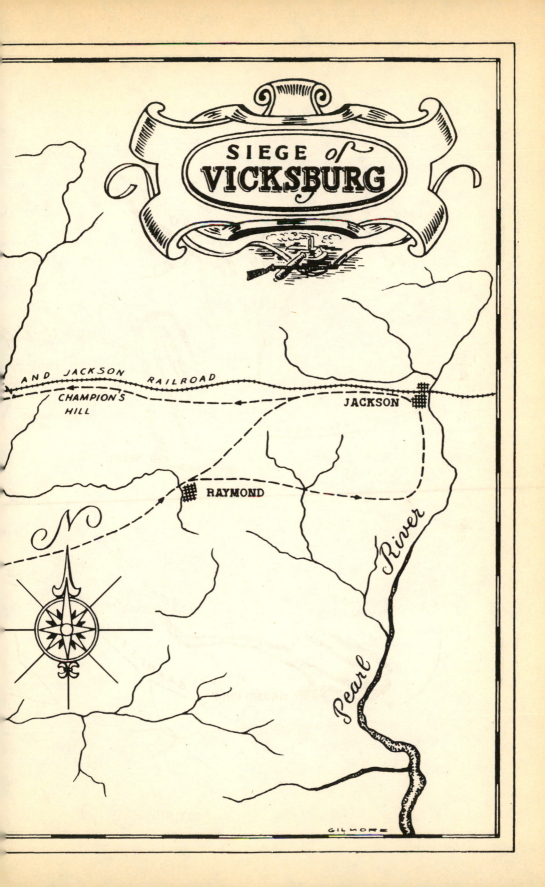

VICKSBURG

47 Days of Siege

★★★ A. A. HOEHLING ★★★

AND THE EDITORS, ARMY TIMES PUBLISHING COMPANY

THE FAIRFAX PRESS • NEW YORK

Copyright © 1969 by A. A. Hoehling and the Editors of the Army
Times Publishing Company
All rights reserved.

This 1991 edition is published by The Fairfax Press, distributed by
Outlet Book Company, Inc., a Random House Company, 225 Park
Avenue South, New York, New York 10003, by arrangement with
A. A. Hoehling and the Army Times Publishing Company.

Printed and bound in the United States of America

Library of Congress Cataloging-in-Publication Data

Hoehling, A. A. (Adolph A.)
    Vicksburg : 47 days of siege / A. A. Hoehling and the editors,
  Army Times Publishing Company.
        p.   cm.
    Reprint. Originally published: Englewood Cliffs, N.J. :
  Prentice-Hall, 1969.
    Includes bibliographical references.
    ISBN 0-517-06008-6
    1. Vicksburg (Miss.) — History — Siege, 1863.   I. Army Times
  Publishing Company.   II. Title.
  E475.27.H64 1991
  973.7'344 — dc20   91-11502
                                                                 CIP

8 7 6 5 4 3 2 1

*. . . well, our beloved Vicksburg has
fallen, the city of a southern heart's pride.
Our own Mississippi is now invaded and what
is to become of us? We must suffer as others
have done long since, our property destroyed
and negroes taken away, etc. I am willing
to work, but oh God, when will this war
end and let . . . families be reunited?*
—MATILDA CHAMPION, *July 10, 1863*

CONTENTS

☆ ☆ ☆ ☆ ☆

THE PEOPLE

Alexander S. Abrams—former soldier, a reporter for the Vicksburg *Whig*.

Dr. Joseph Dill Alison—Confederate Army surgeon from Alabama.

Col. Ephraim McDowell Anderson—with the 1st Missouri Confederate Brigade.

Emma Balfour—the wife of Dr. William T. Balfour, also neighbor and (as she thought) "great favorite" of General Pemberton.

Col. Robert S. Bevier—lawyer from Russellville, Kentucky, serving with the 1st Missouri Confederate Brigade.

Matilda Champion—wife of Sid Champion, a well-to-do planter, whose farm, Champion Hill, was situated east of Vicksburg.

Capt. W. H. Claiborne, aide-de-camp to Col. Alexander W. Reynolds.

Pvt. George Crooke—adjutant with the 21st Iowa Infantry.

Charles A. Dana—former editor, special assistant to the Secretary of War.

Reverend William Lovelace Foster—chaplain with the 35th Mississippi Infantry.

Henry Ginder—civilian construction engineer.

Maj. Gen. Ulysses S. Grant—commanding United States Department of the Tennessee and Army of the Tennessee.

Col. Winchester Hall—of the 26th Louisiana Infantry.

Mrs. A. H. Hoge—of the Sanitary Commission.

Gen. Joseph E. Johnston—senior commander of all Confederate forces in the Department of the West, embracing a vast heartland between the Appalachians and the Mississippi.

Capt. J. J. Kellogg—Company B, 113th Illinois Infantry.

Max Kuner—Austrian immigrant and jewelry store owner.

Mrs. William W. (Margaret) Lord—wife of the northern-born minister of Christ Episcopal Church, who was also chaplain of the First Mississippi Brigade.

Lida Lord—a daughter.

William W. Lord, Jr.—her small son.

Mary Ann Webster Loughborough—wife of an officer stationed in Vicksburg.

Lucy McRae—young daughter of William McRae, Vicksburg commission merchant.

Alfred E. Mathews—an artist with the 51st Ohio Volunteers.

Mrs. Anderson (Dora Richards) Miller—the young wife of a lawyer from New Orleans.

A. Hugh Moss—soldier from Lake Charles, Louisiana.

Col. Osborn Oldroyd—then a sergeant with Company E., 20th Ohio Infantry Regiment.

Lt. Gen. John C. Pemberton—commanding the Confederate Department of Mississippi and Eastern Louisiana, the "defender of Vicksburg."

Rear Admiral David D. Porter—commanding the Mississippi Squadron.

Maj. Gen. William T. Sherman—commanding the 15th Army Corps.

Brig. Gen. Francis A. Shoup—Confederate brigade commander from Florida whose command included Winchester Hall's 26th Louisiana.

Edwin M. Stanton—Secretary of War.

James M. Swords—editor, the *Citizen*.

Dr. Charles Brown Tompkins—surgeon with the 17th Illinois Infantry Regiment.

Ida Barlow Trotter—resident of Vicksburg.

William H. Tunnard—sergeant with the 3d Louisiana Infantry.

Annie Wittenmyer—helping with hospital supplies and diet kitchens.

VICKSBURG

47 DAYS OF SIEGE

FOREWORD

Vicksburg was destined to become a femme fatale among history's strategic cities. The more difficult her possession proved, the more passionate became the Union Army's advances.

"Admirable for defense!" concluded General Grant, the bearded little bulldog. "On the north it is three hundred feet above the Mississippi River at the highest point and very much cut up by the washing rains; the ravines were grown up with cane and underbrush while the sides and tops were covered with a dense forest."

Accustomed to the rolling, wooded battlefields of the past year's campaigns for Donelson and Shiloh, in Tennessee, the Federal soldiers were unprepared for the succession of steep gulleys and minor precipices that flanked the city of 4,500 (next to Natchez, Mississippi's largest) like moats and battlements of King Arthur's time. Col. Robert S. Bevier, a lawyer with the 1st Missouri, added that the half-century-old community established by the Methodist minister, Newitt Vick, was "impressively situated on a tumultous collection of sandhills . . . It overlooks a vast expanse of the great river and a mighty horseshoe bend."

To various historians and for as many reasons, Vicksburg was a Gibraltar, a Sebastopol, a Carthage, Troy, or even a kind of enlarged modernized Fort Defiance.

Spanish soldiers, seventy years earlier, had been equally smitten with the charm of the locale. They established an outpost, Fort Nogales, on what was to become the northern rim of Vicksburg, and one of its outworks later became the site of the Confederate signal battery, Fort Hill.

The caprice of nature in toying with the Mississippi, twisting it at a half-mile waist until it flowed back north, then curved under its own mighty surge that flowed south once more, created an impasse. Now the "father of waters" was closed to United States navigation so long as the Confederates were mounted on that critical "horseshoe."

"The war," Lincoln had stated not long after Manassas in 1861, "can never be brought to a close until that key [Vicksburg] is in our pocket. . . . We may take all the northern ports of the Confederacy and they can still defy us from Vicksburg. . . .

"It means hog and hominy without limit, fresh troops from all the States of the far South, and a cotton country where they can raise the staple without interference."

The "key," if not altogether a grubby place, was nonetheless far from prepossessing: a river town that was kept alive by cotton and the wants of an unending procession of sternwheelers. Long, drab rows of warehouses alternated with rough shacks of Irish laborers beside the river banks. Washington Street, three blocks east and up from the river, was lined with nearly one hundred banks, wholesale grocers, jewelers, photographers, publishers, as well as other stores and businesses.

The Washington Hotel, vaguely suggesting an English tavern, the Prentiss House near the waterfront, and the Commercial Hotel on a hill provided lodging for those who spent time in the city. The patriarch of war correspondents, William Howard Russell, visiting Vicksburg early in the war, recalled the hospitality of Mac Meekan, proprietor of "the Washington"—the goose, apple sauce, oyster pie ("never was better oyster pie") and turkey served on "closely-packed tables." The volume of edibles, however, combined with the density of the dining quarters and zest with which the customers attacked the fare to produce "a semi-barbarous scene," in the Englishman's estimation. And the host's distinctive trademark, singing out the menus like hymns, did not add great class.

To Russell, the Mississippi was "the most uninteresting river in the world—not a particle of romance!"

Atop Vicksburg's higher hills were the irregular battlements of structures dedicated to God: the red brick convent of the Sisters of Mercy, tall-spired St. Paul's Catholic Church, the square Gothic tower of Christ Episcopal Church, and the cupolaed courthouse.

Farther east or obscured in the low ground beneath the rises were the nicer homes, breathing of New Orleans and the Old World with their iron gates and balconies in tribute to the precise art of grillwork. There, too, the smell of oleander, jasmine, and honeysuckle wafted in counterpoint, if evanescent, to Vicksburg's own pervading "perfume": a miasma of the river steamers' coal smoke, tar, mules (beasts almost as common as the roaches and rats), and dirty, muddy streets.

The better side of this municipal Janus was sufficient to inspire a young girl, Lucy McRae, to muse: "On the north, south, and east Vicksburg is girt by hills, while on the west the grand old Mississippi rushes by. It was a place of culture, education, and luxury, almost every man with a family owning his slaves who were proud to serve them."

Lucy was largely correct. Not only was the convent a few blocks up Cherry Street from her own sizable home, but varied learning—parochial and public education—flourished amidst the pedestrian realities of a river port to the measure of five hundred students, enrolled in primary and secondary grades. Approximately one person out of eight in Vicksburg was studying.

This outcropping of "luxury" was no Richmond or Charleston. But it was a fortress, with some forty cannon challenging any gunboats that sought unwelcome passage. Rear Admiral David Glasgow Farragut lost no time in attempting to carry out the President's wishes following his capture of New Orleans the last week of April, 1862. He sailed on up the Mississippi. While he discovered that he could transit the batteries of Vicksburg, their fire was so heavy that he concluded that the port could not be seized by warships alone.

For the ensuing nine months the Union experienced unmitigated defeat in five separate attempts to capture Vicksburg. On the northern approaches, Grant was bogged down by a railroad and by all but impassable bayous extending to the west. Small rebel cavalry detachments and boatmen weaned in the swamp country picked off Grant's soldiers almost at will. A northern Mississippi supply base at Holly Springs was burned by the dashing Mississippi cavalry leader, Maj. Gen. Earl Van Dorn (killed the same year by an irate husband).

The fighters in blue, far from their homes in the "Old Northwest," the west and border states, markedly unconditioned to swamp existence, fell prey to malaria, other fevers, snake as well as insect bites. Sickness and mortality rates soared during a cold, rainy winter and spring.

Northern critics seemingly possessed enough evidence already to claim the scalp of yet another Union general who had failed, one who was manifestly floundering in southern quagmires. Grant, however, had his champions, and the foremost was not the General-in-Chief of the Armies, Henry W. Halleck, but President Lincoln himself.

"Try him a little longer," counseled the ever-patient President. "I can't spare this man. He fights!"

He could remind Grant's defamers that the nickname "Unconditional Surrender," based upon his initials, was not a random pleasantry. The tanner's son from Ohio had earned it by stubbornly following these very terms demanded at the capture of Fort Donelson on the Cumberland River, in February, 1862.

A forty-three-year-old midwesterner, Maj. Gen. William T. Sherman, commanding the 15th Army Corps, was trounced in December, 1862, at Chickasaw Bayou, five miles northeast of Vicksburg. Easily Grant's favorite corps commander, one as flexible and scrappy as himself, this gaunt man with a tousle of red hair had also lost heart in the campaign. He wrote home: "No place on earth is favored by nature with natural defenses as Vicksburg, and I do believe the whole thing will fail."

"Old Tecumseh" nonetheless was one of Grant's strongest admirers, and intensely loyal. He entertained no thoughts of asking for other duties, for his estimate of the Mississippi was no less than Lincoln's. To "secure the navigation" of that river, Sherman had asserted, "I would slay millions; on that point I am not only insane, but mad!"

"Old Brains," Halleck, could not fail to admire such a man, perhaps more so than he did Grant. However, the General-in-Chief of the Armies was committed to support the Vicksburg campaign and this he could continue to do until instructed otherwise by higher authority.

But if Grant was in trouble, Rear Admiral David Dixon Porter, fifty-year-old son of Capt. David Porter (once commander of the *Constellation*) who led the Mississippi Squadron, was faring no better. He had lost several ships including the ironclad *Cairo*. His ironclads and also "tinclads" were mired in the bayous of the Yazoo River (which met the Mississippi just above Vicksburg) and literally ensnarled by hawser-like vines and the huge trunks of cottonwood, oak, and cypress trees. The sailors, as they showed themselves above or outside the armored superstructure or gun ports, were shot by snipers like so many woodchucks.

At one juncture in improvisation, Federal engineers strove to bypass Vicksburg by constructing a canal across the mile-wide De Soto Peninsula, formed by the lumbering, spectacular bend in the Mississippi. For lack of proper equipment and other considerations this otherwise imaginative project proved impractical.

Meanwhile, according to Alexander S. Abrams, a reporter for *The Whig*, the city in returning to a state bordering on normalcy "has assumed a busy appearance—numerous stores were opened and business in a great measure resumed its wonted activity. . . . It was one constant scene of merriment among those who were not devotees to Bacchus and one uninterrupted course of drunken brawls among those who were. Any quantity of officers, dressed up in all the toggery of gold lace and brass buttons, could be seen promenading the streets, and a civilian could scarcely enter a private residence without finding three or four of these gentry on a visit.

"So outrageous had this laxity of discipline become that the press of Vicksburg was at last compelled to call attention to it. . . . The censure had little or no effect."

By spring, observed Abrams, whose health was responsible for his recently being mustered out of the 1st Mississippi Light Artillery, only twenty-three effective guns guarded the crucial bend of the river. On the other hand, Col. Edward Higgins, commanding these river batteries, listed as many as forty-four under his jurisdiction.

Whatever the artillery count, Grant was wary, like a pugilist who has been floored too many times. If he were to take the city at all, he reasoned, he would have to shoot his way in from the one direction not tested—the south.

Porter's large fleet of ironclads, tinclads, wooden gunboats, and assorted flat-bottom transports, supply craft, and skiffs—aggregating sixty-seven vessels—would now serve the function of supporting weapon. Farragut had proven that the Navy could not by itself win the prize. The impressive flotilla would make Vicksburg captive beside the very waterway that had been its reason for existence.

On March 20 Halleck informed Grant, "the great objective of your line now is the opening of the Mississippi River, and everything else must tend to that purpose. The eyes and hopes of the whole country are now directed to your army. In my opinion, the opening of the Mississippi River will be to us of more advantage than the capture of forty Richmonds. . . . Fight the enemy when you please."

Thus the long way around might finally be proven the shortest home. First, however, in mid-April, Grant sent Col. Benjamin Grierson with a small cavalry force galloping down through central Mississippi and westward toward the Louisiana border. His hard-riding horsemen tore up train tracks, burned barns, and generally panicked the countryside. More important, Pemberton, not knowing if this diversionary raid might grow into a major assault, deprived his strategic reserve of needed cavalry and infantry detachments for a pursuit that was almost comic in its futility.

Meanwhile, Grant had started his army southward through the Louisiana parishes, while Porter passed the Vicksburg batteries with a number of his boats. On April 29 Porter's ironclads sought to silence the Rebel batteries at Grand Gulf, twenty-five miles below Vicksburg, to clear the way for Grant's troops to come ashore. After an initial repulse, the fleet, under cover of darkness, passed Grand Gulf and rendezvoused with the army. The next day Grant began ferrying his army from the west bank of the Mississippi to Bruinsburg, on the east shore, a village thirty-five miles below Vicksburg that was completely deserted. Porter's massive fleet became a protective river shield.

Once in Bruinsburg, Grant wrote, "I felt a degree of relief scarcely ever equalled since. . . . I was on dry ground on the same side of the river with the enemy. All campaigns, labors, hardships, and exposures from the month of December previous to this time had been made and endured for the accomplishment of this purpose."

Grant's antagonist, the Philadelphia-born Lt. Gen. John C. Pemberton, commanding the Department of Mississippi and East Louisiana, had real cause for alarm. He telegraphed President Jefferson Davis, in Richmond, and Gen. Joseph E. Johnston, a fifty-six-year-old West Pointer and Mexican War fighter and his immediate superior: "Enemy can cross all his army from Hard Times to Bruinsburg, below Bayou Pierre. Large reinforcements should be sent me from other departments. Enemy's movement threatens Jackson and, if successful, cuts off Vicksburg and Port Hudson from the east. Am hurrying all reinforcements I possibly can."

Midnight had already struck. Grant was gaining momentum for tactics that one day would be known as "blitz." He defeated the enemy at Port Gibson on May 1, then struck toward the Big Black River. He then halted for a week to await General Sherman, who was hurrying south to join him with his powerful 15th Corps.

Accompanying the troops was General Grant's twelve-year-old son, Fred. After the first clash he "joined a detachment which was collecting the dead for burial—but sickening at the sights I made my way with another which was gathering the wounded to a log house which had been appropriated for a hospital. Here the scenes were so terrible that I became faint and ill, and making my way to a tree I sat down, the most woebegone twelve-year-old in America."

Brig. Gen. John E. Smith, who led the 1st Brigade, 3d Division of the 17th Army Corps, was weary but not sickened. The 17th was in turn commanded by Maj. Gen. James B. McPherson, a handsome young Baltimorean.

"Bivouacked near Hankinson's Ferry three days," Smith, a toughened campaigner, reported, "giving the men ample time to rest and clean themselves, which they needed very much after the severe marches in the heat and dust, which at times was suffocating. Nearly one-third of the command at this time had no shoes, having worn them out on the march, and in consequence were very foot-sore. This, together with their want of supplies, which at times were very short, were subjects of pleasantries with the men, who consoled themselves with the prospect of a fight every other day to make amends for their privations."

Max Kuner, an Austrian-born jewelry store owner who had fled from

Vicksburg into the country, himself bore witness to the exhaustion of the victorious armies: "They were so weary that it seemed to us we saw whole companies asleep as they trudged and stumbled—many with cheeks resting upon the gunstocks."

As soon as Sherman arrived, Grant put his army in motion. But he did not move northward toward Vicksburg as Pemberton and his generals expected. Grant struck out toward the railroad linking Vicksburg and Jackson, the capital of Mississippi, forty-five miles northeast of Port Gibson.

Fifteen miles southwest of Jackson, near Raymond, on May 12 in a drenching rain, Grant repeated his performance of Port Gibson, and McPherson defeated a Confederate brigade. Grant then moved on to capture the State capital. It fell on May 14 after a five-hour fight.

Johnston, who had reached the city the previous evening from his headquarters in Middle Tennessee, withdrew north. Seriously wounded at Fair Oaks the year before, the precise, rather short general had little more heart for battle.

The increasingly confident Federal commander had placed his powerful force between two major opposing armies, those of Johnston and Pemberton, which could be hailed as a brilliant accomplishment by any measure. Cut loose as he was from his bases in Tennessee, Grant nonetheless continued his victory march. He abandoned Jackson, which the Confederates then promptly reoccupied. On May 16 he beat Pemberton at Champion Hill (or Baker's Creek, the location of the farm of the affluent Sid Champion, not quite halfway between Jackson and Vicksburg). This furious encounter cost Pemberton 4,800 casualties, about double the number Grant's troops had sustained. The Union general left many of his wounded on the Champion estate, trusting the Confederates to parole them.

After a short engagement at Big Black River Bridge the next day, the 17th, the now-demoralized and sweat-drenched Confederates were toppled in a rout toward long-prepared earthworks of Vicksburg. They barely took time to fire the railroad trestle and the river steamer *Dot* behind them, even though these proved useless gestures.

Army engineers had brought a pontoon train along and the westerners were skilled with the axe. One pontoon bridge and three raft bridges were thrown across the Big Black by morning on the 18th.

By this time the Confederate troops were "so demoralized" in the view of Franc Wilkie, a correspondent for the *Dubuque* (Iowa) *Herald* and the *New York Times*, "that I could alone have captured an army of them—in fact I am not sure that if I had continued directly into Vicksburg I could not have taken the town without difficulty."

Sensing the shadow of defeat, a heartsick Pemberton confided to his chief engineer that his "career" was about to be "ended in disaster and disgrace." He could not halt the "pellmell . . . stampede" of his soldiers, throwing away their rifles and knapsacks as they ran.

The exhausted, frightened men, joined by other retreating battalions from Snyder's and Drumgould's bluffs on the Yazoo twelve miles northeast of Vicksburg, Pemberton's northern anchor, did not stop until they were in the city, "wan, ragged, foot-sore, bloody, unarmed, followed by siege-guns, ambulances, gun carriages, and wagons in aimless confusion," in the words of one citizen. Or, as a Federal private observed in chance understatement, the foe "straggled in a discouraged sort of way inside the fortifications."

This was what Gen. Joe Johnston, the cautious, ailing leader with the trim goatee, did not want. He had urged, if not directly ordered, General Pemberton to save his army by joining up with his own.

"Retreat! Retreat!" was the infectious cry that echoed from house to house above the dust swirls. Not even the brave attempts of regimental bands to inspire courage by tooting "Dixie" or "Bonnie Blue Flag" helped. For the moment the soldiers had lost their nerve—as apparently had those fresh troops in the five brigades stationed in or around the city—and to compound their distress they were obsessed with the conceivable illusion, "we are sold by General Pemberton!"

In eighteen days Grant had marched almost two hundred miles, fought five victorious battles, and captured more than six thousand prisoners and sixty-seven pieces of artillery, plus countless rifles. He had come within an ace of the goal so desperately sought for the past year. The relatively low Union cost was approximately four thousand five hundred casualties. It appeared that Lincoln's faith in the squat, tough Ulysses was amply justified. Lincoln surely knew, at the same time, that Grant was aided, as a ranking Confederate officer had conceded, "by the ablest of the Union generals."

On high ground, north of Vicksburg—Walnut Hills—Sherman, now convinced of the wisdom of his superior's strategy, exclaimed on May 19: "Until this moment I never thought your expedition a success. I never could see the end clearly until now. But this is a campaign; this is a success, if we never take the town!"

However, the victorious general succumbed to overconfidence. He attempted to take Vicksburg by storm in a series of "grand and desperate charges around the entire line," as Colonel Bevier would recall.

The defenses proved too strong, for the defenders had now stiffened their backbones. The cost was not justified.

The Blue lines, along their enveloping twelve-mile semicircle, regrouped and dug in.

"I now determined," wrote Grant, "upon a regular siege, to 'outcamp' the enemy, as it were, and to incur no more losses . . . with the Navy holding the river, the investment of Vicksburg was complete."

And two hundred twenty field artillery pieces were thereupon turned on the back yards and roads of Vicksburg, augmented in the last days of the siege by several clumsy but serviceable cohorn mortars. These were hollowed tree trunks strengthened by barrel straps. Porter at the same time hammered the hapless city with thirteen-inch mortars and several heavy caliber guns mounted on barges.

. . . the purpose of this book is to recount that "regular siege" in the words and thoughts of the participants, insofar as possible, especially of those civilian victims of war. Included in this number—men, women, and children with the foresight to bequeath a written chronicle of the most dramatic days of their lifetime—are "citizen soldiers" (as distinguished from professionals), a young bride, a young girl, a minister's wife and her son and daughter, a reporter, a merchant, the wife of a soldier, and an artist. In sum total they were possibly the random assortment who might be picked to tell the crisis moments in an American city today.

The backdrop for this drama is the contest to the death by opposing armies and their leaders. Ultimately almost 75,000 Federal troops would overwhelm 32,000 Confederates while checkmating Johnston's 30,000 east of the Big Black and 7,000 other enemy troops in the Louisiana parishes.

There was Grant, forty-one years old, short, tenacious, aggressive, ready to adapt his plans to the changing problems and vicissitudes of the battlefield. And there was his long-standing personal challenge—whiskey. As a captain he had resigned from the service, convinced that he could not overcome this all too familiar nemesis. To his profound surprise he had done so, and the Union had called him back to the colors. Again, Lincoln had become a staunch defender. To Grant's jealous detractors, who accused him of being a "drunkard," the Chief Executive had recommended that "a large stock" of the same type of liquor be provided for less aggressive generals, who were in far too ample numbers.

There was Pemberton, almost fifty, a tall, classic prototype of the vanishing southern gentleman, and as such all but consigned to oblivion. Pemberton, who graduated from West Point in the Class of 1837, six years ahead of Grant's class, was somber, moody, inflexible, and, as it turned out, born to lose. His family had pleaded with him not to desert Old Glory for the "Secesh" cause. Perhaps his wife, the brunette Norfolk beauty Martha "Patty" Thompson, had played the strongest role in swaying his emotions. While he tarried in Washington that early, fateful spring of 1861, Patty had written: "My darling husband, why are you not with us? Why do you stay? Jeff Davis has a post ready for you."

. . . although this is the story of war—total war—it is not the story of battle as it might be reconstructed and calipered by any erudite military historian. Nor is it a casual summoning of ghosts, formless and undimensional except by the random happenstance of name and place. This is the story of real people who cannot be relegated to the impersonal limbo of footnotes, whose ordeals and emotional reactions to the challenges are timeless in depth, implication, and likelihood of repetition.

This, further, is not a novel, and certainly not a so-called historical novel, even in minute part. Every quotation is wed to an original source. Every bit of narrative, connective passage, or background represents a culling from authoritative sources.

Such a documentary format, employed in an effort to resummon and recreate yesterday in its full bloom of sight, sound, smell, and the subtler nuances of feeling and emotion, cannot assure the smooth flow of fiction. Nor is it so intended. Life itself cannot be expected unfailingly to scan into the precise and predictable form of a Greek tragedy or, on the other hand, the lighter crescendos of a Shakespearean comedy.

If there are "breaks" in the story, so they must remain. They should not and will not be bridged by fable or even wistful conjecture.

Too, the siege of Vicksburg, except for a few natural demarcations, was not itself chaptered, titled, and leaded, as if by some master printer, with neatly set heads and subheads. This account, following a pattern that was blazed in fire, smoke, and calculated destruction in 1863, is demarked only by dates, newspaper quotes, and army dispatches along with the pertinent and often acute cullings from letters, diaries, or books written after the event when memory was sharpest.

This, then, is the human chronicle—by the participants themselves—

of that "regular siege," one that from the start was so python-like in its encirclement that one Confederate officer wryly observed, "a cat could not have crept out of Vicksburg without being discovered."

The Yankees are come, vile thieves that they are.
Thus are old men and women to wage such a war.
They spoil all our gardens; not a chicken they spare,
To the old sitting hen and the clothes your babes wear.

The Yankees are come! Yes, also it is true,
Each one of them breeched in his sky blue.
I hear their sabers. Clatter, clatter! they go.
How fiendish they look! They're jayhawkers, I know.

The Yankees are come—yes, the worst of the crew,
From Iowa, Kansas and Illinois too.
To restore the blest Union at Abraham's call,
The negroes* set free and drive Secesh to the wall.

The Yankees are come! How madly they rave!
The rebellion they'll crush and Vicksburg they'll have.
In their efforts they say they will never relax
Till Pemberton's whipped, or they die in their tracks.

---

*Not capitalized in the original.

PART 1 *THE*
EYE
OF
THE
STORM

The Yankees had, in truth, "come." For almost a year there had been no doubt as to their intents. But somehow, with all the dramatic repulses and the brave, dashing Southerners who defended their city, the inhabitants of Vicksburg could not believe the worst until the first explosives fell. And these were not the artillery shells from Grant's army but mortar bombs from Porter's fleet, softening up Confederate defenses as the Union soldiers fought their way toward Jackson, then Champion Hill and the Big Black River.

Lucy McRae, the pretty, young daughter of a well-to-do commission merchant, William McRae, who lived in a large house on Monroe Street two blocks north of the Court House with a commanding view of the Mississippi, wrote:

☆ ☆ ☆ One bright afternoon men, women and children could be seen seeking the hill-tops with spyglasses, as from the heights could be seen a black object slowly approaching along the river. Suddenly a shell came rattling over as if to say "Here I am!"

My mother was much alarmed, but, still faithful to womanly curiosity, stood on the upper porch of our house to see the gunboat, if possible. Another shell, and still another, and the hills began to be deserted.

The gunboat, seeing that her shells were falling short, ventured a little closer, and sent a few shells into the town. People sought their homes, but sleep visited few, as the shelling continued until late that night.

The next morning the shelling began very early, and the women and children were to be seen running by every road that led out of the town. A Mrs. Gamble who lived on the edge of town was killed just as she was leaving her gate.

[Another resident, Mrs. Richard Groome, was also aware of the woman's death, if not actually a witness to it. She recalled: "A Mrs. Gamble and her family were leaving the city for a place of safety and were near the city cemetery when a shell struck her in the side, causing immediate death. . . . Mrs. Gamble was buried hurriedly and her heartbroken children lived with kind relatives."]

When the citizens realized that Vicksburg would be a battleground, men sought places of refuge for their families. My father sent his family with all the household furniture into the interior of a small town, Bolton's Depot, some 25 miles from Vicksburg.

Vicksburg, however, put on her war clothes, and cannon were rushed to the river-front; forts sprang into sight in a short time; "Whistling Dick," the rifled 18-pound Confederate gun, sang defiance. Louisiana and Tennessee troops commanded the river-front. My mother, so comfortably fixed in a large suburban house with a friend, considered herself safe. Suddenly, one day, there flashed through the town the news *The Yankees are coming!*

My mother, fearing to be left in the country, decided to go back to Vicksburg. Packing trunks with clothing and what articles of value she could take, she called a negro whom she owned, and said:

"Rice, I will want the dray and surrey ready to make an early start for Vicksburg tomorrow morning."

Very little could be put upon the dray besides trunks, but we began our journey early the next morning. Mother left all of her household goods with the lady at whose house we had been staying, and there everything was destroyed by General Grant's army when it reached the place.

When we drove into the little village of Bolton's Depot, all was confusion. Confederate cavalry and infantry were grouped about. To my young eyes this was exciting beyond expression, and right close did we children huddle to mother as she sat in the surrey, driving as fast as our heavy loads permitted. She inquired as to news, and the reply that the Yankees were close on us caused her much alarm.

Mother kept Rice ahead with his heavy load, and our progress was slow. I shall never forget how my heart would beat as they talked of the Yankees being so close behind us. I do not know what I thought they were, but it was certainly something very dreadful.

We pushed on, being stopped here and there and questioned. When we reached the Joe Davis place (belonging to the brother of the President) we found the plantation deserted, the negroes having been run off to a place of safety. In answer to our request for water, a negro woman told us she was looking for the army every minute. Mother said, "Drive on, Rice!" but Rice was not eager to go.

Mother was constantly saying, "Drive on, Rice, or they will catch us!"

On our journey we could hear the roaring of cannon, and afterward knew it was the battle of Champion Hill. At length we neared Vicksburg. There were no pickets along the road, no guards to ask questions, and we drove right on in town. ☆ ☆ ☆

A bishop, a minister, and the cleric's family also figured in the helter-skelter within Vicksburg those first frantic weeks in May. Perforce, baptisms, marriages, and burials in this war of intensely religious adversaries continued, although very few men of the cloth remained. Most were serving as regimental chaplains on the scattered Confederate fronts.

Bishop William Mercer Green, the first Episcopal Bishop of Mississippi, arrived during the bombardment from the river at the brick-and-stone fastness of Christ Church.

"Although the church has been kept open for the greater part of the time," the bishop penned in diocesan records, "and the attendance larger than usual, it consisted chiefly of the officers and soldiers engaged in defense of the place. It is but reasonable to expect that a church thus situated should share in the general stagnation or state of suspension imposed by the war on business of every kind.

"No place nor employment afforded security from the missiles of the enemy. Their bomb shells greeted my entrance into the town and continued during the three days of my visitation."

The bishop left, however, before he could officiate at two marriages and two burials a few days following his visit. That became the customary duty of the church's pastor, a forty-four-year-old smooth-faced native of Madison County, New York, a studious man of diverse talents. Dr. William Wilberforce Lord, chaplain of the 1st Mississippi Brigade as well as leader of the parish flock, was known to quite another circle outside of the clergy as a poet.

"Christ in Hades" and "Andre," a tragedy in five acts, were the best-known examples of his semireligious, semilyrical, conceivably opaque ventures into verse. An 1851 graduate of Princeton Theological Seminary, the young Lord's poems had been lightly praised by Wordsworth and thumpingly criticized by Edgar Allan Poe.

Caught in Vicksburg with his wife and four children by the approaching siege, Lord left the chronicling of this fateful, dramatic summer to his young son, Bill, Jr., and to his wife, Margaret, and a daughter, Lida. However, the Reverend Lord continued to deliver some memorable requiems for the fallen citizens and soldiers of the city. Bill, Jr., wrote:

☆ ☆ ☆ My first knowledge of the siege was gained in sitting all night on a pile of coal, which had been overspread with rugs and blankets in the cellar of Christ Church . . . and to this cellar he [Dr. Lord] took his family for refuge when the opening fire of the Union fleet was turned upon the forts and the town.

With the deep but muffled boom of the guns reaching us at intervals in our underground retreat, my mother and sisters huddling around me upon the coal-heap, my father, in clerical coat, and a red smoking-cap on his head, seated on an empty cask and looking delightfully like a pirate, our negro servants crouching in a neighboring coal-bin, and all lighted by the fitful glow of two or three tallow candles, the war became for the first time a reality and not the fairytale it had hitherto seemed.

The next day, taking advantage of a cessation in the bombardment, our entire household, excepting only my father, who remained in the city as chaplain of the First Mississippi Brigade, departed for [Uriah] Flowers' plantation near the Big Black River where shelter and entertainment had been offered us in anticipation of the shelling of the city.

Our most valued household effects, including my father's library, reputed to be the most scholarly and largest private collection in the Southwest, followed us in a canvas-covered army wagon. The family silver, however, destined to other strange vicissitudes later, we buried under the grass-grown sod of the [St. Albans Parish] churchyard, which was laid out in parklike fashion and was in no sense a cemetery or graveyard.

Mr. Flowers—a patriarchal bachelor of the old school—gave us a planter's cordial welcome. The suite of apartments placed at our disposal was on the first floor of the family mansion, opening upon the cool and roomy reception hall, and fronting on three sides upon a wide piazza which ran entirely around the house.

Here we were most pleasantly domiciled, to remain undisturbed, as my father hoped, as long as the siege should last.

But I was not destined long to enjoy the delights of this plantation paradise. My mother was so constituted that when separated from those she loved her imagination constantly drew the most painfully realistic pictures of possible disaster. As she was of a high-strung temperament, this continual agonizing in an atmosphere of apprehended misfortune so told upon her health that my father reluctantly gave his consent to our return to the city.

On our return journey to Vicksburg we rode in state in the Flowers' family carriage, but left behind us, alas! the priceless library, our household treasure of art and bric-a-brac, and the greater part of my

18

mother's dainty wardrobe; all, by the courteous permission of our host, stored, safely, as we supposed, in the apartments we had occupied on the ground floor of the plantation mansion. As it happened, this was about the worst possible disposal of our treasures. ☆ ☆ ☆

Mrs. Margaret Lord postscripted:

☆ ☆ ☆ We started for town about 3 o'clock in the afternoon, first Flora Tulley, myself with the children and George Tulley in the carriage, then the wagon with provisions and the servants and behind that Mr. Lord (who had driven out as escort) and Washington in the buggy—at almost every turn we looked around in apprehension of the Yankee cavalry—when almost eight miles from town we were overtaken by a servant who said the Yankees were already at Parson Fox's. This redoubled our anxiety, and I had a hushed heart, for our horses had left the wagon and buggy long behind. ☆ ☆ ☆

Near the road to Bovina the Lords encountered a hollow-eyed cavalryman who reined back on his overheated horse and blurted, "Madam, I am ashamed to tell you we have been terribly whipped . . . the enemy are pursuing us to the Big Black and to Bridgeport Ferry!"
Mrs. Lord continued:

☆ ☆ ☆ My heart sank . . . I never had such feelings in my life . . . that we should be so dreadfully defeated when so sure of victory!
We reached town at 10 o'clock at night. You cannot imagine what a scene—from the time we met our pickets stationed about a mile or a mile and a half from town there was a constant succession of camps and the whole town and hills seemed all aglow with fires of the camps: soldiers, soldiers at every step . . . for two hours I waited to throw myself upon my knees (by the four little ones sleeping, hungry as they were) and prayed oh! how earnestly that my husband might be saved. At 12 he arrived and we all with Major Williams and Mrs. Merriam congratulated ourselves on our escapes.
I found our church gallery filled to overflowing with sleeping soldiers and the street full of wagons and artillery. ☆ ☆ ☆

The First Day

"A citizen just up from Jackson reports
that the enemy abandoned Vicksburg on
Sunday (May 17), retreating up the ridge
northwest to Livingston, which is 20
miles north northeast of Jackson."
—NEW YORK *Tribune*

Pemberton's men continued, quite contrary to the "citizen's" report, to tumble back into the trenches, breastworks, and redans of the city as though obtaining shield at last from the onrushing, apparently invincible Blue tidal wave. Nor had the flood yet crested. If this flotsam of battle were disquieting to the southern military, it was no less shattering to everyone who called Vicksburg home.

"We are defeated!" wailed Emma Balfour, the forty-five-year-old brunette wife of socially prominent Dr. William T. Balfour. The Balfours and several of their six children lived in a two-story mansion on the corner of Cherry and Crawford streets, next door to Pemberton's headquarters and two blocks south of the Court House. She wrote:

☆ ☆ ☆ My pen almost refuses to tell of our terrible disaster. . . . From 6 o'clock in the morning until five in the evening the battle raged furiously. We are defeated—our army in confusion and the carnage—awful! awful!

. . . I hope never to witness again such a scene as the return of our routed army. From 12 o'clock until late in the night the streets and roads were jammed with wagons, cannons, horses, men, mules, stock, sheep, everything you can imagine that appertains to an army—being brought hurriedly within the entrenchments. Nothing like order prevailed, of course, as divisions, brigades and regiments were broken and separated.

As the poor fellows passed, every house poured forth all it had to refresh them. I had every one on the lot and there were some visitors carrying buckets of water to the corner for the men. Then in the back gallery I had everything that was eatable put out—and fed as many as I could. Poor fellows, it made my heart ache to see them, for I knew from all I saw and heard that it was want of confidence in the General commanding that was the cause of our disaster. I cannot write more—but oh! there will be a fearful reckoning somewhere. This has been brooding, growing and many fears have been felt for the result. General Pemberton has not the confidence of Officers, people or men judging from all I am compelled to see and hear. I would rather not have heard if I could have helped it.

What is to become of all the living things in this place when the boats begin shelling—God only knows! Shut up as in a trap, no ingress or egress—and thousands of women and children who have fled here for safety.

The Yankees are at our entrenchments and we hear firing. Mrs. Luke's place, where Mollie [a daughter] was, is outside and, sick as Mollie was, she has had to come in. Mrs. L. has lost all her corn and a great many other things, and I fear some of her negroes. The firing seems all along toward the Jackson road to the graveyard. Major General [Martin L.] Smith's division are now actually in the field, a general battle is expected at daylight.

There is firing all along the left wing toward the graveyard and toward the center, but not yet on the left. Brigadier General Stephen D. Lee is on the right near the center, his brigade not yet engaged. Last night we saw a grand and awful spectacle. The darkness was lit by burning houses all along our lines. They were burnt so that our firing would not be obstructed.

It was sad to see.

Many of them we knew to be handsome residences put up in the last few years as country residences—two of them very large and handsome houses, but the stern necessity of war has caused their destruction. We have provided ourselves with a cave as General Lee says there will be no safety elsewhere. Our entrenchments are from a mile and a half to three miles from town, varying with the nature of the country. (And 9 miles in perimeter.)

Of course shells and balls from these will reach any part of the town and the gunboats from the other side can throw to beyond our entrenchments in many places. When the General asked me if we were provided with a rat hole, I told him it seemed to me that we were all caught in a rat hole. ☆ ☆ ☆

The military truly shared that hopeless rathole. Col. Winchester Hall of the 26th Louisiana Infantry Regiment was summoned to the window of his boarding house "early on Sunday, May 17 [as] Mrs.

Hall called my attention to scattered bodies of troops coming in on the Jackson Road, which ran near my quarters."

Hall, a thoughtful, studious Louisianan, had quit his partnership in the law firm of Bush and Hall, in Thibodaux, to assume active duty in a volunteer militia, the "Allen Rifles," which was then incorporated in the 26th. He sent for his wife and children when it became apparent that he would be defending the Mississippi for some time, and settled them in the house of a Mrs. Downs outside of Vicksburg until the fighting neared. Then he moved his family to Mrs. Hansford's lodgings within the city limits, where Cemetery Road met the Jackson Road, near the Phoenix No. 2 firehouse.

He continued:

☆ ☆ ☆ I saw at once it was our army in retreat, and in utter confusion—a long line of stragglers. There would be a squad of infantry, a horseman—a gun—a few more infantry, and so on; with no more order than travelers on a highway, seeking Vicksburg as a shelter. This stream of stragglers continued nearly all day. After breakfast, I went down town to hear the news.

It was all one story, a fight, a repulse and a retreat. Every one I met had the gloomiest forebodings. I felt some of the "stern joy" warriors feel. My spirits rose as much above their normal condition as others were depressed. In the afternoon an order came to move the regiment at once to a point of the outer line of fortifications, where we slept on our arms in the trenches.

On Monday, May 18, news reached headquarters that a force of the enemy was moving toward us, on a road north of the city. The 27th and 26th Louisiana were ordered out to impede its progress. We took a position on the outer fortifications, and awaited, in vain, their approach; although we were annoyed by sharpshooters concealed by a forest in front; we lay behind a spur of a ridge, and were not pleased by their attentions, particularly as we could not place them.

After some time Captain Lovincy Hymel came to me and said, "Colonel, I will show you where they are."

He took me over the spur, pointed to some trees in the distance, and said, "They are there!"

We must have been fully exposed to their fire, at the place where we stood, for three bullets whizzed near to us in quick succession. I saw at once they were not only concealed, but too far away to enable us to return the compliment, and not relishing the position of being made a target, I sought shelter behind the spur, with as much elasticity in my step as my rank would allow, the captain following, as unconcerned as if they had been shooting peas.

We bivouacked near the outer works. ☆ ☆ ☆

Immediately to the east, refugees such as Max Kuner, the Austrian immigrant (who previously with his three brothers had sold pianos in New Orleans) were having their own troubles with the Union forces. The abandoned planter's house and one-time school into which they had moved was bad enough: "a family of hogs" were living in the basement, beds were fashioned from weather-beaten fence palings from an old graveyard, paper peeled in every room. Max wrote:

☆ ☆ ☆ We were just off one of the main roads to Vicksburg; consequently we were exposed to the depredations of everybody, blue or gray, who chanced to be travelling by. We had, in the beginning, three cows; one was stolen; another was killed, and only a steak cut out of her. We had chickens, which speedily learned to roost very high.

The house was open to a visit from whosoever chose. Our hours were not our own. One night I was aroused by the negro whistling the peculiar signal used by the race when something was to be communicated. I stepped out on the porch and asked him what was the matter.

"Any Yanks in theah?" he queried.

I told him no.

"They's some Confederate officers out heah who want to come in, if they's no Yanks about," he explained. The Federal troops had closed in so fast that many Confederates were caught within the lines; and these were some. They were about famished. They said that they were determined to get into Vicksburg; but whether they did I do not know.

Again, we were aroused by the clank of bridle chains, and by orders, in our yard. My wife went out; I followed. The approach to the house was an avenue of trees, great poplars; and we could descry a party of Federal soldiers leading away our horse. This was a thoroughbred horse bought by me from [Brigadier] General [Thomas H.] Taylor of the Confederate Army.

The General had used him as his personal mount; but in the battle of Chickasaw Bayou the horse had been mired, and in pulling free had sprained his foreleg. He was valued at several thousand dollars.

"Here!" we called. "What are you men doing?"

They began to joke us.

"Why, hello, old woman!" they retorted, seeing my wife. "What are you doing up? Where's your nightcap?"

"Bring back that horse!" we cried.

They good-naturedly explained. They said they knew they ought not to take such a fine horse, but the orders against stealing had become very strict and yet they wanted some chickens. We had chickens, and if we would give them all they could take, they would return the horse! Certainly, anything rather than to have the horse removed. So they brought back the horse and put him in the stable; and producing sacks, they proceeded to grab the poor chickens from the limbs of the trees, wring their heads off, and stuff the bags. With sacks filled, they rode away, engaging to come back again the next night. But they didn't.

We tried to bear patiently with the depredations; but when one night marauder broke into the barn and took every bridle, leaving me none, I revolted. From some carpet yarn and an old bit my wife made me an apology for a bridle; and using this I rode into the Federal camp, sought the officer in command of the District, and complained. He immediately gave me an order upon the quartermaster, which procured me a good, new bridle—but with a big U.S. upon the buttons. However, I put it on my horse and started back for home.

I had gone but a short distance through the Federal camp, when suddenly a soldier sprang up and stopped me. "Well, if here isn't a dashed Johnny Reb going off with a U.S. bridle!" he remarked. And he coolly divested my horse of it! So I rode home with the old rope yarn contraption after all. ☆ ☆ ☆

MAY 19

The Second Day

"The evacuation of Vicksburg! It would
mean the loss of valuable stores of
munitions of war collected for its defense,
the fall of Port Hudson, the surrender of
the Mississippi River, and the severance of
the Confederacy . . . !"

—PEMBERTON

Col. Winchester Hall of the 26th Louisiana Infantry continued:

☆ ☆ ☆ . . . 3 A.M., Tuesday, May 19, we moved back to the inner line
of fortifications. I had ordered out the band, and intended to give
our opponents "Dixie" at daylight, but Brigadier General Francis S.
Shoup, who now commanded our brigade, considered it untimely to
make overtures to the enemy.

When we reached the position assigned to us, I found rifle pits for
two companies only. The remainder of the ground to be covered by
us was on a ridge of gentle slope fully exposed to a fire from the
front. I had ordered spades and picks to be sent out the evening previous.

We got to work at once making pits, nor did we commence too
soon; we had nearly completed what would have served a temporary
purpose, when Dorneville Fabre of Company A was killed while at
work. I ordered the work to cease. ☆ ☆ ☆

These fortifications, as all others, were, according to Colonel Bevier,
"hastily and irregularly constructed entrenchments, circling the other
side of the city with the curve of a jagged 9-mile crescent, but so badly
engineered that in some places an enfilading fire would sweep us for
regiments in length, and in others palings, loosely erected, would cause
more damage from wooden splinters than could have resulted from iron
balls."

On the other hand, the attackers had their own troubles with
cotton-bale bulwarks from which bullets often bounced back. They
also experienced some confusion from old but still effective hoaxes:

25

the Confederates' use of logs painted as cannon, drawing fire away from the real batteries.

Colonel Hall went on:

☆ ☆ ☆ There were several mounted officers of the enemy now seen on a distant hill, out of range of our rifles, apparently taking observations with their field glasses. The troops of the enemy were well covered, and soon began to annoy us with artillery, and sharpshooters. I hitched my horse in a depression out of harm's way, as I believed. My eldest son now appeared with my breakfast, and I took a nap as I had slept little the night before.

The firing continued. It was Lieutenant [Richard C.] West's first experience under fire. He was excited. He stood up fully exposed and, in language not held orthodox, solicited his adversary to come out.

I called out "Get down, Lieutenant!"

He turned to me, "Colonel, do you order me to get down?"

"Yes."

"Well, if you order me to get down, I will get down," and suiting the action to the word, protected himself in the trenches.

I walked up and down the line about fifteen paces in the rear, protected by the crest of the ridge, as I supposed, from the fire of the enemy. About noon, under cover of a heavy artillery fire, the enemy assaulted the position of the 27th Louisiana, which was next to us in line, on our right; they were checked, however, aided, to some extent, by a flank fire of the 26th.

About two hours later, a charge was made against that portion of the line held by the 26th and 27th Louisiana. The column which emerged from the woods in front of us, for that purpose, was driven to cover by the fire of both regiments, although a color-bearer stood his ground concealed in a clump of bushes, above which he waved his colors as though he would stay there.

[One Union regimental flag, that of the 13th United States Infantry, was riddled by 55 bullets. The standard was saved through the furious action at a cost of 43 percent casualties. The regiment's performance, as Sherman extolled, was "unequalled in the army.]

After this repulse the enemy stood at a prudent distance and maintained a heavy artillery and musketry fire. ☆ ☆ ☆

At the same time, General Shoup, Hall's immediate superior who had posted the latter's 26th "in the gorge," reported:

☆ ☆ ☆ I was advised that it had been determined to abandon the advanced line on the left, and was ordered to withdraw Colonel Hall's regiment as soon as the troops of that line had fallen back, which was accomplished quietly at dawn. I caused Colonel [L. D.] Marks' regiment [the 27th Louisiana] to close to the right, to make the line more complete, and placed Colonel Hall's regiment on its left. The latter regiment found its position almost without intrenchments. Few tools could be had, but in a surprisingly short time a very tolerable cover was constructed.

At daylight the enemy had taken possession of the heights abandoned a few hours before by our troops, from which position he soon opened upon us with artillery. By 10 a.m. he had placed his batteries in our front, as well as on the right and left of my position, the line making a very decided salient. The fire from artillery and sharpshooters soon became very heavy. We made little reply, waiting for further developments.

About 1 p.m. the enemy debouched in force from a gorge in front of the center of my position. We opened on him. He broke and fled to the cover of the hills. After a time he reappeared in greater force.

. . . the enemy continued a terrific fire until dark. In this attack the enemy lost several prisoners, a stand of colors, and many stand of arms. Our loss was heavy.

Colonel Hall, 26th Louisiana, was severely wounded while in the gallant discharge of his duty. . . . ☆ ☆ ☆

☆ ☆ ☆ . . . about 2 p.m. [Hall estimated] I was walking slowly up to the right of the line, watching the movements in front, when I felt something strike the calf of my right leg, as though a clod had been thrown against it; in a moment I became dizzy. I sat down on a bank of earth near to me. A deathly faintness came over me.

My orderly came up. I sent him for some whiskey, and took enough to revive me. Major William Martin came up to know the extent of the injury. All I could say or knew was that I had been struck, and was disabled.

Colonel William C. Crow came up, and had me moved on a stretcher to a less-exposed place. As the fire of the enemy covered our rear, I could not be moved from the field; so I laid in the rut of a wagon road, with my body close to the bank; even here a spent minié struck me in the side.

I was exceedingly nervous. I knew the regiment was hotly engaged, and my anxiety was strung to its highest pitch. . . .

I remained in this wagon rut until dark, the firing had not ceased, but I sent for a stretcher, and with bullets whistling all about us, I was taken to our improvised hospital, whence I was taken in an ambulance to my quarters, which I reached about midnight. I saw Mrs. Hall at the door waiting for me. I cried out "Hurrah for Vicksburg and the Southern Confederacy."

She quietly gave orders to move me to a cot she had made ready for me, and soon I was as comfortable as circumstances allowed, but I passed *une nuit blanche*, as the shelling about us was terrific and incessant. Mrs. Hansford's house which we occupied was in the acute angle of the Cemetery Road and the Jackson Road. The enemy had a floating mortar battery in the river opposite to us. His efforts were directed to shelling these two roads thoroughly; so that these roads, and any place near to them, were unsafe for any living thing. The grounds about the house, as well as the house, bore many marks of the shelling but were uninjured. ☆ ☆ ☆

MAY 20

The Third Day

"A Washington special to the *Herald* says
  that up to a late hour tonight nothing
  additional was received from Grant. . . .
  The rebel papers are filled with gloomy
  and despondent articles on the position
  of affairs at Vicksburg and evidently
  anticipate the worst from that quarter."
  —NEW YORK *Herald*

Colonel Hall continued to describe the treatment of his wound:

☆ ☆ ☆ The next morning Dr. [Alfred] Hall, an assistant surgeon, examined the limb, but not being well, felt unequal to the task of deciding what to do with it; he called in a surgeon who considered amputation proper. Dr. Hall not coinciding with him, they agreed to leave the decision to Dr. Winn, the brigade surgeon, who had called in the meanwhile. Dr. Winn declared in favor of an attempt to save the limb.

I was put under the influence of chloroform. On return to consciousness I found a slit three inches long had been made on the shin-bone, the minié ball which had been split in two, extracated, several pieces of bone taken out, and the skin sewed together. It proved to be a compound, comminuted [shattered] fracture of the tibia.

As the shelling was vigorously kept up, it was deemed prudent to move behind a hill in the rear of Mrs. Hansford's dwelling. Here two tents were pitched, and occupied by Mrs. George Marshall and her child, and my family. It seemed to protect us from the mortar battery across the river, whence the heaviest shelling proceeded, as the hill had been partially cut away, almost perpendicularly, and our tents were pitched close to the cut.

A portion of this cut had been scooped out sufficient to hold one or two persons, and to this scooped-out place, my youngest children learned to run for safety, on the approach of a shell.

During the afternoon a shell was heard. A soldier passing at the same moment, seeing this scooped-out hole in the upright bank of the hill, sought shelter in it from the coming shell. It exploded directly over him, the concussion killing him instantly, in the very spot my children had sought shelter frequently during the day. Fortunately, they were, at that time, occupied with their dinner in Mrs. Marshall's tent, and were not aware of the coming of the shell.

The tent I occupied was thrown down by the concussion. I was covered with earth, and it gave me a considerable shock.

I resolved to strike our tents for a more secure position, if practicable. We pitched them behind Sky-parlor hill [one of Vicksburg's highest hills—three blocks from the waterfront and four blocks south of the Court House—used as a signal tower]. Just as I reached there I heard a shell crash through a dwelling, near the tents. I determined we could not remain.

Colonel Henry A. Clinch of the heavy artillery called. Noting the forlorn condition of my family, and my own helplessness, he started off to look up a better place for us, and soon returned, stating he had found rooms for us, on the second floor of the dwelling of Tim Dowling, on the river just below the built portion of the city [to the south of the Marine Hospital].

Thither went Mrs. Marshall and her child and my family. I followed on a stretcher. ☆ ☆ ☆

As the wounded Louisianan tried to make himself comfortable in Tim Dowling's place, the shadows of evening lengthened and the smell of burnt gunpowder mixed with the persistent humid if now somewhat more cooling air. By 1 A.M. "the silence of the starlit night was broken by the roar of heavy guns," in the words of a soldier thus far luckier than Winchester Hall.

Tough, wiry Sgt. William H. Tunnard, twenty-six, of the "Pelican Rifles" of Baton Rouge, a company in the combat-tested 3d Louisiana Infantry Regiment, had the good fortune to be assigned to the commissary. This kept him out of the rifle pits but close enough, most of the time, to maintain tally of the days' duelings. (His father, W. F. Tunnard, was a Major with the same regiment.) The New Jersey-born younger Tunnard had graduated from Kenyon College in Ohio, where he had been active in fraternity work and journalism. A newspaperman after graduation, he saw his first active military service when his regiment participated in the capture of John Brown at Harpers Ferry. Sergeant Tunnard wrote about Vicksburg:

☆ ☆ ☆ A huge ironclad approached from below, and commenced a furious bombardment of the city, which was rapidly responded to by our heavy batteries.

Below lay the fleet of the enemy, and above, the river was dotted with a huge fleet of transports and war vessels. On the peninsula the white tents of the enemy's encampment were plainly visible.

Such was the panoramic view in front of Vicksburg on the third morning of the siege. At early dawn the mortar fleet of Commodore Porter opened fire on the beleaguered city, adding to the tremendous din their hoarse bellowing, accompanied with the fearful screams and tremendous concussions of their huge exploding missiles.

[" . . . dropping into every part of the city, from over the clouds, huge iron spheres that looked like big potash kettles until they burst, when they behaved as one would imagine of an aerial powder magazine," observed Colonel Bevier of the naval mortar bombardment.]

The place was a perfect pandemonium from early dawn. The hoarse bellowing of the mortars, the sharp report of rifled artillery, the scream and explosion of every variety of deadly missiles, intermingled with the incessant, sharp reports of small-arms, made up a combination of sounds not such as described by the poet as being a "sweet concord." A trip through Vicksburg exhibited some strange spectacles.

Huge caves were excavated out of the precipitous hillsides, where families of women and children sheltered themselves from the hurtling shot and the descending fragments of exploding missiles. Fair ladies, in all the vigor and loveliness of youth, hurried with light tread along the torn-up pavements, fearless of the storm of iron and lead, penetrating every portion of the city, as they attended to the necessities of their brave, wounded, and dying protectors. The annals of history can furnish no more brilliant record than did the heroic women of Vicksburg during this fearful siege.

Regardless of personal danger, they flitted about the hospitals or threaded the streets on their missions of love, utterly forgetful of self in their heroic efforts to relieve the sufferings of those who so gallantly defended their hearthstones.

Many, very many heroic spirits bade farewell to earth amid the thunder and din of the siege, feeling the soothing pressure of soft hands upon their clammy brows, and the glance of tender, pitying eyes gazing into the failing light of their glazing orbs, as these ministering angels hovered about the lowly cots of the dying soldiers. No pen can describe in sufficiently glowing colors; no human language find words brilliant, forcible enough to do justice to the unwearying attentions, tender compassion, soul-felt sympathy, unvarying kindness and unceasing labors of love, of the tender-hearted, heroic and fearless ladies of Vicksburg toward their suffering countrymen. ☆ ☆ ☆

MAY 21

The Fourth Day

"Vicksburg is closely besieged, the
enemy closing in on every side . . . !"
 —MOBILE *Advertiser and Register*

Late News from Cairo
"The gunboat *Cricket*, from Young's
Point, with Government dispatches from
Admiral Porter, has arrived. Several
ironclads were stationed at various points
in the Red River.
 —*New York Times*

The week in which Vicksburg's doom might be sealed at almost any given hour continued into this Thursday, as the Confederates hung on grimly. Grant kept boring in, with a steamroller's imponderability and disinterest.

☆ ☆ ☆ The firing, wrote Will Tunnard, continued rapid and heavy all day, the mortar shells tearing the houses into fragments, and injuring several citizens, including one lady. The enemy, in front of the Third Regiment, were slowly but surely contracting their lines, and the fire of their sharpshooters was particularly accurate and deadly. Their batteries concentrated their fire on every one of our guns that opened on their lines, and speedily dismounted them. A splendid piece of ordnance, protected by cotton bales, was thus dismounted by the skillful fire from the enemy's rifled pieces, their balls striking the bales, upsetting them on the gun carriage, setting fire to them at the same time, and thus burning them to the ground.

It was a foolhardy piece of business to expose the least portion of the person above the breastworks, as a hundred rifles immediately directed their missiles upon the man thus showing himself. No less than five cannoneers were thus shot in an attempt to apply a lighted fuse to the vent of a loaded gun.

The members of the Third Regiment suffered severely in their reckless exposure of their persons to the fire of the enemy's sharpshooters, and the list of casualties rapidly increased.

In conversation with the enemy [a common occurrence because of the proximity of the lines] a member of Company E, by the name of Masterton, a Missourian of huge dimension and familiarly known in the regiment as "Shanghai," found some acquaintances, and was invited into the enemy's lines, with the assurance that he would be allowed to return. The invitation was immediately accepted, and he trusted himself to the honor of the foe.

He was cordially welcomed, and all the delicacies and substantials, which the Federals possessed in such profusion, were furnished him. After a feast, accompanied with a sociable chat and several drinks, he was permitted to return, very favorably impressed with the generosity of the Yankees.

The evening chats, after the day's deadly sharpshooting, revealed the fact that there were members of both armies who were personally acquainted, and, in one instance, two members of the Third Regiment found a brother in the regiment opposed to them. ☆ ☆ ☆

A Confederate officer later recounted to Emma Balfour that he had overheard his own men calling across the lines, "Lend us some coffee for supper, won't you, we will pay you when Johnston comes!" And the reply had come back, "Never mind the coffee, but Grant will take dinner in Vicksburg tomorrow."

Emma continued:

☆ ☆ ☆ The battle raged again all day yesterday, again on the right. They seem determined to have that point. Last night after all was quiet, the Doctor [her husband] went out to know how it had gone with us and our friends.

He found the General [Pemberton] at his dinner in good spirits and confident of holding his position. He [Pemberton] told me when he got here from Big Black that he did not believe his [soldiers] would ever behave badly again, that he had been around and talked to them all and he thought they would fight next time.

I believe I did not tell you he [General Lee] had his coat sleeve all torn by a passing bullet and another spent ball struck his arm making it black from the shoulder to the elbow. Then at Big Black, or rather in falling back from Edward's to Big Black, he and Captain Elliott came near being captured by a ruse, the Yankee cavalrymen all about them and they had ridden on some distance in advance of the brigade to look out.

33

They saw two horsemen in Confederate uniform approaching and called out "Who are you?"

They answered, "Who are you?"

General Lee answered, "I am General Lee."

They called out, "All right, General, come on!"

Immediately he suspected something and noticing at the same time that they had their pistols in their hands, he waved his hand to them with a smile, saying, "No you don't," put spurs to his horse and was off.

They fired their revolvers and six pieces of artillery in the woods opened on them—but strange to say not a thing touched them or their horses!

10 P.M. Heavy firing still on the right and heavy shelling from the line. This went on all night [from the line]; our batteries have been firing now for an hour and I think the evening's firing is ceasing. We have driven them back from above and below repeatedly in the last two days.

They have one of those terrible [gunboats] and day before yesterday she tried to come near our batteries. They let her approach until within good range and then fired and fortunately the first shot struck her. She retired at once. Yesterday she approached again and after shots retired. Those behind seem more determined but after a shot or two tells they retire.

Last night Mrs. Higgins and myself sat up until after eleven o'clock making cartridges. We get no help from the outside world now and have to help ourselves.

One of their [Federal] lieutenants we took yesterday says that Grant has a hundred and thirty thousand men. I don't think this can be so.

I have sad intelligence of Winston Reese. As soon as our men got to the trenches, the Doctor went all around himself till he found a young man who said he knew him well—that he was wounded near Edward's and captured. Then he saw another who said he assisted in carrying him off the field and he was wounded in the knee. I only hope he was able to telegraph his father from Jackson.

What they have done with the wounded ones we do not know, we know nothing outside, but the prisoners are supposed to have been carried up the river, as several transports passed up from the point opposite their wood yesterday. Duncan Green is safe. I have seen him. ☆ ☆ ☆

MAY 22

The Fifth Day

"Vicksburg has not fallen—is not going
to fall. It is not in so much danger now as it
has often been before, and the Federal
army . . . is in a very dangerous situation."
—RICHMOND *Examiner*

"If this is not a hot place I hope I may
never see one . . . !"
—DR. JOSEPH DILL ALISON

On Friday, the 22d, Grant made one last attempt. He decided to do so even though his skirmish line and other frontal units, infantry as well as artillery, were becoming short—momentarily—of ammunition.

"At exactly ten o'clock," telegraphed a correspondent with Grant's troops, "the whole Federal army was transformed into a monster serpent, which began to writhe and twist and turn and undulate. Brigades broke off and advanced right or left oblique—divisions moved up squarely to the front, cannon began to thunder, the hoarse shouts of officers were echoed along the line, columns closed up, the earth began to shake and tremble—the curtain had gone up on the tragedy of war."

Maj. Gen. John A. McClernand's 13th Corps, hammering forward on the southern wing of the Federal line, gained partial possession of the railroad redoubt, while his men occupied the ditch fronting the 2d Texas lunette. But he could not hold what he had won. As one witness flippantly observed, these light advance units "had no more show of carrying them [the enemy's major works] than Porter had of running his fleet over the housetops of the city."

Sergeant Tunnard wrote:

☆ ☆ ☆ The bombardment continued unabated from all sides of the beleaguered city, and was more rapid and furious than heretofore. Nearly all the artillery along the lines was dismounted. The report of a single gun within the breastworks was the signal for a concentrated fire of the enemy's batteries, which poured a perfect storm of solid shot and shell upon the fated point, resulting, usually, in the destruction of the battery, and killing and wounding numbers of artillerymen.

35

The fire was terrific, and the fearful list of casualties in the regiment much depressed the spirits of the men. The enemy made an assault on the right of the line, but were repulsed with terrible slaughter, and two hundred of them taken prisoners. This creditable affair was due to the unflinching bravery of the Second Texas Infantry —a gallant and noble regiment. About 10 A.M., four gunboats steamed up the river from below, and engaged our batteries. They were soon compelled to retire, badly damaged, with but few casualties among our skillful artillerists." ☆ ☆ ☆

"The air," reported Maj. Gen. John S. Bowen, one of Pemberton's five division commanders, "was literally burdened with hissing missiles of death . . . . from the enemy's numerous batteries of shell, grape, and canister. . . . Colonel [W. R.] Gause of the Third Missouri Infantry procured some fuse shell and, using them as hand grenades, threw them into the ditch, where they exploded, killing and wounding some twenty-two of the enemy."

At the same time, Osborn Oldroyd, a sergeant with Company E, 20th Ohio Infantry Regiment, was witnessing the "tragedy" and majesty of war from the attackers' side:

☆ ☆ ☆ The boys were expecting the order and were busy divesting themselves of watches, rings, pictures, and other keepsakes, which were being placed in the custody of the cooks, who were not expected to go into action. I never saw such a scene before, nor do I ever want to see it again. About 11 o'clock came a signal for the entire line to charge the works of the enemy. Our boys were all ready, and in an instant leaped forward to find victory or defeat. The 7th Missouri took the lead with ladders which they placed against the fort [the "Great Redoubt"] and then gave way for others to scale them.

Those who climbed to the top of the fort met cold steel, and when at length it was found impossible to enter the fort that way, the command was given to fall back, which was done under a perfect hail of lead from the enemy. The rebels, in their excitement and haste to fire at our retreating force, thrust their heads a little too high above their cover—an advantage we were quick to seize with well-aimed volleys. . . .

Thus ended another day of bloody fight in vain, except for an increase of the knowledge which has been steadily growing lately, that a regular siege will be required to take Vicksburg. ☆ ☆ ☆

The assault was enough to test the sense of humor of the happiest man. Capt. J. J. Kellogg of Company B, 113th Illinois Volunteer Infantry, was tried and found not wanting.

☆ ☆ ☆ While waiting the charge of the storming party and watching their progress across the field to the enemy's works, I noticed a group of general officers close to our left, composed of Grant,* Sherman, and Giles A. Smith, with their field glasses, watching the little storming party painting a trail of blood across that field. Those distinguished commanders, unlike ourselves, were standing behind large trees, and squinted cautiously out to the right and left, exposing as little of their brass buttons as possible, and I think I saw them dodge a couple of times. I thought of the convincing speech the officer made to his command on the eve of the battle, when he assured them that he might be killed himself, as some balls would go through the biggest trees.

General [Hugh] Ewing's brigade led the assault [on stockade Redan] after the storming party had sped their bolts, and advanced along the crown of an interior ridge which partially sheltered his advance. This command actually entered the parapet of the enemy's works at a shoulder of the bastion,† but when the enemy rose up in double ranks and delivered its withering fire his forces were swept back to cover, but the brave and resourceful old Ewing shifted his command to the left, crossed the ditch, pressed forward, and ere long we saw his men scrambling up the outer face of the bastion and his colors planted near the top of the rebel works.‡

Our brigade was formed in a ravine threatening the parapet, 300 yards to the left of the bastion, and we had connected with [Brig. Gen. Thomas E. G.] Ransom's brigade. From that formation we fixed bayonets and charged point blank for the rebel works at a double quick. Unfortunately for me I was in the front of the rank and compelled to maintain that position, and a glance at the forest of gleaming bayonets sweeping up from the rear, at a charge, made me realize

*Grant was at the Jackson Road at this time, not with this group.
†Kellogg's memory played tricks on him. Ewing's men reached only the ditch fronting stockade Redan.
‡Actually, Ewing's headquarter's flag was planted on the superior slope of the work.

that it only required a stumble of some lubber just behind me to launch his bayonet into the offside of my anatomy, somewhere in the neighborhood of my anterior suspender buttons.

This knowledge so stimulated me that I feared the front far less than the rear, and forged ahead like an antelope, easily changing my double quick to a quadruple gait, and most emphatically making telegraph time. During that run and rush I had frequently to either step upon or jump over the bodies of our dead and wounded, which were scattered along our track.

The nearer the enemy we got the more enthusiastic we became, and the more confidence we had in scaling their works, but as we neared their parapet we encountered the reserved fire of the rebels which swept us back to temporary cover of a ridge, two-thirds of the way across the field, from which position we operated the rest of the day. ☆ ☆ ☆

There was also one civilian, at least, who managed a smile through the armageddon. Mrs. Groome, who had known of Mrs. Gamble's tragic death, was using a makeshift shelter of cotton bales in a small depression behind her house. She recalled a conversation between her mother and aunt.

"Oh, sister, are you killed?" her mother asked, following a near miss that had showered everyone with dirt and cotton fluff.

"No," replied her aunt with equal solicitude, "are you?" And soon the huddled occupants of the cotton-bale sanctuary, realizing the absurdity of the conversation, were all laughing.

Dr. Joseph Dill Alison, a Confederate army surgeon from Dallas County, Alabama, formerly stationed in Pensacola, still could not find anything funny about this Friday, in postscripting to his previous observation: "Firing today has been terrible, but gunboats have come up and engaged our batteries, the mortars continue shelling in an unending roar all along our lines. We are penned in two square miles and fighting all around.

"It is decidedly unpleasant to be cut off from the world and know that important movements are going on outside without being able to learn the nature of them. . . ."

Emma Balfour wrote of the day's assault:

☆ ☆ ☆ This part of the town is just southeast and east of us, and of course very near so we had the full benefit. It is just where the railroad crosses our lines. I was up in my room sewing and praying in my heart, oh so earnestly for our cause when Nancy rushed up, actually pale, exclaiming:

"Oh Mistress, the Yankees are pouring over the hill and our men are running! Just come to the gallery and you can see!"

It brought before me forcibly what a state of excitement we were living in when I found that this coincidence did not startle me. I got up, but I suppose slowly because she exclaimed:

"Mistress, just hear them, the shells are falling all round you! You will stay up here until you are killed!"

I went on the back gallery with my glass and saw some men pouring over the hill as the negroes were darting through the shells, a brigade running past towards this point—so I thought perhaps it might not be so bad as she thought, and quieted her a little. I found out that I was right—that point was hotly pressed and reinforcements were being sent from other points there.

They were repulsed and three times again during the day at the same point the same thing took place. General Lee's praise is in everyone's mouth.

Some gentlemen tried to go there but had to jump off their horses and into the ditches for safety. About nine o'clock in the morning the gunboats towed some mortars into range, and then there was a rushing into caves. Mrs. Higgins came up and then we went into a cave for the first time. Colonel Higgins [the river battery commander] thought we ought to go.

Just as we got in, several "machines" exploded, it seemed, just over our heads, and at the same time two riders were killed in the valley below us by a twenty-four pound shell from the east side, so you see we were between two fires.

As all this rushed over me and the sense of suffocation from being underground, the certainty that there was no way of escape, that we were hemmed in, caged:—for one moment my heart seemed to stand still. Then my faith and courage rose to meet the emergency, and I have felt prepared ever since and cheerful.

I preferred to risk the danger in a house rather than in a cave with so many, so we are having a cave of our own made, but I certainly shall stay out as long as I can. All night the fleet fired but I was sick and in bed. Nearly all the families in town spent the night in their caves. . . .

I have a piece of one of their flags taken at General Lee's position.

They stormed his ranks, got within [the Railroad Redoubt] and planted their flag on the breastwork. Then there was more work. They were not inside but in the ditch on the outside.

The General called for volunteers to drive them out and took all of them prisoners and captured their flags. You must know this was a dangerous thing to do, when their sharpshooters kill nearly every man that puts his head above the works. ☆ ☆ ☆

A young bride, Mrs. Anderson Miller, found that she was subjected to a continuous "fiery shower of shells." The former Dora Richards, of San Croix in the West Indies, Mrs. Miller had been married on January 18, 1862, in Trinity Episcopal Church, New Orleans. Then, with her lawyer-husband, Dora, who had long thought of herself as "a rather lonely young girl," had gone on to a small town in Arkansas, Anderson's home. She became lonelier yet. Nor could they escape the war in Arkansas.

The Millers then moved east to Vicksburg, and found disruption even more acute. They arrived in time for the Battle of Chickasaw Bayou. Not only was there no law practice in the embattled city but the couple soon became "utterly cut off from the world." Now, "surrounded by a circle of fire," Dora, an indefatigible diarist, penned:

☆ ☆ ☆ H's [her husband] occupation, of course, is gone, his office closed. Every man has to carry a pass in his pocket. People do nothing but eat what they can get, sleep when they can, and dodge the shells. There are three intervals when the shelling stops, either for the guns to cool or for the gunners' meals, I suppose—about eight in the morning, the same in the evening, and at noon. In that time we have both to prepare and eat ours.

Clothing cannot be washed or anything else done. On the 19th and 22nd, when the assaults were made on the lines, I watched the soldiers cooking on the green opposite. The half-spent balls coming all the way from those lines were flying so thick that they were obliged to dodge at every turn.

At all the caves I could see from my high perch, people were sitting, eating their poor suppers at the cave doors, ready to plunge in again. As the first shell again flew they dived, and not a human being was visible.

The sharp crackle of the musketry-firing was a strong contrast to the scream of the bombs. I think all the dogs and cats must be killed or starved, we don't see any more pitiful animals prowling around. . . . The cellar is so damp and musty the bedding has to be carried out and laid in the sun every day, with the forecast that it may be demolished at any moment. The confinement is dreadful. To sit and listen as if waiting for death in a horrible manner would drive me insane. ☆ ☆ ☆

Margaret Lord, however, as befitting a clergyman's wife, was of more optimistic mind than Dora Miller. She wrote: "Toward evening the glorious news was brought in: three tremendous charges by the enemy! They had been repulsed with terrific slaughter. Then began the reincarnation of our army—men who had been gloomy and despondent once more stood erect and hurled defiance at the foe!"

Counting four thousand fresh casualties from the bloody assaults of the 19th and 22d, General Grant concluded that this was no way to take Vicksburg. He reasoned, "as long as we could hold our positions, the enemy was limited in supplies of food, men, and munitions of war to what they had on hand. They could not last always."

And the commanding general decided upon orders for a "regular siege."

MAY 23

The Sixth Day

> Our latest information from Vicksburg
> and its vicinity, although not so clear as
> we would wish it to be, yet encouraging
> enough. . . . We are pretty sure that General
> Pemberton will hold the place in spite of all
> that Grant can do against it.
> —PETERSBURG (VA.) *Express*

Saturday dawned overcast and raining. Pvt. Seth Wells of Company G, 8th Illinois Infantry, feeling dank and dirty, scrawled in his small diary, "how I wish I had a clean shirt or time to wash this!"

Sgt. Will Tunnard, not a great distance across the ravines from where Wells had slept on the steamy ground, rubbed his own sore muscles, and noted, "the shadows of night, falling over the beleaguered city, brought no repose to the weary soldiers. Heavy details were made to rebuild and repair those portions of the works ploughed up and torn down by the heavy firing of the enemy's batteries during the day."

It was no light task, after fighting all day beneath the rays of the summer's sun, thus, amid the shadows of night, to use pickax, spade, and shovel, carrying heavy sandbags, strengthen the torn-down breast-works with heavy timbers and cotton bales, in order to be protected during the approaching day's combat. Rations at this period were plentiful, and were distributed to the men, already prepared by details made for this purpose. General Grant sent in a flag of truce, asking permission to bury his dead, which were lying unburied in thick profusion outside of the entrenchments, where the enemy had assaulted the lines.

General Pemberton refused to grant the request, replying that the battle was not yet decided. The Federal trains and troops were observed moving away from the camps, while rumors prevailed that Johnston was fighting their rear at Big Black. Yet no definite news of succor reached the besieged army.

And so "shovel and pick are more in use today," it was apparent to Osborn Oldroyd, from Illinois, "which seems to be a sign that digging is to take the place of charging at the enemy. We think Grant's head is level, anyhow: The weather is getting hotter, and I fear sickness; and water is growing scarce, which is very annoying. If we can but keep well, the future has no fears for us."

"I had to stop writing on Thursday," Emma Balfour continued. "The shells exploded so thickly all around us all day." She went on:

☆ ☆ ☆ About five o'clock there was a lull and we hoped to get some rest at night but at six o'clock as we sat on the gallery a mortar shell exploded in the shed in front making me involuntarily jump from my seat. Then another and another from all directions. The gunboats came and engaged in battling, and such a time as we had watching the shells, you cannot imagine.

We were thankful when dark came for we could better avoid them. We sat or stood in front of the house until eleven o'clock knowing that it would never do to go to bed as several houses had already been struck, Mrs. Peyer's and Mrs. Willis'. We concluded as we had to be up, it was as well to see all that was going on, so we went down and paid Mrs. Peyer a visit in her cave back of the Roman C. [Catholic] Church. Then on to Sky Parlor Hill and stayed there until one o'clock.

You must understand that it was not in the usual way we walked down the street, but had to take the middle of the street, when we heard a shell and watch for it, and this was about every half minute. You may imagine our progress was not very fast.

As soon as a shell gets over your head you are safe for even if it approaches near, the pieces fall forward and do not touch you, but the danger is that sometimes while watching one—another comes and may explode or fall near you 'ere you are aware.

Twice while we were on the hill the boats came up and attacked, but a few shots drove them back. Soon after we got home Mrs. Crump came from some cave where she had been quite exhausted. We made her come and lie down while we watched and she got a little sleep, but I don't think many eyes closed in town that night.

Poor May Green with her little ones was running from place to place all night and finally went into a cave. While we stood watching the shells, while Mrs. Crump slept, one fell as we thought right into Mrs. Peyer's and another just at the same time into Major Grimes' and another into Major General Carter L. Stevenson's. The Dr. ran down to see and found the only one that did much harm was the one that struck Mrs. Peyer's.

It took both of us busily engaged to keep a proper lookout. I shall have to close now as they are falling so thickly both from the battle-field in the east and the river. Yesterday we picked up five powder shells unexploded, and today they are falling thickly. ☆ ☆ ☆

Another prominent woman of Vicksburg, a physician's daughter, Mary Ann Webster Loughborough, also was keeping meticulous diary notes. Her husband was Maj. James M. Loughborough, formerly an attorney and now a staff adjutant in the defending army. Mary, the mother of a two-year-old daughter, was born in New York City but raised in St. Louis after her father, Dr. A. W. Webster, moved there.

Mary, who was twenty-seven years old, had "heard that Vicksburg would not in all probability hold out more than a week or two, as the garrison was poorly provisioned; and one of General Pemberton's staff officers told us that the effective force of the garrison, upon being estimated, was found to be fifteen thousand men; [Major] General [William W.] Loring having been cut off after the battle of Black River, with probably ten thousand.

"The ladies all cried, 'Oh, never surrender!' but after the experience of the night, I really could not tell what I wanted, or what my opinions were." Then she added:

☆ ☆ ☆ How often I thought of M—— [her husband] upon the battle field, and his anxiety for us in the midst of this unanticipated danger, wherein the safety lay entirely on the side of the belligerent gentle-men, who were shelling us so furiously, at least two miles from the city, in the bend of the river near the canal.

So constantly dropped the shells around the city, that the inhabit-ants all made preparations to live under the ground during the siege. M—— sent over and had a cave made in a hill near by. We seized the opportunity one evening, when the gunners were probably at their supper, for we had a few moments of quiet, to go over and take possession. We were under the care of a friend of M——, who was paymaster on the staff of the same General with whom M—— was Adjutant. We had neighbors on both sides of us; and it would have been an amusing sight to a spectator to witness the domestic scenes presented without by the number of servants preparing the meals under the high bank containing the caves.

Our dining, breakfasting, and supper hours were quite irregular. When the shells were falling fast, the servants came in for safety, and our meals waited for completion some little time; again they would fall slowly, with the lapse of many minutes between, and out would start the cooks to their work.

Some families had light bread made in large quantities, and subsisted on it with milk (provided their cows were not killed from one milking time to another), without any more cooking, until called on to replenish. Though most of us lived on corn bread and bacon, served three times a day, the only luxury of the meal consisting in its warmth, I had some flour, and frequently had some hard, tough biscuit made from it, there being no soda or yeast to be procured . . . we could, also, procure beef.

A gentleman friend was kind enough to offer me his camp bed, a narrow spring mattress, which fitted within the contracted cave very comfortably; another had his tent fly stretched over the mouth of our residence to shield us from the sun; and thus I was the recipient of many favors, and under obligations to many gentlemen of the army for delicate and kind attentions; and, in looking back to my trials at that time, I shall ever remember with gratitude the kindness with which they strove to ward off every deprivation.

And so I went regularly to work, keeping house under ground. Our new habitation was an excavation made in the earth, and branching six feet from the entrance, forming a cave in the shape of a T. In one of the wings my bed fitted; the other I used as a kind of a dressing room; in this the earth had been cut down a foot or two below the floor of the main cave; I could stand erect here; and when tired of sitting in other portions of my residence, I bowed myself into it, and stood impassively resting at full height—one of the variations in the still shell-expectant life. M——'s servant cooked for us under protection of the hill. Our quarters were close, indeed; yet I was more comfortable than I expected I could have been made under the earth in that fashion.

We were safe at least from fragments of shell—and they were flying in all directions; though no one seemed to think our cave any protection, should a mortar shell happen to fall directly on top of the ground above us. We had our roof arched and braced, the supports of the bracing taking up much room in our confined quarters. The earth was about five feet thick above, and seemed hard and compact; yet, poor M——, every time he came in, examined it, fearing, amid some of the shocks it sustained, that it might crack and fall upon us.

One afternoon, amid the rush and explosion of the shells, cries and screams arose—the screams of women amid the shrieks of the falling shells. The servant boy, George, after starting and coming back once or twice, his timidity overcoming his curiosity (I was not at all surprised at it), at last gathered courage to go to the ravine near us, from whence the cries proceeded, and found that a negro man had been buried alive within a cave, he being alone at that time.

Workmen were instantly set to deliver him, if possible; but when found, the unfortunate man had evidently been dead some little time. His wife and relations were distressed beyond measure, and filled the air with their cries and groans.

This incident made me doubly doubtful of my cave; I feared that I might be buried alive at any time. Another incident happened the same day: A gentleman, resident of Vicksburg, had a large cave made and repeatedly urged his wife to leave the house and go into it. She steadily refused and, being quite an invalid, was lying on the bed when he took her by the hand and insisted upon her accompanying him so strongly that she yielded; and they had scarcely left the house when a mortar shell went crashing through, utterly demolishing the bed that had so lately been vacated, tearing up the floor and almost completely destroying the room.

That night, after my little one had been laid in bed, I sat at the mouth of the cave with the servants drawn around me, watching the brilliant display of fireworks the mortar boats were making—the passage of the shell, as it travelled through the heavens, looking like a swiftly moving star. As it fell, it approached the earth so rapidly that it seemed to leave behind a track of fire.

This night we kept our seats, as they all passed rapidly over us, none falling near. The incendiary shells were still more beautiful in appearance. As they exploded in the air, the burning matter and balls fell like large, clear blue-and-amber stars, scattering hither and thither.

"Miss M——," said one of the more timid servants, "do they want to kill us all dead? Will they keep doing this until we all die?"

I said most heartily, "I hope not."

The servants we had with us seemed to possess more courage than is usually attributed to negroes. They seldom hesitated to cross the street for water at any time. The "boy" slept at the entrance of the cave, with a pistol I had given him, telling me I need not be "afeared—dat any one dat come dar would have to go over his body first."

He never refused to carry out any little article to M—— on the battle field. I laughed heartily at a dilemma he was placed in one day: The mule that he had mounted to ride out to the battlefield took him to a dangerous locality, where the shells were flying thickly and then, suddenly stopping, through fright, obstinately refused to stir. It was in vain that George kicked and beat him—go he would not; so, clenching his hand, he hit him severely in the head several times, jumped down, ran home and left him. The mule stood a few minutes rigidly, then, looking around and seeing George at some distance from him, turned and followed, quite demurely. ☆ ☆ ☆

The Seventh Day

"The Federal and Rebel soldiers are not
twenty-five feet apart, both powerless
to inflict much harm. Each watches the
other, and dozens of muskets are fired as
soon as a soldier exposes himself above the
works on either side."

—CHICAGO *Times*

"The Federals were in rifle pits or behind
cover and in some cases near enough to
have killed a sparrow resting on the
Confederate works."

—CINCINNATI *Commercial*

"Sunday dawned clear and beautiful, yet its holy quiet was disturbed by the fierce storm of war, which swept over the city of hills, and thundered in angry surges around its whole circumference," Sergeant Tunnard wrote with some enthusiasm. "The houses of worship were deserted, and women and children sought shelter from the exploding shells in their underground habitations." He continued:

☆ ☆ ☆ The enemy had succeeded in establishing themselves directly beneath one of our parapets, above which stood the undaunted and heroic men of the Third Regiment. They immediately commenced undermining this portion of the line, with the intention of blowing it up.

As the sound of their voices could be distinctly heard, our brave boys began to annoy them, by hurling upon them every species of deadly missile which human ingenuity could invent. Twelve-pounder shells were dropped over the breastworks among them, and kegs, filled with powder, shells, nails, and scraps of iron. A more deadly, vindictive, and determined species of warfare was never waged. The chief aim of both combatants seemed to be concentrated in the invention of apparatus for taking human life. ☆ ☆ ☆

However, bulky or complex "apparatus" was but one instrument of life-taking before Vicksburg. The minié ball, as it had done in the two years of war, continued to claim by far the majority of casualties, killed and wounded. There were those riflemen, for that matter—hill boys or squirrel hunters from midwest farms—who had come to obtain a fierce joy from this human game.

Col. Manning Force, commanding a brigade in McPherson's 18th Corps, reported that a young sharpshooter, Private Ruggles of Company H, 20th Ohio Infantry, formerly a spy in the Union Army, had approached him, "quite dejected." General Grant had personally sent Ruggles one of the new Henry rifles as a reward for his information-gathering.

"Sir," the private said, "I ain't had no kind of luck today. I ain't killed a feller."

Meanwhile, little Lucy McRae was settled in one of Vicksburg's largest caves, located on an exceptionally high hill in the northeastern part of the city, uncomfortably close, however, to Sherman's pickets. She wrote:

☆ ☆ ☆ It had four entrances, dug in the form of arched hallways, coming to a common center, at which point was dug a room which was curtained off. In this cave my mother took refuge with her three young children, my father having such an aversion for a cave that he would not enter one. My two older brothers were in the army, one in Vicksburg, the other with General Lee in Virginia.

Mother took pillows, comforts, provisions and clothing into the cave with her. There were about two hundred persons in this cave, mostly women and children (some men, of course, too). The mortars, which were planted just opposite the city on the Louisiana side, kept up a continual fire upon us. All along on the ground in this cave planks were laid, that our beds might be made as comfortable as possible under the circumstances.

Mother had a negro girl who took care of me in my playtime. I remember her name was Mary Ann. She was short and stout and so black that her skin was glossy. One night, soon after entering our cave home, mother fixed our beds for us, putting my brothers on a plank at one side, and putting me near Mary Ann; but, spoiled and humored child that I was, I decided not to stay near Mary Ann, so proceeded to tear up my bed.

The Rev. Lord, of the Episcopal Church, and at the time rector of Christ Church, was suffering with a sore foot and leg, which was all bandaged and propped on a chair for comfort. He said, "Come here, Lucy, and lie down on this plank."

Dr. Lord was almost helpless, but he assisted me to arrange my bed, my head being just at his foot. The mortars were sending over their shells hot and heavy; they seemed to have range of the hill, due, it was said, to some fires that a few soldiers had made on a hill beyond us. Every one in the cave seemed to be dreadfully alarmed and excited, when suddenly a shell came down on the top of the hill, buried itself about six feet in the earth, and exploded. This caused a large mass of earth to slide from the side of the archway in a solid piece, catching me under it.

Dr. Lord, whose leg was caught and held by it, gave the alarm that a child was buried. Mother reached me first, and a Mrs. Stites, who was partially paralyzed, with the assistance that Dr. Lord, who was in agony, could give, succeeded in getting my head out first. The people had become frightened, rushing into the street screaming, and thinking that the cave was falling in. Just as they reached the street over came another shell bursting just above them, and they rushed into the cave again. Then came my release. Mother had cried in distressing tones for help, so as soon as the men could get to me they pulled me from under the mass of earth. The blood was gushing from my nose, eyes, ears, and mouth.

A physician who was then in the cave was called, and said there were no bones broken, but he could not then tell what my internal injuries were. Just here I must say that during all this excitement there was a little baby boy born in the room dug out at the back of the cave; he was called William Siege Green.

The firing continued throughout the night, and early the next morning a shell struck and closed one of the entrances of the cave in which were some sick soldiers. Mother instantly decided to leave the cave, and, calling Rice and Mary Ann, she gathered clothing and bedding, determined to risk her life at home with father. We left the cave about eight o'clock in the morning, having some distance to go to reach home. I was bent over from my injuries, and could not run fast, though between the shells we would make the fastest time possible; watching the shells, we learned to run toward them, to let them go over us if they would. As a great mortar-shell would come over with its rumbling noise, which I shall never forget, one of my brothers would say "Run along, poor little thing," and my remembrance is that I was indeed a poor little thing.

Father was horrified when he saw us, and immediately made an effort to secure us another hiding place. Within two squares of home was a small hill in which some parties had dug a cave, digging down into the ground so as to make the earth above too deep for a shell to pass through. A number of steps led down into this cave. Mother had a tent pitched outside, so that when the mortars did not have the range we could sit there and watch the shells as they came over. They were beautiful at night.

Mother and I were standing in the tent, she brushing my hair, when we heard the report of the mortar, heard the shell rattling over, and knew it was near. We looked at each other, and mother exclaimed, "That sounds very near; get into the cave!"

She did get in, but I had only time to jump into a small hole we children had dug out in the side of the hill when a piece of the shell came down into the tent, demolishing the wash-stand by which we had stood.

I felt the heat as it came down. Mother's face, white with anxiety for me, peeped out from the cave door. There I sat, stunned with fear.

One morning fire was opened all around the lines. The shot fell thick and fast. We sat, or stood, under the ground, looking at one another in speechless fear, for the booming cannon sounded terrible. It seemed so long that we were there, thinking that each moment would be our last. When we could look out upon the daylight it was with thankful hearts that we had been spared through that battle.

The Federal forces had Parrott guns on the Peninsula opposite the different streets, and could see persons crossing the street, and fire on them. These guns [mounted in casemates] they would run out from behind the trees, fire, and then run them back into the clump of trees so that the Confederate batteries could not play on them. The limbs of the trees would be cut, and fall in front or behind us, as we would cross the street, for we had learned to run between fires. ☆ ☆ ☆

And so distracted had Emma Balfour become during the past two days that she had to confess to her diary:

☆ ☆ ☆ There is no possibility of writing regularly. Several times I have attempted to write but been compelled to stop. We have spent the last two nights in a cave, but tonight I think we will stay at home. It is not safe I know, for the shells are falling all around us, but I hope none may strike us.

Yesterday morning a piece of a mortar shell struck the schoolroom roof, tore through the partition wall, shattered the door, and then went into the doorsill and down the side of the wall. Another piece struck in the same room and a third in the cement in front of the house.

Such a large piece struck the kitchen also, but we see them explode all around us and as this is all the harm done to us yet, we consider ourselves fortunate. Mrs. Hawkes' house is literally torn to pieces, and Mrs. Maulin's was struck yesterday evening by a shell from one of the guns east of us, and very much injured. In both of these houses gentlemen were sick and in neither case was anyone hurt. It is marvelous. Two persons only that I have heard have been killed in town, and a little child. The child was buried in the wall by a piece of shell, pinned to it.

Today a shocking thing occurred. In one of the hospitals where some wounded had just undergone operations, a shell exploded and six men had to have limbs amputated. Some of them that had been taken off at the ankle had to have the leg taken off to the thigh and one who had lost one arm had to have the other taken off. It is horrible and the worst of it is we cannot help it.

I suppose there never was a case before of a besieged town when the guns from front and back met and passed each other. The other day while standing on Sky Parlor Hill a shell exploded and pieces struck in the flag near the steps. This was from a mortar. Then a Parrott shell from the eastern side passed over us and into Washington Street between them. A shot from a gun boat missed the house batteries and struck the hill just below where we were standing. At that moment there was firing all around us—a complete circle from the fortification above all around to those below and from the river. . . .

I have quite a collection of shells which have fallen around us and if this goes on much longer, I can build a pyramid. I realize that we are a people yesterday when I saw seven hundred mules in the morning and eight or nine hundred in the evening driven beyond our lines given to the Yankees—because we have not the food to feed them, or are afraid to use it for that purpose. No corn is issued for horses, except those of officers in the field. ☆ ☆ ☆

MAY 25

The Eighth Day

"A dispatch from Mr. Fuller, the manager
of the telegraph at Memphis, dated late in
the night, says the Stars and Stripes float
over Vicksburg and the victory is complete.
I have held this message, hoping to get
confirmation, but the line has been
interrupted. . . . I think the wires will be
all right soon. . . .
—NEW YORK *Herald*

"Vicksburg is cleared for action, stripped
for battle, glaring defiance all around. . . .
Our flag flies hastily over the invincible
bluff, and Johnston is coming."
—RICHMOND *Enquirer*

Emma Balfour knew which flag flew over the city, although she had reason to wonder just how long it would be unfurled there. Facing her desk once more, she commenced:

☆ ☆ ☆ Monday, May 25. For the first time in a week there is comparative quiet. All night the mortars shelled and though they fell around and near us I slept at home almost soundly, after commending my soul and body to my heavenly Father.

This morning at five o'clock fresh firing commenced along the right wing and from the mortars but at this time there is only about a shell in every few minutes and the firing on the lines is distant. Yesterday afternoon we heard that Johnston had attacked Grant in the rear, but I do not know whether it is so. Oh! how we all look to him as our saviour!

The enemy are moving from our left [up the river] to . . . [positions down the river]. What is their object? None can tell. Whether it is to be more convenient to water or to throw their whole force against one point is only surmise.

In the midst of all this carnage and commotion, it is touching to see how every work of God save man gives praise to Him. The birds are singing as merrily as if all were well, rearing their little ones,

53

teaching them to fly and fulfilling their part in nature's program as quietly and happily as if this fearful work of man slaying his brother man was not in progress. The heavy firing gives us showers every day and nature is more lovely than usual. The flowers are in perfection, the air heavy with the perfume of jasmine and honeysuckle, and the garden bright and gay with all the summer flowers. The fruit is coming to perfection, the apricots were abundant and more beautiful than I ever saw them. Nature is all fair and lovely—"all save the spirit of man seems divine."

Later—General Lee and Captain Elliott have just left here. They came in and took lunch. They say the greater part of the [Union] army have left—they suppose to meet General Johnston. At any rate we have cooperation—rest none. Though they keep up sufficient firing to prevent our men having rest, still all are not needed, as when an assault is momentarily expected.

Thank God for this respite. They have left their dead thick in the field and General Pemberton is about sending out a flag of truce to ask them to bury them or to offer to do so for them. ☆ ☆ ☆

"The 'effluvia,'" Sgt. Tunnard explained, in confirmation of Emma's intelligence, "from the putrefying bodies had become almost unbearable to friend and foe alike," which resulted in the three-hour truce. Suddenly, "the usual music along the lines"—from musket and cannon both—was stilled.

Pvt. Ephraim McDowell Anderson, from Middle Grove, Missouri, with the 1st Confederate Missouri Brigade, at eighteen one of the youngest in his company, added:

☆ ☆ ☆ Some of the enemy's wounded lay in sight and died for want of attention. One poor fellow in full view of our regiment, about seventy-five yards from the works, although never heard to call out, yet was seen repeatedly raising both his arms and legs for nearly two days, when he became still, was dead, most probably from want of timely and proper attention.

Now commenced a strange spectacle in this thrilling drama of war. Flags were displayed along both lines, and the troops thronged the breastworks, gaily chatting with each other, discussing the issues of the war, disputing over differences of opinion, losses in the fight, etc. Numbers of the Confederates accepted invitations to visit the enemy's lines, where they were hospitably entertained and warmly welcomed.

They were abundantly supplied with provisions, supplies of various kind, and liquors. Of course, there were numerous laughable and interesting incidents resulting from these visits.

The foe were exultant, confident of success, and in high spirits; the Confederates defiant, undaunted in soul, and equally well assured of a successful defense. The members of the Third [Missouri] Regiment found numerous acquaintances and relatives among the Ohio, Illinois, and Missouri regiments, and there were mutual regrets that the issues of the war had made them antagonistic in a deadly struggle. As a general rule, however, the Southerners were the least regretful, and relied, with firm confidence, on the justice of their cause.

Among the numerous incidents that occurred, none seemed to afford more amusement than the one related of Captain F. Gallagher, the worthy commissary of the regiment. The Captain had been enjoying the hospitalities of a Yankee officer, imbibing his fine liquors, and partaking of his choice viands. As they shook hands, previous to separating, the Federal remarked:

"Good day, Captain; I trust we shall meet soon again in the Union of old."

Captain G., with a peculiar expression on his pleasant face, and an extra side poise of his head, quickly replied:

"I cannot return your sentiment. The only union which you and I will enjoy, I hope, will be in kingdom come. Goodbye, sir." ☆ ☆ ☆

And one of the "Yankee generals" who wanted to be "very civil" to General Lee, Emma Balfour was subsequently told, "invited him to go over and drink with him, which the General declined. Then he tried to converse in a very friendly way, regretting that during the truce they had shown bad faith in permitting the mortars still to fire in the city, said it was a misunderstanding, and he deeply regretted it. Emma continued to relate:

☆ ☆ ☆ The general knew this was not so, for they had signals and in an instant fire or stop as signaled but treated it as of no importance —told him oh! it was of no consequence. There was no one in the city but the women and children and the sick and they were accustomed to it.

He wanted to know then how long the truce continued (he knew very well it was until nine o'clock); General Lee told him it made no difference how long it continued, the purpose for which it was asked was accomplished so far as his lines were concerned and if he saw proper, he could withdraw his men and let hostilities commence at once.

He was only trying to be agreeable. He seemed deeply mortified, made many apologies, said the general misunderstood him entirely, then remarked, "General, your lines seem very strong!"

"Yes sir," the General said, "I think I can hold them."

Conversations occur nightly between friends on the opposite sides. Two missionary brothers held a conversation, very friendly—one sent the other coffee and whiskey. Then they parted with an oath and an exclamation from one that he would "blow the other's head off tomorrow." How unnatural all this is. The commanders object to this intercourse, but it is impossible they say in two armies so near to prevent it altogether. . . . ☆ ☆ ☆

Just off the Jackson Road, Maj. Samuel H. Lockett, Pemberton's chief engineer, recognized the ruddy hair and stubbled chin of General Sherman, standing nearby. Then he was more startled yet when a Federal orderly asked if he would accompany him to the not unfamiliar Union commander.

"I saw that you were an officer by your insignia of rank," Sherman asserted when Lockett was brought before him, "and have asked you to meet me, to put into your hands some letters intrusted to me by northern friends of some of your officers and men. I thought this would be a good opportunity to deliver this mail before it got too old."

Lockett then replied:

"Yes, General, it would have been very old, indeed, if you had kept it until you brought it into Vicksburg yourself."

"So you think then," said the General, "I am a very slow mail route."

"Well, rather," was the reply, "when you have to travel by regular approaches, parallels, and zigzags."

"Yes," he said, "that is a slow way of getting into a place, but it is a very sure way, and I was determined to deliver those letters sooner or later."

Then the two officers sat down on a log and, as Lockett recalled, "the rest of the time was spent in pleasant conversation." The Confederate engineer concluded:

☆ ☆ ☆ The General remarked, "You have an admirable position for defense here, and you have taken excellent advantage of the ground."

Intentionally or not, his civility certainly prevented me from seeing many other points in our front that I as chief engineer was very anxious to examine.

The truce ended, the sharpshooters immediately began their work and kept it up until darkness prevented accuracy of aim. Then the pickets of the two armies were posted in front of their respective lines, so near to each other that they whiled away the long hours of the night-watch with social chat. Within our lines the pick and shovel were the weapons of defense until the next morning. ☆ ☆ ☆

"At the expiration of the appointed time," Sergeant Tunnard postscripted, "the men were all back in their places. The stillness which superceded the fierce uproar of battle seemed strange and unnatural. The hours of peace had scarcely expired 'ere those who had so lately intermingled in friendly intercourse were once again engaged in the deadly struggle. Heavy mortars, artillery of every caliber, and small arms once more with thunder tones awakened the slumbering echoes of the hills surrounding the heroic city of Vicksburg."

The Ninth Day

"Corps commanders will immediately
commence the work of reducing the enemy
by regular approaches. It is desirable that no
more loss of life shall be sustained in the
reduction of Vicksburg and the capture of
the garrison . . . (By Order of General
Grant)."

—COL. JOHN A. RAWLINS,
ASSISTANT ADJUTANT GENERAL

As part of the "regular approaches" and possibly, as well, the "zigzags" to which Pemberton's chief engineer had alluded, a renewed bombombardment—sixty-five shells in forty-five minutes, by her count—shook Emma Balfour's house Tuesday "like a cradle."

☆ ☆ ☆ Once or twice we were sure the other side of the house was struck. They were at it again this morning but more along the lines from the river and the guns seemed nearer.

Yesterday there was comparatively no firing along the lines. General Lee and Captain Elliott came in to see us. They took lunch and seemed to enjoy it very much, poor fellows! It was the first time in a week they had eaten without an accompaniment of minié balls and Parrott shells. They seemed in fine spirits.

General Pemberton was here yesterday. He seems very hopeful. Says we can hold the place 60 days and even more by living on very short rations. We heard from the Yankees who were burying the dead that [Gen. Braxton] Bragg had whipped [Maj. Gen. William S.] Rosecrans [Commanding the Department of the Cumberland] and Lee had another battle and defeated Hooker, but we don't know whether to believe it or not. We hear also from them that General Johnston is in the rear but General Pemberton says he has had no news from outside since the 18th, Thursday week.

The Yankees, after leaving our left, are going to the right. Yesterday marched again in force to the left. Also many transports are seen crossing troops over and going towards Yazoo, but as we can have no scouts out there we know nothing of what is going on. We evacuated Snyders Bluff when we fell back to Vicksburg. ☆ ☆ ☆

Reporter Alexander Abrams of the Vicksburg *Whig*, critical of the winter and spring "laxity" of the troops, had turned from writing— since his newspaper's office had been burned down by arsonists in early May—to the defense of Vicksburg. The trained writer, however, maintained a day-by-day chronicle of what was happening in his city:

☆ ☆ ☆ The enemy, finding that our position could not be taken by storm, commenced mining. The reason of the enemy's coming so close to our works as to be able to dig under them was the want of foresight in General Pemberton's order prohibiting the expenditure of ammunition. Not being permitted to use the artillery or to return the fire of the sharpshooters, our men were compelled to see the enemy approach nearer every day, until they had worked their way to within thirty yards of our breastworks.

That this could have been prevented, was the opinion of many prominent officers of the garrison, who favored our throwing out a body of picked men every day to act as sharpshooters, and prevent the enemy from making his approaches. If this could not have prevented them entirely from approaching, it could have, at least, prevented their mining our works.

The enemy, having been permitted to approach as near as above described, went vigorously to work, mining our line of entrenchments at various places, the principal point being on the left of the Jackson road, held by the Third Louisiana, of Hébert's brigade. The means at our disposal for annoying them in their labor were limited to throwing a few hand grenades at their working parties, but these had little or no effect, as the fuses attached to them being very often too long, the enemy would pick them up before they exploded, and throw them back.

The enemy, at first, worked only in the night, but pushed on their operations with untiring energy and determination. Had the sharpshooting been less severe, some effort would have been made to drive them out with musketry; but the minié balls swept the line of entrenchments night and day, making it almost certain death for any of the men to show their bodies above the parapet of our works; at the same time, the greater portion of our artillery had been dismounted or disabled by the fire of the enemy. This was occasioned from the open condition of our works, the positions for the guns being all exposed, while the guns themselves were all *en barbette*, which rendered them easily dismounted by the fire of the enemy, and prevented our gunners from working them.

It was about this period that the hardships and privations of a siege began to be comprehended and experienced. From the smallness of the garrison, and the extent of our line, it required every available man to occupy the works. The troops were thus compelled to remain behind the breastworks and in the riflepits for weeks without removing from their crouching positions, and subject to the different changes of weather. Very often a storm would rise, and the rain come pouring down, drenching them to the skin, and they would be unable to leave the works for the purpose of changing their clothing, but were compelled to remain in their damp and unhealthy garments, until the sun shone again and dried them.

It is, therefore, no surprise that the list of sick in the garrison was large and daily increasing. Their food had to be cooked by details of men from each company, and brought to them at the breastworks, and they remained for weeks together without either washing their clothes or bathing themselves. Under this accumulation of hardships, they bore themselves manfully, and although it was apparent that the life they were leading would soon break down their constitutions, and weaken them beyond the powers of endurance, not a murmur was heard.

The cannonading and sharpshooting continued at times severely; while at other times it would slacken considerably.

Shut up as the garrison was, and completely surrounded by the enemy, we were completely ignorant of everything transpiring outside of the city, except on the safe arrival of a courier in our lines. As these were of rare occurrence, we remained in profound ignorance of the true state of affairs outside nearly all the time. As will be found in all places, rumors of every kind and any quantity were circulated among the garrison, tending for a while to elate them with the hope of a speedy relief. All of them however turned out false, much to the chagrin of the soldiers whom the reports had deceived.

In the night the pickets of both armies would abstain from firing, and would sit down and engage in conversation, with bragging of their ability to whip the other. Many of these interviews were very amusing, and the incidents that occurred were the source of much laughter to our men, who would show their wit at every opportunity, for the purpose of exasperating the enemy.

At one time, so familiar had the pickets become that they would meet one another on the neutral ground between the two armies and discuss the merits of the war.

The defense on both sides would be carried on with considerable vehemence, until argument failed on one side or the other, when they would separate to avoid, as a Yankee told one of our men who had argued him beyond reply, any fighting over the subject! As soon as this familiarity was discovered, strict orders were given to prohibit its continuation, and in a measure it was stopped; nevertheless, some "good joke" occurring between them would leak out now and then, but as the parties with whom it took place could never be discovered, the officers were obliged to laugh at the joke and leave the disobedient party unpunished. In these conversations the different motives which occupied the opposing forces and impelled them to fight would be apparent and form a striking contrast.

The conversation of the Yankee would be principally directed to the fine country they had gone through and its capacity for making money, while that of the Confederate soldier would be a defense of his country, and his determination never to go back into their accursed Union. ☆ ☆ ☆

The Tenth Day

"Damage to Vicksburg occasioned by the
fire of our guns is immense. He [a deserter]
estimates that at least 1/5 of the city is
destroyed . . . the names of 100 women and
children were reported at the provost
marshal's office who were killed by the
explosion of our missiles. Among these is
said to be the wife of General
Pemberton. . . ."

—CHICAGO *Tribune*

Most interested to learn this news would undoubtedly have been Martha "Patty" Pemberton herself. She had fled from her home in Jackson to Gainesville, Alabama, when Grant crossed the Mississippi at Bruinsburg. With her—in good health—were the five Pemberton children, including an infant.

Emma Balfour, the physician's wife, continued her chronicle:

☆ ☆ ☆ Wednesday. Nothing from the outside world yet. All day and all night the shells from the mortars are falling around us and all day from the guns around the fortifications.

No rest for our poor soldiers who have to stay down in the trenches all day in the hot sun. It is a most discouraging sort of warfare, the enemy shoot from their muskets and Parrott guns all day; if a head, even a hand appears above the breastworks it is fired on, and we do not fire in return except from artillery unless they attempt an assault.

Of course many of our men and many of our officers are killed and wounded every day. We do not fire because we have no ammunition to waste and must save it to repel assaults, but it is very discouraging to the men. I have stayed at home every night except two.

I could not stand the mosquitoes and the crowd in the caves. Most people spend their time entirely in them, for there is no safety anywhere else, indeed there is no safety there. Several accidents have occurred. In one cave nearly a whole family were killed or crippled.

Mrs. Luke and all their family survived and all live entirely in caves.

Last night I thought we would have to go somewhere, but at last worn out with watching we retired and slept as if we were in safety. Now and then when a shell exploded nearer than usual or the house shook more than usual we would listen for awhile and then sleep again.

The Doctor says he begins to realize now that we can get used to anything—to think of one's sleeping with these 12 and 13-inch shells, three inches in thickness, falling and exploding all around, now and then tearing a house to pieces and knowing that yours may be the next; seems strange, but so we are constituted!

Poor Mrs. Crump does not get used to it, and it is pitiable to see her at every shell jumping up and crouching with fear.

This morning the firing is heavy along our right wing. I send out buttermilk every day to General Lee and staff, and yesterday when Joe (Lee's slave) came for it I told him to go over and give my compliments to General Grant and ask him to send me some newspapers and to tell him not to shoot these shells so near here that they might break some of my flower pots.

Joe took it all in earnest and Nancy told me he said he would tell the General what I said; but he did not believe he would send him over there to those Yankees.

Major Grimes had a tent put up for me yesterday, close under the hill, a very safe place; but I have only been down to look at it. He wanted us to sleep there last night. In some parts of the town, the streets are literally ploughed up. Many narrow escapes have been made, but I have only heard of three deaths of citizens from shells.

Later—we went to see another gunboat fight, five boats from below and one a terrible monster from above engaged our batteries. In a very short time we perceived that the monster was disabled and a tug from above came to her relief. Later, men were seen to leave her side. There she drifted over to the Mississippi shore, and then arose the glad shout:

"She is sinking!"

Sinking indeed she was and there she lies under water except her chimneys and her horn! Those from below retired when they saw this, so the battle is over for today and we are again victorious on water!

There is a curious craft above which looks like a regular man-of-war from the distance we see her. She is up near the transports. I don't think any of them will be so anxious to try our batteries again. The impression is that this gunboat was trying to get to the fleet below to operate with them in a general attack. ☆ ☆ ☆

Earlier that Wednesday, Dr. Richard R. Hall, an acting assistant surgeon from Fairfield, Indiana, one of those aboard that "monster," the Union ironclad *Cincinnati*, was starting a letter home:

☆ ☆ ☆ Dear Anna and Mother: Again I write for the satisfaction of my loved ones at home and in this respect you will not charge me with neglect. I am done, I am not well this morning; my system is relaxed. It is so warm and suffocating in my room on the gundeck that I have been compelled to sleep in the turret over the pilot house. Sleeping on the hard floor has made me quite sore all over. I intend having a hammock prepared for me today. Maybe I will then rest easier—hope so. We did not run the batteries on the night that we expected.

Our orders were revoked and we became servant maid of all work. Sherman's divisions have silenced three of the enemy's batteries and Sherman has advanced and taken three of them. Today we are ordered to run down to Vicksburg and take a 200-pound English parrott (cannon with a rifled bore) that has been a great bar to our progress. It goes by the name of "Whistling Dick," a sobriquet given it by our boys from the peculiar noise its balls make as they hurtle through the air.

We have also to destroy a masked battery that holds General Sherman in check and shells our rifle pits that bar his progress. This masked battery has destroyed a great number of his brave boys; they have made two charges and both times have been repulsed. He says that if the *Cincinnati* will take the battery and shell the pits that he and his men will go into Vicksburg. Well, we will do it for him and give him a chance. The battle still rages at all points with unstinted fury. I am thinking there will be no stop until Vicksburg is taken or we are all worse than whipped.

It is very hot down here so I sleep on the hurricane deck for the past three nights. With the ethereal blue for my curtains, whilst the beautiful stars held their silent vigils. . . . Dear ones, we are now under way, where to I am unable to say. I must close my letter. . . . ☆ ☆ ☆

A "ball" penetrated the hull of the *Cincinnati*, "one of the finest ironclads in the enemy fleet," Sergeant Tunnard had learned.

☆ ☆ ☆ This combat was witnessed by hundreds of ladies, who ascended on the summits of the most prominent hills in Vicksburg. There were loud cheers, the waving of handkerchiefs, amid general exultation, as the vessel went down.

Notwithstanding positive orders prohibiting the fair ladies from needlessly exposing themselves to the flying missiles, they fearlessly sought some prominent position to witness combats whenever an opportunity presented itself. Many despondent soldiers gained renewed courage from the example thus given them by the heroic women of the Hill City.

This disastrous termination of the gun-boat fight seemed to satisfy the enemy in front, and they were quiet during the remainder of the day. The intention of this attack was for the gunboats to engage and silence our upper batteries, while General Sherman assaulted the works on the extreme left of the line, from the direction of Snyder's Bluff. The whole plan failed most signally.

A large number of articles from the sunken boat were picked up in the river, including hay, clothing, whisky, a medical chest, letters, photographs, etc. We often wonder if the surgeon of the *Cincinnati*, who so comfortably penned a letter to his affectionate wife as the boat neared our batteries, escaped unhurt. ☆ ☆ ☆

James M. Swords, middle-aged editor of Vicksburg's sole remaining newspaper, the *Daily Citizen*, publishing at irregular intervals from its beleaguered office on Crawford Street two blocks west of Dr. Balfour's home, now wrote: "It is a high honor to Colonel Ed Higgins and his command of heavy artillery [the Water and Wyman's Hill Batteries in this case] as well as to the country generally that this giant, the boasted monster and terror of the western waters, is now a total wreck in view of both friend and foe. It is one of those achievements, and when fully detailed in history will be appreciated by futurity as well as it is at present. . . ."

The Eleventh Day

> "Spades are once more trumps. We are
> erecting earthworks to protect men and are
> moving to blow the face out of one or two
> of the rebel forts that are unapproachable
> otherwise."
> —NEW YORK *World*

> "I never saw such a line of defenses as are
> in front of Gen. Sherman's lines. At some
> places our parallels are within 50 yards of
> the enemy's works, and our men lie down
> directly under the guns of the rebels. If an
> assault is made, with 10 thousand men
> they cannot help taking the city."
> —*National Intelligencer*

The weather remained clear, hot, and sweaty. A "courier," Sergeant Tunnard learned, succeeded in reaching the city with 18,000 rifle caps.

(Not all runners, nonetheless, got through with percussion caps. Federal troops had just captured eight Confederates purportedly carrying 200,000 of these essentials of infantry ammunition. Hidden in the bundles were crudely encrypted messages that turned out to be from General Johnston, east of the Big Black River, to Pemberton advising, "Bragg is sending a division. When it comes I will come to you. How and where is the enemy encamped?")

Tunnard continued:

☆ ☆ ☆ Heretofore, the Third Louisiana were armed with the Confederate Mississippi rifles furnished them at Snyder's Mill. These arms were almost worthless, often exploding, and so inefficient that the enemy boldly exposed themselves, and taunted the men for their unskilled shooting. On this day, however, the regiment was supplied with Enfield rifles, English manufacture, and Ely's cartridges, containing a peculiarly shaped elongated ball, and the finest English rifle powder. These guns had evaded the blockade at Charleston, and had never been unboxed.

Beside the rifles, every man was furnished with a musket loaded with buckshot, to be used in case of an assault and in close quarters. The men were so elated at the change in their weapons that they began a brisk fire in their eagerness to test their quality. The foe soon discovered the change, and there was a hasty retreat to the shelter of their rifle-pits, and the protection of their earthworks.

They wished to know where in the devil the men procured these guns, and were by no means choice in the language which they used against England and English manufacturers. Not a single casualty occurred in the regiment. As night approached there was the usual cessation of hostilities, and interchange of witticisms and general conversation between the belligerents.

The mortars seldom ceased their work all day, and through the still hours of the night spoke their thunder voices, and the concussions of their explosions shook the buildings to their very foundations.

There was a strange fascination in watching these huge missiles at night as they described their graceful curves through the darkness, exploding with a sudden glare, followed by the strange sounds of their descending fragments. The spectacle to the eyesight was quite agreeable, but to the other senses anything but pleasant. ☆ ☆ ☆

And now that there was respite these final days of May in the desperate, hand-to-hand fighting, Ephraim Anderson, of the 1st Missouri Brigade, took time to assess the moment, both as to the complexion of the Confederate works and the changing visage of the city itself.

☆ ☆ ☆ The artillery was mounted in parapets composed of timber and earth, with proper elevation and embrasures for the guns. On the river-side there were four batteries that occupied positions of this character. The guns were generally of heavy calibre, being thirty-two pounders, or thereabouts, and were either rifled or columbiads.

The rifled pieces shoot conical balls, and have the advantage of greater force and accuracy, and at the same time carry a longer distance, while the columbiads are smooth-bore, charged with round balls or shell, and are not equal in force or precision. Either can be used for the discharge of canister or grape.

The celebrated Blakely guns had not long before been brought to Vicksburg, and one of them placed in battery on the river line. It was found to be very effective against the iron-clad vessels, and discharged a steel-pointed ball with great accuracy of aim and extraordinary power.

The upper battery was a mile above, commanding the bend of the river, and one stood immediately on the edge of the town; two others were lower down, on the first slope of the bluff from the river. The number of guns on this line was about twenty-five or thirty.

Aided by darkness, many of the enemy's vessels had succeeded in passing with impunity. Calcium lights had recently been introduced, by the use of which the river could be lighted up in a few minutes almost as bright as day, and the danger of attempting to pass in the night was greatly increased.

The defences on the land side commenced at the river, a short distance above the battery which commanded the bend, and made a circuit of about five miles, coming to the Mississippi nearly a mile and a half below the town. For some distance on the south side, next to the river, approach with any considerable force was scarcely practicable, on account of the low and swampy character of the ground.

This line was covered by batteries placed on favorable elevations and at proper intervals; the calibre of the guns was generally from six to twenty-four pounders. Among them were a few heavy pieces, not more, however, than three or four, and all were in position in parapets of timber and earth.

At short distances between the artillery were rifle-pits around most of the circuit, which commanded to a considerable extent the points of attack. These were very indifferently constructed, and afforded insufficient and inadequate protection: the earth was not properly thrown up on the outside, and the ditches were altogether too shallow; at some points where pits should have been dug, it had not been done, and important positions were left exposed.

Our first employment was to improve all the defenses and keep a vigilant look-out around us, and to this end the work began. Surrounded by an immense force, five times our number [*Note*: Two times would be more accurate], it was necessary to be ever on the *qui vive*, and the soldiers with cheerfulness and spirit performed the labors and duties assigned them.

The city had already been bombarded, at different periods, for some months, by the fleet now lying in sight, both on the opposite side of the peninsula and below, at the mouth of the canal, and had also been attacked by forces from the land. The people had become familiar with the deafening thunder of the mortar-boats, and accustomed to the loud and terrific explosions of their monstrous and massive shells, many of which ornamented the gate-posts of the citizens.

The weight of these shells varied from a hundred and twenty-eight to two hundred and forty pounds; they were thrown high in the air from the distance of four miles, describing nearly a half-circle in their flight, and either bursted in large fragments hundreds of feet above the earth, or, failing to explode, buried themselves deep in its surface, where they frequently blew up and tore immense holes in the ground, or, the fuse having been extinguished, they remained whole and self-deposited in these silent and undisturbed recesses.

The streets were filled with excavations made by the falling and explosions of these missiles, and the people of the town had provided themselves with holes in the neighboring hills, around which they sought refuge during the enemy's heaviest bombardments. These holes, or underground houses, were of considerable extent, and frequently had several rooms in them, which were provided with beds and furniture—often carpeted—and were, for the time, the principal abodes of many of the inhabitants. ☆ ☆ ☆

Actually, how strong were Vicksburg's defenses?

Richard T. Colburn, a correspondent for the New York *World*, had the unique experience of imprisonment for two days in the city's "common jail" after a barge of Porter's flotilla, on which he had been a passenger, was sunk. He had been rescued by the Confederates.

"We believe," Colburn wrote for his paper upon his release, "the strength of Vicksburg in men, guns and works, and native conformation to have been overrated. The site is admirable especially for river defense. The batteries fronting the river are neither so numerous nor dangerous as commonly supposed . . . it is astonishing how long and how much the enemy has, here as elsewhere, befooled and thwarted us by an empty show of strength. It is admitted by those who have lived in and defended Vicksburg that it might have been taken at any time since the fall of Memphis [one year previously]."

The Twelfth Day

"An official telegram from General Joseph
E. Johnston states that General Stevenson
reports that hard fighting has been going
on at Vicksburg since Tuesday of last week
with continuing success and that our men
are confident and in fine spirits."
—RICHMOND *Enquirer*

"Clear and warm," Sergeant Tunnard observed. "The cannonading was again very heavy and continuous. A gunboat engaged the lower batteries without any material results. There were no casualties in the regiment."

Federal gunners stepped up their rate of shelling. For four hours the cannonade from land and river pummeled the city without interruption, ruining and setting fire to a large number of buildings and causing casualties among both civilians and soldiers.

The composition of the incendiary shells was analyzed by a *Citizen* reporter, commenting at the same time that "they have thus far proved ineffective in destroying any property." The article added, "these shells contain a small tin tube, about the size of an ounce vial, which appears to be filled with some ignitable fluid, and is wrapt around on the outside with several layers of paper. Upon the bursting of the shell, the top of the tube is blown off and the fluid ignited. When it falls upon the ground it burns with a blue, flickering blaze some two minutes and seems to possess intense heat, consuming the green grass within its reach."

On May 29, Emma Balfour heard that Pemberton had received word from a courier, luckier than those who had been captured, that Johnston and Loring, the testy First Division commander, with perhaps 22,000 effective combined, were coming to Vicksburg's relief. Both generals, together with most of their armies, had been separated from Pemberton after the battles of Jackson and Champion's Hill. Emma picked up at the same time an even more remarkable bit of gossip: "Lee had driven the Yankees across the Potomac and . . . burned Long Bridge (into Washington) and were in possession of Arlington Heights," adding:

☆ ☆ ☆ . . . in addition to this, he [the courier] brought us 18,000 rifle caps which we greatly need and says two million are on the way!

You may judge we were excited. This, the first piece of news from the outside world we have had in 10 days, was glorious. I had laughed at General Pemberton the other day for being gloomy and told him the ladies were not despondent, so he told Colonel Higgins to tell me he thought things looked brighter now. The Doctor invited Colonel Higgins and some of the battery officers and General Pemberton and a few others to come up to lunch, and such a thanksgiving for this good news and the sinking of the boat the day before! So we made merry over it.

Pemberton said that the Yankees if they could look in would not think that we minded the siege very much.

I have so many things to tell you all. Some very amusing letters which were taken from the trunk of an officer from the gunboat. It was the *Cincinnati* of 14 guns. We got various things from her.

General Lee took tea with us last night. The second time he has been in since he took the field. He told us he was afraid our house would be too hot for us today. He intended to open a large gun ["Whistling Dick"] he had put up on them this morning and as it is exactly in range of our house and they would attempt to silence it, we must look out.

Sure enough, after passing a bad night, from the bursting of bombs around us, we were roused this morning by the whistling of Parrott shells and I assure you we dressed hurriedly. They came so thick and fast that it seemed a miracle that none came in the windows or against the house.

I found the servants all in consternation as they had seen them striking in many places. One struck Mrs. Lawrence, one Mrs. Peyers, and after knocking the chimney off killed a mule in the yard. None have struck us as yet, partly owing to the protection of Mrs. Willis' house, but far more to the mercy of God.

Yesterday evening [Thursday] Mrs. Luke and Lee walked around during a lull in the shelling for Alice who had spent the day with me. While here the mortars opened again and they were very much alarmed. While the Doctor and Major Devereaux were standing outside the library window talking to them a bomb exploded overhead scattering pieces all around us. One struck Major Devereaux on the arm, but it was fortunately a very small fragment, one piece fell in our vegetable garden as large as the whole diameter of the shell—

twelve inches. They started home and while going up Cherry Street four shells exploded in front and behind them.

It is the last time they will come in this part of the town I expect. Just as many fall near them but they are in the cave and do not see them. We have been mercifully preserved so far. For an hour or more there has been no firing. I don't know what it means. General Lee told us there are twenty-four guns opposite his lines, and I can believe it from the specimens we had this morning. ☆ ☆ ☆

MAY 30

The Thirteenth Day

"We gave two chances for the women and
children to leave the city and they would
not accept the offer, but since we have passed
them so closely and shelled the city they came
with a flag of truce and asked to pass our
lines, but Grant told them that they were too
late. He only wished that there were 50
thousand of them and they would then
surrender. . . . I spent four days and nights
in front of the city just across the river,
opposite the court house, doing picket duty
and helping to run the mortars. . . . I was
close enough to tell a white man from a
black man and heard them talk in their
streets and yards. . . . Vicksburg is quite a
fine city and we are desirous of taking it
without destroying it if possible."

—LETTER FROM A SOLDIER AT A" CAMP
NEAR YOUNG'S POINT," PRINTED
IN THE WASHINGTON *Evening Star.*

Emma awoke Saturday to remark on the "comparative quiet yesterday
after the morning till 5 o'clock when the most fearful cannonading
commenced from the lines."

She continued:

☆ ☆ ☆ I never saw anything like it. People were running in every
direction to find a place of safety. The shells fell literally like hail.
Mrs. Willis' house was struck twice and two horses in front of her door
killed.

General Pemberton and staff had to quit it.

I made the servants crouch under the alley wall and all the couriers
got under there with them. I took my knitting and went into the parlor
as I did not think the shells would do me much harm, by the time
they had passed through three brick walls they would not hurt me,
but some gentlemen who came in when it was over told me I had
been very rash. However, I felt safe and I should feel safe there again.

73

It only lasted an hour and a great deal of damage was done in that time. Three persons in town were killed, all servants.

General Pemberton received another message from Johnston last evening; very encouraging, and this courier brought 20 thousand more caps. He [Pemberton] very kindly came in to tell me of it. I think he is inclined to be rather despondent, and very persistent hopefulness cheers him.

I hear I am a great favorite with him.

Yesterday evening Captain Elliott brought in Lieutenant Martin with a high fever for us to nurse. The Doctor thinks it was produced by the bursting of a shell so near him, as to produce deafness and a violent headache, and that he will be better in a few days. He is quite sick this morning, however.

Just after he came, the chaplain of [an] Artillery [regiment] came to ask if I would take Lieutenant [Charles E.] Hooker of their regiment who had his arm taken off by a shell and who is in a highly excited nervous state. He said he knew there was danger here from Parrott shells and bombs, but he heard I was the coolest lady in town, never discomposed by the shelling and he thought my calmness would keep him cooler and so prevent any future effects.

I could but laugh but I told him I would take him with a great deal of pleasure and do my best for him. However, he has not been brought yet and I fear he is too ill to be moved.

The shelling from the mortars was worse than usual last night. It kept me from sleeping and Lieutenant Martin passed a bad night. I hear this morning that a bomb exploded in the court house killing two men and wounding seven,* and in another house several were injured. I could hear the pieces falling all around us as the shell would explode, and once I thought our time had come. ☆ ☆ ☆

But Dora Richards was neither "cool" nor happy about any of the privations spelled by the siege. She kept at her diary nonetheless, in spite of the distractions from land and from water. She had already become "so tired of corn bread, which I never liked, that I eat it with tears in my eyes." She forced down the dry meal as she passed the endless hours reading "a lot of Dickens 'novels' or the 'rehash of speculations which amuses half an hour'" from the *Citizen*, selling at fifty cents a copy. She continued:

*This turned out to be no more than rumor.

☆ ☆ ☆ We are lucky to get a quart of milk daily from a family near who have a cow they hourly expect to be killed. I send five dollars to market each morning, and it buys a small piece of mule meat.

[Her mention was the first that mules were now being slaughtered.]

Rice and milk is my main food; I can't eat the meat. We boil the rice and eat it cold with milk for supper. Martha [a slave] runs the gauntlet to buy the meat and milk once a day in perfect terror. The shells seem to have many different names. I hear the soldiers say, "that's a mortar shell. There goes a Parrott. That's a rifle shell."

They are all equally terrible.

A pair of chimney swallows have built in the parlor chimney. The concussion of the house often sends down parts of their nest, which they patiently pick up and reascend with.

[In the cellar] H. said he must take a little walk, and went while the shelling had stopped. He never leaves me alone long, and when an hour had passed without his return, I grew anxious; and when two hours, and the shelling had grown terrific, I momentarily expected to see his mangled body.

All sorts of horrors fill the mind now, and I am so desolate here; not a friend. When he came he said that passing a cave where there were no others near, he heard groans, and found a shell had struck above and caused the cave to fall in on the man within. He could not extricate him alone, and had to get help and dig him out. He was badly hurt, but not mortally. I felt fairly sick from the suspense.

Yesterday morning a note was brought H. from a bachelor uncle out in the trenches, saying he had been taken ill with fever, and could we receive him if he came? H. sent to tell him to come, and I arranged one of the parlors as a dressing-room for him, and laid a pallet that he could move back and forth to the cellar. He did not arrive, however.

It is our custom in the evening to sit in the front room a little while in the dark, with matches and candles held ready in hand, and watch the shells, whose course at night is shown by the fuse.

H. was at the window and suddenly sprang up, crying, "Run!"

"Where?"

"Back!"

I started through the back room, H. after me. I was just within the door when the crash came that threw me to the floor. It was the most appalling sensation I'd ever known. Worse than an earthquake, which I've also experienced.

Shaken and deafened I picked myself up; H. had struck a light to find me.* I lighted mine, and the smoke guided us to the parlor I had fixed for Uncle J. The candles were useless in the dense smoke, and it was many minutes before we could see. Then we found the entire side of the room torn out. The soldiers who had rushed in said,

"This is an eighty-pound Parrott."

It had entered through the front and burst on the pallet-bed, which was in tatters; the toilet service and everything else in the room was smashed. The soldiers assisted H. to board up the break with planks to keep out prowlers, and we went to bed in the cellar as usual.

This morning the yard is partially plowed by two shells that fell there in the night. I think this house, so large and prominent from the river, is perhaps mistaken for headquarters and specially shelled. As we descend at night to the lower regions, I think of the evening hymn that grandmother taught me when a child:

> Lord, keep us safe this night,
> Secure from all our fears;
> May angels guard us while we sleep,
> Till morning light appears. ☆ ☆ ☆

Dr. Alison could conceive of "no safe place" in all of Vicksburg, as he wrote, "shot and shell crash in every direction. Occasionally the wounded are killed in the hospitals."

But even though the scores of surgeons on both sides were daily in peril of their own lives, their death rate was not high. Dr. Edmund Andrews, with the 1st Regiment, Illinois Light Infantry, wrote, however: "A few of the assistant surgeons who were sent under fire became so exhilarated at the music of the bullets as to expose themselves to an unnecessary amount of danger, but not a man of them proved cowardly."

*Probably the common, large glue-and-phosphorous matches originally manufactured in Germany and Austria and which had been in use for about three decades.

MAY 31

The Fourteenth Day

"You have heard that I was incompetent
and a traitor—that it was my intention to
sell Vicksburg. Follow me and you will see
the cost at which I will sell Vicksburg! When
the last pound of beef and bacon and flour
—the last grain of corn, the last cow and
the last man shall perish in the trenches,
then and only then will I sell
Vicksburg. . . !"

—PEMBERTON TO HIS TROOPS,
PUBLISHED IN THE
NATCHEZ *Daily Courier*

The concluding day of May, "the month of smiling skies and budding flowers," Sergeant Tunnard observed, "was clear blue overhead, the usual struggle around the works. Sunday brought with it no cessation of hostilities. Fourteen long days and wearisome nights had passed away and still no prospects of relief to the defiant troops. The mortar fleet concentrated their fire on the courthouse, near the central portion of the city." He continued:

☆ ☆ ☆ The constant daily fighting, night work and disturbed rest began to exhibit their effects on the men. They were physically worn out and much reduced in flesh. Rations began to be shortened, and for the first time a mixture of ground peas and meal was issued. This food was very unhealthy, as it was almost impossible to thoroughly bake the mixture so that both pea flour and meal would be fit for consumption. Yet these deficiencies were heroically endured, and the men succeeded by an ingenious application of the culinary art in rendering this unwholesome food palatable, calling the dish "cush-cush."

Another messenger arrived with dispatches and a supply of percussion caps. While the news from without seemed cheering, not an item of intended succor reached the undaunted soldiers who so heroically defended Vicksburg against the overwhelming forces of the enemy. ☆ ☆ ☆

And, "how unlike Sunday" it was to Emma Balfour—"Trinity Sunday, all nature wears a Sabbath calm, but the thunder of artillery reminds us that man knows no Sabbath—Yankee man at least." She went on:

☆ ☆ ☆ Mr. Lord at the particular request of Alice Luke and myself held service. There was not much firing, though, and the ringing of the bell only commenced service. There were thirty persons. I walked there and back, but I was glad to do so for the sake of worshipping once more.

The church has been considerably injured and was so filled with bricks, mortar and glass that it was difficult to find a place to sit. Next Saturday I intend sending out another petition. . . .

Two gunboats came up and commenced shelling the woods below here, and the mortars—all of them—opened in the city and kept it up all night. We soon perceived that we could not retire while they fired as they had changed the range and every shell came either directly over us or just back or front of us. So we made up our minds to sit up and watch, hoping, however, that they would cease about midnight, as they sometimes do and commence about light. But no, all night it continued to add to the horrors.

At 12 o'clock the guns all along the lines opened and the Parrott shells flew as thick as hail around us! Then there was commotion. We had gone upstairs determined to rest, lying down but not sleeping, but when these commenced to come it was not safe upstairs. So we came down in the dining room and lay down upon the bed there, but soon found that would not do as they came from the southeast as well as east and might strike the house. Still, from sheer uneasiness we remained there until a shell struck in the garden against a tree, and at the same time we heard the servants all up and making exclamations.

We got up thoroughly worn out and disheartened and after looking to see the damage, went into the parlor and lay on the sofas there until morning, feeling that at any moment a mortar shell might crash through the roof, though we felt comparatively safe from the others. ☆ ☆ ☆

That final day of May, two other writers were transferring their thoughts to paper. One was already famous in the world of letters and opinion-forming, while the other was unknown other than in his immediate medical circles.

Charles A. Dana, former abolitionist editor for the New York *Trib-*

une, telegraphed Secretary of War Stanton, for whom he was a special adviser:

☆ ☆ ☆ The siege progresses satisfactorily. Sherman has his parallels completed to within 80 yards of the rebel fortifications. He is able to carry artillery and wagons with horses under cover to that point.

McPherson's rifle-pits are at about the same distance from the forts in his front. On both these lines our sharpshooters keep the rebels under cover and never allow them to load a cannon. It is a mistake to say that the place is entirely invested.

I made the complete circuit of the lines yesterday. The left is open in direction of Warrenton, so that the enemy have no difficulty in sending messengers in and out. Our force is not large enough to occupy the whole line and keep the necessary reserves and outposts at dangerous and important points; still, the enemy cannot either escape by that route or receive supplies.

An officer who returned yesterday from a visit to Jackson with a flag of truce to take supplies to our wounded found Loring there with his force, apparently reorganizing and ready for movement. The number he could not ascertain, but thought it was 5,000 at least. Loring, you may remember, escaped to the southeast with his division after the battle of Baker's Creek [or, Champion Hill].

The gunboat *Cincinnati* was disabled in a sharp engagement with the enemy's upper water battery, on Steele's front. She was compelled by discharges of grape to close her bow port holes, and in endeavoring to get away, swung her stern around toward the battery, when she was so badly hit that her commander ran her ashore, and she sank in shoal water. Some twenty-one lives were lost. She may be raised and saved.

The weather is hot, but not at all oppressive. ☆ ☆ ☆

Then, looking toward his own future authorship, Dana scribbled in an ever-swelling ledger book:

☆ ☆ ☆ We had not been many days in the rear of Vicksburg before we settled into regular habits. The men were detailed in reliefs for work in the trenches, and being relieved at fixed hours everybody seemed to lead a systematic life.

My chief duty was a daily round through the trenches, generally with the corps commander or some one of his staff. As the lines of investment were six or seven miles long, it occupied the greater part of my day; sometimes I made a portion of my tour of inspection in the night. One night in riding through the trenches I must have passed 20,000 men asleep on their guns. I still can see the grotesque positions into which they had curled themselves.

The trenches were so protected that there was no danger in riding through them. It was not so safe to venture on the hills overlooking Vicksburg. I went on foot and alone to the top of a hill, and was looking at the town when I suddenly heard something go whizz, whizz, by my ear.

"What in the world is that?" I asked myself. The place was so desolate that it was an instant before I could believe that these were bullets intended for me. When I did realize it, I immediately started to lie down. Then came the question, which was the best way to lie down?

If I lay at right angles to the enemy's line the bullets from the right and left might strike me; if I lay parallel to it then those directly from the front might hit me. So I concluded it made no difference which way I lay. After remaining quiet for a time the bullets ceased, and I left the hilltop. I was more cautious in the future in venturing beyond cover.

I lived in General Grant's headquarters, which were on a high bluff northeast of Sherman's extreme left. I had a tent to myself, and on the whole was very comfortable. We never lacked an abundance of provisions. There was good water, enough even for the bath, and we suffered very little from excessive heat. [Toiletry was an especial blandishment for Dana, who had a massive beard to keep trimmed.]

The only serious annoyance was the cannonade from our whole line, which from the first of June went on steadily by night as well as by day. The following bit from a letter I wrote on June 2d, to my little daughter, tells something of my situation:

"It is real summer weather here, and, after coming in at noon today from my usual ride through the trenches, I was very glad to get a cold bath in my tent before dinner. I like living in tents very well, especially if you ride horseback all day. Every night I sleep with one side of the tent wide open and the walls put up all around to get plenty of air.

Sometimes I wake up in the night and think it is raining, the wind roars so in the tops of the great oak forest on the hillside where we are encamped, and I think it is thundering till I look out and see the golden moonlight in all its glory, and listen again and know that it is only the thunder of General Sherman's great guns, that neither rest nor let others rest by night or by day." ☆ ☆ ☆

The other writer, the unknown Dr. Charles Brown Tompkins, twenty-three-year-old surgeon with the 17th Regiment Illinois Infantry, in McPherson's corps, was becoming an almost daily correspondent himself, but on more personal chords. Nightly or whenever he could seize moments from his all-too-many patients, he poured out much of his heart to his bride, the former Pennsylvania schoolteacher Mollie Gapen, a raw-boned but equally emotional woman ten years her husband's senior.

"Since Dr. Stephenson's death (killed by a musket ball)," wrote Dr. Tompkins to "my dearest wife Mollie," in Lewiston, Illinois, "our boys have been more careful. I have my tent in quite a secure place now and it is only fun to hear the balls whistle over without hurting anyone. We have had killed of our Regiment, 5, wounded, 30. We are living very well here. We have very good potatoes, pickles and kraut or, rather, pickled cabbage, fresh ham as we prefer, dried apples and peaches, and biscuits and good butter. It is the first good butter I have seen down here. It is only 60 cents per pound.

"This morning from 3 o'clock until 4 an incessant roar of cannoning shook the earth and air, but since then it has been very quiet. . . ."

Dr. Tompkins' letters were answered in complementing detail and volume by Mollie. Thus far childless, she had the time to write and did so with a lonely passion interspersed with homilies:

☆ ☆ ☆ . . . the bird had fallen over in its cage and died unexpectedly from "a spasm."

. . . there had been "a strawberry supper at Eichelberger's," and the next night "auntie came to supper.

. . . "It is awful hot. I don't see how you can stand it down there!" ☆ ☆ ☆

JUNE 1

The Fifteenth Day

"A body of Yankees went upon the plantation
of President Davis and rifled it completely,
destroying every implement of husbandry,
all his household and kitchen furniture,
defacing the premises and carrying and
driving off every negro upon the place. The
plantation of Mr. Joe Davis, brother of the
President, was treated in the same way, if
we except four or five domestic servants
which the robbers left."
            —VICKSBURG *Daily Citizen*

(Davis, who had become President of the
provisional Confederate States in
Montgomery, Alabama, in February, 1861,
had long owned extensive cotton plantations
in Mississippi.)

Monday, June 1, arrived "clear and unusually warm." Sergeant Will
Tunnard and his regimental buddies "sought shelter from the sun's
scorching rays beneath the shade of outstretched blankets, and in small
excavations and huts in the hillsides."

Osborn Oldroyd "stayed in camp all day much to the enjoyment of
the boys. Sergeant Hoover and I got a horse and mule and rode down
to Chickasaw Bayou where the supplies for our army around Vicksburg
are received . . . if our poor foes could see our piles of provisions
on the river landing they might hunger for defeat. . . ."

And Captain Alonzo Brown of the 4th Minnesota Volunteer Infantry
Regiment reported a cornucopia from home: a box of preserved
"peaches." When the containers were opened, the "fruit" proved to be
whiskey—a beverage otherwise prohibited in the Union camp.

Ephraim Anderson, not quite ready to "hunger for defeat" and not
a recipient of "peaches," nonetheless *was* hungry for good food. He
commented on the progress of the indigestible pea bread:

☆ ☆ ☆ . . . a well-known product of several of the Southern States called "cow peas," which is rather a small bean, cultivated quite extensively as provender for animals. When properly and well prepared, it makes, what I consider, a very poor vegetable for the table, though some persons profess to be fond of it. Being introduced as a ration into the army, it was always our principal and regular vegetable; occasionally, we received rice and sweet potatoes.

There was a good supply of this pea in the commissariat at Vicksburg, and the idea grew out of the fertile brain of some official, that, if reduced to the form of meal, it would make an admirable substitute for bread. Sagacious and prolific genius! whether general or commissary—originator of this glorious conception! this altogether novel species of the hardest of "hard tack!" perhaps he never swallowed a particle of it. If he did, the truth and force of these comments will be appreciated.

The process of getting the pea into the form of bread was the same as that to which corn is subjected: the meal was ground at a large mill in the city, and sent to the cooks in camp to be prepared. It was accordingly mixed with cold water and put through the form of baking; but the nature of it was such, that it never got done, and the longer it was cooked, the harder it became on the outside, which was natural, but, at the same time, it grew relatively softer on the inside, and, upon breaking it, you were sure to find raw pea-meal in the centre. The cooks protested that it had been on the fire two good hours, but it was all to no purpose; yet, on the outside it was so hard, that one might have knocked down a full-grown steer with a chunk of it.

The experiment soon satisfied all parties, and, after giving us this bread for three days, it was abandoned. But it had already made a number of us sick. Peas were afterwards issued, boiled in camp, and still constituted about half our subsistence.

We did not really suffer for provisions, and got enough to live on sparingly. The corn having given out, four ounces of flour and the same of bacon were issued to us daily, with "cow peas"—about a quarter of the regular army rations. Not taking very active exercise, we managed to get along tolerably well; and, though I ate no peas, it cannot be said that I actually suffered from hunger, but some of the hearty feeders of the mess did. It was better, perhaps, for the garrison that short rations were issued, as eating heartily in hot weather might have produced a greater amount of disease than actually existed.

The Federals found out, by some means, through deserters I suppose, that we were eating pea-bread, and hallooed over for several nights afterwards, enquiring how long the pea-bread would hold out; if it was not about time to lower our colors; and asking us to come over and take a good cup of coffee and eat a biscuit with them. Some of the boys replied that they need not be uneasy about rations, as we had plenty of mules to fall back upon.

During the siege our brigade was held in reserve a considerable portion of the time, and was ordered wherever it was thought our services would be most needed, so that we occupied several positions, both in the ditches and in the hollows, in their rear, and were, at different times, over the whole interior enclosed by the lines, except the fortifications immediately on the river above and to the extreme left.

The grounds all over the enclosed space now bore the marks of battle: the trees around, near the works, were stripped of their foliage, riddled with bullets, torn and cut to pieces by cannon balls. Some large honey-locusts exhibited nothing but bare trunks, literally in shreds —the bark and all, save the stoutest limbs, had been clipped by the constant fire of the enemy. A large poplar, over four feet through, which must have been struck from top to bottom by more than two hundred cannon balls, had finally given way and fallen: it was almost entirely severed in a number of places, and shells were buried and still remained in its huge trunk.

This tree was about three hundred yards to the left of the Jackson Road, in a hollow behind a parapet and to the left of a short piece of stockade, in the rear of which was the position occupied chiefly by our regiment and the Twenty-Seventh Louisiana. A party of the Twenty-Seventh Louisiana built up a fire against this tree one morning, and several of them were stooping over and around it, frying their meat for breakfast in the blaze, when a shell buried in the wood was ignited, and exploded in their midst, about ten steps from the line occupied by our company.

Many were knocked down and I thought, at the moment, killed, as the shell bursted within three feet of nearly a dozen of them. But all got up except two—some with whiskers and hair considerably singed, and others slightly scratched. None had been badly hurt. The two on the ground lay apparently lifeless for a minute, when one of them came to, and had received no serious injury, though for the while stunned and senseless.

The other finally revived, but was severely wounded and sent to the hospital. It was a very remarkable incident, that a shell should explode in the center of a large group of men, and in the very faces of some, without killing any, and only wounding one dangerously, and he was standing near the outside of the circle.

There was a considerable quantity of rice in the town, owned by a private party, from whom we were in the habit of purchasing a supply to fill out our rations. One morning, a pot of it having been boiled, several of the boys were sitting 'round eating it, when John Hanger's spoon was struck while just in the act of putting it into his mouth, by a small piece of shell, which tore a hole through the spoon and splattered the rice all over his face. John quietly observed "that was cool," and continued to finish his breakfast.

When stopping for several days at the same place, we were accustomed to dig holes to sleep in during the night, and generally had a blanket stretched over, or a covering of cane, bark, or anything else that was suitable and convenient to keep the sun out in the day. They were easily made by cutting down about two feet into the side of the hill and throwing off to a level below, which made an even and smooth surface to lie upon, somewhat more protected and decidedly more comfortable than the natural face of the ground.

. . . it became so that we could find these holes at almost every place to which we were ordered, and were spared the trouble of constructing them. The regiment on one occasion laid for three or four days in pits of this kind, near the site of a house that had been burnt, and which had stood on the top of a hill about three hundred yards off.

Each morning we had been greeted by the crowing of a cock in that quarter, and, as we were not very bountifully supplied with meat, Joe Kennedy, now in our mess, and myself, concluded that he was a waif, and we would go up the next morning and take possession: we already indulged anticipations of what a splendid feast was before us, and the important matter, as to the style in which he should be cooked and dressed, was discussed and settled. . . . ☆ ☆ ☆

Anderson never caught his rooster, but, in trying, almost lost the seat of his pants to the two bulldogs belonging to the Irishman who also owned the chicken coop. Thievery was becoming far from an exception to any rule. Tunnard, himself on commissary duty, reported:

☆ ☆ ☆ . . . several forms could have been seen stealing away from the entrenchments occupied by the Third Regiment, as if bent on some mysterious mission. Not far distant, a commissary of one of the other regiments had snugly ensconced himself in a secure position near some deserted cabins. Some of the Argus-eyed boys discovered that his quarters contained more provisions than the "regulations" allowed. It required only a few moments for the discoverer of this fact to gather a few choice friends from the groups of hungry men to make a raid on the hoarded treasure.

Like a spirit, we follow their footsteps as they approached the victim of their wiles. They soon surrounded his quarters and watched his movements. He was preparing his supper. Savory bacon, and, *actually*, *"slap-jacks"* made of flour, with molasses to give them an additional flavor. Had he peered into the darkness, while thus cooking his fine meal, he would have seen eyes, glittering in the darkness like a fierce tiger's, glaring at him—eyes brilliant with the fires of starvation and hunger.

All unconsciously, he completed his cooking, ate a portion of his food, then carefully placed the remainder safely away for his morning meal. Alas! for the uncertainty of human expectations. After arranging everything to his entire satisfaction, the occupant of the tent laid down on his humble couch to seek repose. . . .

Imagine the surprise of some of the Mississippians the next morning, when they beheld the Louisianians bountifully supplied with delicious biscuits and bacon. . . .

A starving soldier is the very worst of all moralists, and it is as useless to expect the habitual robber to desist from plundering, when gold is placed in his way, as to anticipate that a hungry soldier will not steal food when others have. . . .

A successful "foraging" party was always welcomed with great demonstrations of joy, for supplies thus procured were generously distributed among their comrades. ☆ ☆ ☆

The Sixteenth Day

3 P.M. Washington, to Maj. Gen. John M. Schofield
        St. Louis
      (Commanding, Department and Army
        of the Missouri)
". . . send everything you can to General Grant.
Send those nearest and replace them from the
interior. It is all-important that Grant have early
assistance."

                        —HALLECK

"Our telegrams from the southwest still continue
to be of the most cheering character. The brave
garrison of Vicksburg is as confident and determined
as ever, and [Lt. Gen. Edmund] Kirby Smith,
with 10 thousand men, is said to occupy Milliken's
Bend, some 20 miles above Vicksburg. It will be
noticed that all the reports concur in their
statement that the Yankee losses at Vicksburg and
Port Hudson have been enormous. No wonder
that Grant calls for reinforcements."

              —RICHMOND *Dispatch*

It was a blistering Tuesday, unbearable as had been Monday and Sunday for the more sensitive Navy men, accustomed to some river breezes. "Admiral Porter," Sherman advised Grant, "with some of his junior officers, was here on horseback, the day before yesterday, the same on which I found you complaining of illness.

"I took the party forward to the trenches, the sun glaring hot, and the admiral got tired and overheated so that, although we proposed coming to see you, he asked me to make his excuses and say he would come again to make you a special visit."

The enemy "kept up a heavy fire," wrote Abrams, the former reporter for the *Whig*, "both in front and rear, from his mortars, Parrotts, and other guns, and his sharpshooters poured thousands of minié balls into our line." Abrams continued:

☆ ☆ ☆ The enemy's sharpshooters were all splendid marksmen, and effectually prevented any of our men from rising above the parapet on pain of certain death, while it was an utter impossibility for our cannoneers to load the guns remaining in position on our line, without being exposed to the aim of a dense line of sharpshooters.

Our line of works, as planned by Major General M. L. Smith, was as good as could be desired, but the execution of his plans was the most miserable ever performed by men claiming to be engineers. There were several faults in the construction of these works, the principal of which were: first, they were not high enough; second, they were not built sufficiently thick; and third, the bastions on which the guns rested were entirely too much exposed, and afforded no protection to the gunners.

There was a hill on the immediate left of the Jackson Road, which ought to have been occupied by our forces, as it commanded that portion of our works afterwards held by the Third Louisiana regiment. Brigadier General Louis Hébert, one of our ablest and most gallant officers, desired to hold this hill at the commencement of the siege, and before the enemy had invested us, but was prevented from so doing, we suppose, by order of his superior officers. This position appears to have been entirely overlooked by our engineers, or its importance was very much undervalued.

So badly were the works erected, that three days after the siege commenced the enemy had enfiladed us, and a few days after that, opened a fire in reverse. We were thus subject to a continual fire from all quarters. The number of pieces of artillery brought to bear upon our defenses, could not have been less than from two hundred and fifty to three hundred of all descriptions and calibres.

This large number of guns, keeping up a constant fire on our lines, naturally created an uproar almost deafening, and as a result thousands of shells were poured into our works. There was no portion of the space of ground in our lines but where whole shells and fragments of shells could be seen, while at the line, and about one hundred yards from it, thousands upon thousands of minié balls covered the road and woods. Enough of these little missiles could have been picked up in half an hour to have supplied our army for a day. ☆ ☆ ☆

Part of Washington Street had caught fire and blazed through the night out of control. There was some speculation that it had been kindled not by the bombardment but by enemy agents in the city.

"The mortar boats were unusually active last night," reported Seth Wells, "and part of the town was burned. It made a grand illumination."

On the other side, it was a far from "grand" sight. "The whole block from Brown and Johnston to Crutcher's store burned," according to Emma Balfour. "Only two houses left. It is the third fire that has taken place in that neighborhood and it is doubtless the work of an incendiary." Emma further reported:

☆ ☆ ☆ There is a magazine near and the burning up of that would ruin that part of the town. It was an awful and strange sight . . . [a] night long to be remembered in the annals of our little city.

As I sat at my window, I saw the mortars from the west passing entirely over the house and the Parrott shells from the east passing by—crossing each other and this terrible fire raging in the center. . . .

I have almost made up my mind not to think of retiring at night. I see we are to have no rest. They are evidently trying to harrass our army into submission. All night they fired so that our poor soldiers have no rest, and as we have few reserves it is very hard on them. ☆ ☆ ☆

Tunnard, agreeing that the cause must be "incendiarism," observed:

☆ ☆ ☆ The sky was overcast with dull, leaden clouds, the glare of the conflagration, the bombs' meteoric course through the air, the heavy concussions of the mortars, the sharp reports of rifled-guns, and the shrill scream of the shells, made up a grand and gloomy scene of warfare, during a siege such as is seldom witnessed. Captain J. Beggs, appointed Chief of the Fire Brigade, was promptly on hand directing the operations which soon stayed the progress of the flames.

There was the usual heavy cannonading at early dawn, and dusk. During the hottest portion of the day the enemy seemed content to seek shelter from the sun's scorching rays, but in the morning they exercised their skill by pouring a rapid and heavy fire into the breast-works. ☆ ☆ ☆

Dr. Alison thought that an entire "fine block on Washington Street" was destroyed before the fire "could be outed."

JUNE 3

The Seventeenth Day

"Fire as usual. We lose a number of men
each day. Last night, enemy was at work
within 150 yards of redan. Feel the want of
light balls; have no means of lighting up.
The nature of the ground, being very broken,
permits the enemy to work so near us; are
not strong enough to drive him away."

—GENERAL SHOUP

The third of June dawned "against the usual music of sharpshooting and cannonading." Sergeant Tunnard continued:

☆ ☆ ☆ Seventeen days and nights the fierce conflict has continued, and still no definite news of succor reached the undaunted troops who held at bay the powerful forces of the foe. True, reports reached the besieged, that General J. Johnston was concentrating troops at Clinton, with a view of succoring the heroic garrison of Vicksburg, yet it seemed a slender thread of hope.

The Third Regiment was becoming sadly decimated in numbers, yet the survivors fought with the same determined, unconquerable, valorous spirit that had always distinguished them. They had promised to hold that portion of the lines entrusted to them, and accumulating disasters unnerved not a single brave spirit or filled a single soul with despair.

The tremendous storm of iron and lead continually poured upon them was received with an indifference to danger worthy of the heroic self-sacrificing devotion that distinguished the Spartans at Thermopylae. Though their thinned ranks required an increased amount of exertion and labor, and consequently augmented the burden of their accumulated hardships, there were no complaints, a reckless disregard to peril, and a spirit of heroism manifesting itself by the men composing and singing, with harmonious voices and enthusiastic chorus, songs regarding their situation. What a strange spectacle! These unsheltered, half-fed men amid the din and uproar of a furious siege, thus manifesting a spirit of reckless disregard for their perilous surroundings. ☆ ☆ ☆

They *were* "half-fed," echoed reporter Abrams, who wrote:

☆ ☆ ☆ For a period of about five days after the siege commenced, the garrison was pretty comfortable, so far as food was concerned, as they were allowed full rations. At the expiration of that time, however, Major General C. L. Stevenson, who had been appointed Chief of Subsistence, perceived that the supply of provisions on hand at that time would not last many days, if the soldiers continued to receive the allowance provided for them by the regulations. The rations were then gradually reduced, until it reached the following small amount of food, issued daily to each man as rations for twenty-four hours:

Flour, or meal	4 ounces.
Bacon	4 "
Rice	1½ "
Peas (scarcely eatable)	2 "
Sugar	3 "

the whole making a total of fourteen and a half ounces of food per day, or less than one-quarter the amount of rations usually issued to the men as full allowance. This small amount naturally brought the men to the verge of starvation, and was entirely inadequate to supply the cravings of nature. Though the men felt that such was the case, and saw that, under this partial starvation, their strength would soon fail, all cheerfully submitted to the inexorable necessity that had reduced them to such a strait. ☆ ☆ ☆

He also noted he had expected "a second general assault on our works" during the past twenty-four hours. "Certain suspicious movements" had been detected in the opposing lines.

"In accordance with this," he added, "preparations were immediately made to meet the threatened attack, and to give the enemy a warm reception on his assault. The day passed, however, without their attempting anything more than the customary bombardment, except on the peninsula, where the enemy appeared to slacken their fire somewhat, not caring to strain their mortars too much."

And like so many of Vicksburg's residents, he continued to muse upon the origin of Monday night's fire. Almost certain, however, that those responsible were "spies and emissaries of the enemy in the city . . . as we were informed by a gentleman of reliability, that two or three days before the incendiarism narrated above took place, a man clad in the enemy's uniform, and to all appearance a stranger in Vicksburg, was observed walking about the city; several questions he propounded excited the suspicions of the party to whom he addressed them, and after answering them in an evasive manner, the party hastened to give information to the provost guard respecting the singular appearance of this man, and the suspicious questions he had asked." Abrams went on:

☆ ☆ ☆ A guard was immediately started after him, and after awhile discovered him walking up one of the streets. As soon as he observed them approaching him with the party he had previously questioned, he must have divined what they were coming for, for he immediately started off at a run, pursued by the guard for some distance, until he arrived at some deserted building, which he entered. When the guard arrived they went into the building after him, but he could not be discovered.

That he was a spy is evident, and we feel sure that he was well acquainted with the building he entered, otherwise he would have been captured.

The damage done to the city up to this date was small, when we consider the amount of shells that had been thrown into it. It is true that a great many buildings had been struck, but none demolished; all of those struck were still tenable, and were occupied by the different families during the brief moments that the enemy's mortars were silent. After the first excitement was over, the citizens became quite hopeful of the result, and from the exaggerated reports brought by couriers of the strength of Johnston's army, it was confidently believed that the day of relief would soon come, and that the siege would be shortly raised.

Not the slightest fear was expressed of the city ever falling into the hands of the enemy; not a man, woman, or child believed such an event at all likely to occur, but all anticipating the defeat and destruction of Grant's army as soon as Johnston arrived with the fifty thousand men he was reported to have under his command.

The same course of shelling and sharpshooting continued, without anything of importance being attempted by the enemy. They had now decided on a regular investment of the city, and determined upon making gradual approaches by means of their engineers and sappers and miners, until they could come up close to our works, when they would make another endeavor to storm our lines; if unsuccessful, they would then keep us penned up until starvation compelled the garrison to capitulate. That such was their idea we were repeatedly informed by their pickets. ☆ ☆ ☆

Grant's engineers were completing no fewer than thirteen approach trenches toward the Confederate positions, probably more than Abrams realized were under way. Countermining and flaming "thunderball" barrels of powder that were rolled down ravines annoyed, angered, occasionally killed, but did not stop the ever-encroaching Blue hordes.

Everything—not strength of numbers alone—was in the Union's favor these scorching days. Their officers seemed to know as much about what was going on in Pemberton's army and in the city itself as did the Confederates. The primary, visual information was gleaned through signal and observation towers, manned all day and night in spite of the perils from sharpshooters.

Nor had the Federal signalmen made any effort to hide their flag messages between corps positions or between Grant's headquarters and Porter's fleet. They relied on the encrypting of every dispatch. Unknown to the attackers, however, the enemy had already broken the cipher, having merely referred to Edgar Allan Poe's "Gold Bug" on the crude science of substituting numerals for letters. Thus the Union forces themselves held few secrets from the Confederates.

In this early period of the siege a private from the 4th Minnesota Infantry noted a slovenly dressed soldier exposed with far too much *savoir faire* atop a tower near the strategic Jackson road.

"Say!" he shouted, "you old bastard, you better keep down from there or you will get shot!"

The other paid no heed, but when the soldier started to shout a second time he was grabbed by an officer from the same regiment, Capt. Alonzo Brown, recipient of the "peach whiskey," who remonstrated:

"That's General Grant!"

It was true. The Union commander, who looked as disheveled as though he had slept in his clothes, possessed the further distressing habit of slouching around the front, often unescorted, wearing a private's uniform. He was incognito to the bulk of his own armies.

Signal towers were but one source for intelligence-gathering. More detailed information about the Confederates was obtained from the *Citizen* (commanding a rapt and increasing, if not necessarily credulous, northern readership), and from paid, semiprofessional spies as well as from deserters. The latter, disenchanted southerners, were surrendering each day in ever-mounting numbers to Federal soldiers, as well as sailors.

"Six deserters have just come in," Admiral Porter wrote Grant this Wednesday. "One, who has been in the trenches, says that if you were to fire more at night it would prevent the Rebels from working and resting. They are moving some heavy guns to the rear which they could not do if the artillery kept at work . . . we get about 15 deserters a day who all tell the same story—shortness of food and intention to hold out 10 to 20 days.

"Our mortar shells have given out but I hope to have a fresh supply in a day or two. Our mortars have killed a great many cattle of all kinds. . . . I would have been over to see you the other day, but after going over Sherman's works I was so sick I had not the strength to go farther. I will be up in a day or two."

The inhabitants of Vicksburg, however, were hardly aware of this shell shortage. Those engaged in tending the sick and wounded were especially sensitive to the continuing cascade of explosives.

"I have been closely occupied in nursing Lieutenant Martin who is very sick, and the bursting of shells near keeps him so nervous that he cannot sleep," reported Emma Balfour, who continued:

☆ ☆ ☆ We have slept scarcely none now for two days and two nights. Oh! It is dreadful. After I went to lie down while the Doctor watched every shell from the machines* as it came swishing down like some infernal demon. They seemed to me to be coming exactly on me and I had looked up then so long that I can see them just as plainly with my eyes shut as with them open.

They come, gradually making their way higher and higher, tracked by their firing fuse until they reach their greatest altitude, then with a rush and whiz they come down furiously, their own weight added to the impetus given by the powder. Then look out, for if they explode before reaching the ground, which they generally do, the pieces fly in all directions, the very least of which will kill one, and most of them of sufficient weight to tear through a house from top to bottom.

The Parrott shells come directly so one can feel somewhat protected from them, by getting under a wall, but when both come at once and so fast that one has not time to see where one shell is going before another comes, it wears one out. The general impression is

*Emma tended to use "machines" interchangeably with "mortars."

that they fire at the city in that way thinking that they will wear out the women and children and sick, and General Pemberton will be obliged to surrender the place on that account. But they little know the spirit of the Vicksburg women and children if they expect this.

Rather than let them know they are causing us any suffering I would be content to suffer martyrdom!

Some few timid ones started a petition last week asking General Pemberton to grant a flag of truce to send the women and children beyond the lines. He said he could not do it for an individual but if the majority of the citizens would sign it, he would do so. Judge Barnett who started it tried to get signatures but did not get one except the three persons who had gotten it up. I told General Pemberton I hoped he never would grant anything of the kind as we had all been sufficiently warned. ☆ ☆ ☆

(The policy or lack of one for safe conduct remained confused. Hugh Moss, for example, wrote the same day, "several women and children were crossed over the river today—their provisions having given out, were compelled to ask quarters somewhere else. The Yankees took them in charge. I hope they meet with good treatment.")

Emma would have no more time to write in her diary. The women of Vicksburg were desperately busy with the sick, wounded, and dying. Young Pvt. Ephraim Anderson himself recorded the increasingly critical hospital situation:

☆ ☆ ☆ As the siege rolled on, the enemy's efforts to reduce the city redoubled: the thunder and roar of artillery, both night and day, were incessant and the rattle of musketry was unremitting. The hostile lines gradually approached ours and the fire of their sharpshooters became more and more effective. We were losing daily many of our men, who were becoming very reckless and exposed themselves constantly; indeed, there were few positions near the lines that could be considered at all secure, and the ditches were about as safe as any other places.

The soldiers had become crowded in the hospitals and in them were seen the forms of women clad in simple, dark attire, with quiet steps and pale faces, gliding about and hovering around the beds of the sick and wounded. They seemed to know no cessation in their days and nights of watchfulness and care. Without noise—without display—meekly and faithfully they went forth upon their pious and holy mission, like ministering angels, carrying balm and healing to the poor soldier, cheering his hope of recovery or soothing the last moments of expiring life. These were "Sisters of Mercy"—a sisterhood of the Catholic Church.

Our hospitals being situated in the town and occupying the courthouse and other buildings were exposed to the fire of the mortar boats. Hospital flags waved over them, and Federal wounded were sheltered within, but still the enemy's fire was indiscriminately and mercilessly directed. Several of the shells fell upon and came crashing down through these asylums, and those already suffering from wounds, bleeding, mutilated and helpless, were slain upon their sick beds.

It was stated to me by physicians on duty there that this shelling caused the death of many not immediately and directly killed by the missiles. A wounded man is naturally nervous, and the constant explosions of these immense bombs around the hospitals and sometimes in them kept the inmates in a feverish state of excitement and constantly in alarm. They were confined to their beds, without the chance of getting out of the way or escaping, and were compelled to submit to the consequences of their inevitable helplessness. This, of course, irritated their wounds and increased their tendency to fever, and death resulted in numerous cases in which comparative repose and quiet would have effected a recovery.

Messages, I understood, were sent and humanity and the usages of civilized warfare were invoked, in vain: the wounded and sick occupants could be saved, neither by remonstrance nor by the yellow flag which waved above them, from daily and nightly subjection to this dangerous and torturing fire. ☆ ☆ ☆

JUNE 4

The Eighteenth Day

"The bombardment of Vicksburg continues. All
the guns in position opened fire at midnight and
continued their fire until daylight. The rapidity
of the firing was unparalleled.
"It is believed great damage was inflicted by
the fire . . . one of the rebels, a boy, came out
of the city 10 days ago, took the oath of
allegiance and was allowed to go home, 5 miles
back. He will probably be condemned as a spy."
—*New York Times*

Not many yards east of Ephraim Anderson's position, his hurt and
sick enemies experienced fears and anguish in their own front-line
hospitals that were surprisingly the same as those of the "helpless"
Southerners the Missouri soldier had described.

Mrs. Annie Turner Wittenmeyer, thirty-six-year-old widow and
mother of two children, from Keokuk, Iowa, was one of many who
bore such testament. Upon visiting the Union lines in connection with
her duties in administering hospital supplies and diet kitchens, she
wrote:

☆ ☆ ☆ There was little level ground on which to camp about the
lines. Excavations had to be made to get a level place to sleep. So all
the bluffs around Vicksburg were catacombed to afford sleeping apartments. No wonder there was sickness—no wonder Death held high
carnival on both sides of the lines. It was not only dangerous, but almost impossible to reach the little hospitals under the shadow of the
guns. Very many times driven at full speed I reached them, but it
was at great peril.

At one point I went down under the guns of the fort at one of
the most exposed places, with a carriage-load of supplies for the little
fort hospital under the bluff, just behind the heavy guns. I found
when I reached there that the position was so dangerous that it
would be madness, so the officers said, to try to get out of there till
I could go under the cover of darkness. But the afternoon was well

spent in making lemonade and ministering to the men who had been stricken down with fever and hardships.

The ceaseless roar of artillery, and scream of shot and shell; the sharp whiz and whirr of small shot just over our heads, the June sun blazing down upon us with torrid heat, and no shelter for the sick but the white canvas tents, perched on the sides of the bluffs in places excavated for them, the bank cutting off the circulation of air—were almost unbearable. How the poor fever-racked heads and fainting hearts ached amid the ceaseless din and the dust and heat of these little camp hospitals! One poor fellow, with parched lips and cheeks red with the fever that was burning through every vein, said, "I got a little sleep a while ago, and I dreamed that I was at the old spring; but just as I was taking a good cool drink I waked up."

I partially met his cravings for a drink from the well at the old home by giving him generous draughts of lemonade, but when night came on I had to leave him. . . . There was no cool water there to allay his burning thirst. One of the hardships of that long summer campaign was the lack of good cool water. There were some springs, and a few wells were dug; but at points water had to be hauled long distances. Think of thousands of men to be supplied—of the thousands of horses and mules, the great burden-bearers of the army, that must have their thirst quenched.

Most of the water for the use in camp was hauled up from the Mississippi River or the Yazoo, through the hot sun in barrels, and stood in camp all day.

During that dreadful day I sat down in one of the tents for a little while; there was a patch of weeds growing near the tent door. I noticed the weeds shaking as though partridges were running through them. I called attention to the matter, which made the surgeon smile, as he explained,

"Why, those are bullets!"

"Bullets? Do bullets come so near as that?"

"Oh, yes," he answered cheerfully; "they are flying around here quite thick."

"Do you consider yourself safe while in this tent? It seems to me the bullets are coming very close."

"It is considered very safe. The bullets fall a little short, you see."

All the while I sat there I watched the bullets coming over and clipping through the weeds.

Three days from that time an officer was killed while sitting in the same chair on the same spot where I had sat and watched the bullets shaking the weeds. ☆ ☆ ☆

To soldiers such as Will Tunnard, possessing robust health and a manifestly charmed life, the ever-magnifying daily need for food was of more immediacy than hospitals.

☆ ☆ ☆ The ration furnished each man was: peas, one-third of a pound; meal, two-thirds or five-sixths of a pound; beef, one-half of a pound, including in the weight bones and shanks; sugar, lard, soup, and salt in like proportions. On this day all surplus provisions in the city were seized, and rations issued to citizens and soldiers alike. To the perils of the siege began now to be added the prospect of famine. The gaunt skeleton of starvation commenced to appear among the ranks of the brave defenders.

It seemed wonderful that human endurance could withstand the accumulated horrors of the situation. Living on this slender allowance, fighting all day in the hot summer sun and at night with pick-axe and spade, repairing the destroyed portions of the line, it passed all comprehension how the men endured the trying ordeal. ☆ ☆ ☆

The Nineteenth Day

"... the surrender of the place will be a
mere question of time."
— JOHNSTON TO SECRETARY OF WAR
JAMES E. SEDDON, IN RICHMOND.

"The siege," wrote Osborn Oldroyd on June 5, "still progressing
favorably. There is joy in our camp for Uncle Sam has again opened
a clothing store, which we shall patronize, asking nothing about
price or quality. The boys cheered lustily when they saw the teams
drive in and heard what they were loaded with."

But there was not much jubilation in the Confederate camp, especially since civilians were themselves on the firing line. Sergeant Tunnard reported "a citizen and a little girl . . . killed in the city by a
Parrott shell from the breastworks. The gunboats above and below remained quietly anchored in the stream, evidently indisposed to make
any demonstrations after the warm reception which they had already
received." Then he mused, as an afterthought, "not a rumor was
afloat, for a wonder."

Perhaps it was the human's capacity for adaptation to the most dire
of circumstances that helped soldier and civilian alike to exist amid
the exploding Union shells. Many of the caves, for example, had been
fitted out quite comfortably with walls already carpeted against the
dampness or plastered with newspapers, the floors planked, and kitchen
facilities often available. Some boasted an eighteen-foot thick covering
of "loess soil," a clay-like substance, relatively easy to scoop out. Shells,
however, could blast down to a depth of eight feet, injuring and
deafening the occupants by their concussion. But against the swarms
of gnats and mosquitoes there could be no defense whatsoever.

Mary Loughborough, whose husband remained in Maj. Gen. John H.
Forney's division, had already learned to bake bread in her cave and
brew sweet potato coffee.

☆ ☆ ☆ Each day, as the couriers came into the city, M—— would
write me little notes, asking after our welfare, and telling me of the
progress of the siege. I, in return, would write to him of our safety,
but was always careful in speaking of the danger to which we were

exposed. I thought poor M—— had enough to try him, without suffering anxiety for us; so I made light of my fears, which were in reality wearing off rapidly. Every week he came in to make inquiries in person. In his letters he charged me particularly to be careful of the provisions—that no one could tell what our necessities might be.

In one of his letters, he says: "Already I am living on pea meal, and cannot think of your coming to this." One thing I had learned quite lately in my cave was to make good bread: one of my cave neighbors had given me yeast and instructions. I, in turn, had instructed a servant, so that when we used the flour it could be presented in a more inviting form.

. . . after breakfast, the shells began falling so thickly around us, that they seemed aimed at the particular spot on which our cave was located. Two or three fell immediately in the rear of it, exploding a few moments before reaching the ground, and the fragments went singing over the top of our habitation. I, at length, became so much alarmed—as the cave trembled excessively—for our safety, that I determined, rather than be buried alive, to stand out from under the earth; so, taking my child in my arms, and calling the servants, we ran to a refuge near the roots of a large fig tree, that branched out over the bank, and served as a protection from the fragments of shells. As we stood trembling there—for the shells were falling all around us—some of my gentlemen friends came up to reassure me, telling me that the tree would protect us, and that the range would probably be changed in a short time.

While they spoke, a shell that seemed to be of enormous size fell, screaming and hissing, immediately before the mouth of our cave, within a few feet of the entrance, sending up a huge column of smoke and earth, and jarring the ground most sensibly where we stood. What seemed very strange, the earth closed in around the shell, and left only the newly upturned soil to show where it had fallen.

Long it was before the range was changed, and the frightful missiles fell beyond us—long before I could resolve to return to our sadly threatened home.

I found on my return that the walls were seamed here and there with cracks, but the earth had remained firm above us. I took possession again, with resignation, yet in fear and trembling. My past resolution having forsaken me, again were the mortar shells heard with extreme terror.

This night, as a few nights before, a large fire raged in the town.

I was told that a large storehouse, filled with commissary stores, was burning, casting lurid lights over the devoted city; and amid all, fell—with screams and violent explosions, flinging the fatal fragments in all directions—our old and relentless enemies, the mortar shells.

The night was so warm and the cave so close that I tried to sit out at the entrance, George [a slave] saying he would keep watch and tell when they were falling toward us. Soon the report of the gun would be heard and George, standing on the hillock of loose earth, near the cave, looked intently upward; while I, with suspended breath, would listen anxiously as he cried,

"Here she comes! Going over! Coming—falling—falling right dis way!"

Then I would spring to my feet, and for a moment hesitate about the protection of the cave. Suddenly, as the rushing descent was heard, I would beat a precipitate retreat into it, followed by the servants.

That night I could scarcely sleep, the explosions were so loud and frequent. Before we retired, George had been lying without the door. I had arisen about twelve o'clock, and stood looking out at the different courses of light marking the passage of the shells, when I noticed that George was not in his usual place at the entrance. On looking out, I saw that he was sleeping soundly, some little distance off, and many fragments of shell falling near him.

I aroused him, telling him to come to the entrance for safety. He had scarcely started when a huge piece of shell came whizzing along, which fortunately George dodged in time, and it fell on the very spot where he had so lately slept.

Fearing to retire, I sat in the moonlight at the entrance, the square of light that lay in the doorway causing our little bed, with the sleeping child, to be set out in relief against the dark wall of the cave—causing the little mirror and a picture or two I had hung against the wall to show misshapen lengths of shadows—tinting the crimson shawl that draped the entrance of my little dressing room, with light on the outer folds, and darkening in shadow the inner curves;—beautifying all, this silvery glow of moonlight, within the darkened earth—beautifying my heart with lighter and more hopeful thoughts.

Whatever the sins of the world may have brought us to, however dark and fearful the life to which man may subject us, our Heavenly Father ever blesseth us alike with the sun's warmth and the moon's beauty—ever blesseth us with the hope that, when our toil and travail here are ended, the peace and the beautiful life of heaven will be ours. . . .

The mortar shells had passed over continually without falling near us, so that I became quite at my ease, in view of our danger, when one of the Federal batteries opposite the entrenchments altered their range. At about six o'clock every evening, Parrott shells came whirring into the city, frightening the inhabitants of caves woefully. ☆ ☆ ☆

By this time a cave had come to mean many things to the people of Vicksburg. To Dora Miller, wife of a Vicksburg lawyer, her cave, in addition to bulwark, was a place endowed with water. And to children a cave could connote a wonderland of adventure and imagination. Wrote Dora:

☆ ☆ ☆ I feel especially grateful that amid these horrors we have been spared that of suffering for water. The weather has been dry a long time, and we hear of others dipping up the water from ditches and mud-holes. This place has two large underground cisterns of good cool water, and every night in my subterranean dressing-room a tub of cold water is the nerve-calmer that sends me to sleep in spite of the roar.

One cistern I had to give up to the soldiers, who swarm about like hungry animals seeking something to devour. Poor fellows! my heart bleeds for them. They have nothing but spoiled, greasy bacon and bread made of musty pea-flour, and but little of that. The sick ones can't bolt it. They come into the kitchen when Martha puts the pan of corn bread in the stove, and beg for the bowl she has mixed it in.

They shake up the scrapings with water, put in their bacon, and boil the mixture into a kind of soup, which is easier to swallow than pea-bread. When I happen in they look so ashamed of their poor clothes. I know we saved the lives of two by giving a few meals. Today one crawled upon the gallery to lie in the breeze. He looked as if shells had lost their terrors for his dumb and famished misery.

I've taught Martha to make first-rate corn meal gruel, because I can eat meal easier that way than in hoe-cake, and I prepared him a saucerfull, put milk and sugar and nutmeg—I've actually got a nutmeg. When he ate it the tears ran from his eyes.

"Oh, madam, there was never anything so good! I shall get better."

The churches are a great resort for those who have no caves. People fancy they are not shelled so much, and they are substantial and the pews good to sleep in. We had to leave this house last night, they were shelling our quarter so heavily. The night before, Martha forsook the cellar for a church.

We went to H.'s office, which was comparatively quiet last night.

H. carried the bank box, I the case of matches, Martha the blankets and pillows, keeping an eye on the shells. We slept on piles of old newspapers.

In the streets the roar seems so much more confusing, I feel sure I shall run right into the way of a shell. They seem to have five different sounds from the second of throwing them to the hollow echo wandering among the hills which sounds the most blood-curdling of all. ☆ ☆ ☆

Willie Lord's cave, an "Arabian nights" of mystery and excitement, was "shaped like the letter L" with five separate excavations from the street terminating in a long central gallery, allowing a choice of refuge or escape should one area collapse. A "shorter cut" to this immense sanctuary—which could and several times did hold sixty-five persons, including wounded soldiers—was an overhead hatchway, a hole in a hillside with a ladder for stairs.

The vertical means of access also was responsible for keeping the minister's dugout "remarkably well ventilated." The air in turn enhanced the dryness, a quality not associated with most caves, which were humid, clammy, mosquito-infested purgatories.

Willie recalled:

☆ ☆ ☆ The entrance galleries at either end were reserved for servants and cooking purposes and the intervening galleries and inner central gallery were occupied as family dormitories, separated from each other by such flimsy partitions of boards, screens, and hangings as could be devised.

In caves of this description a common danger abolished the unwritten law of caste. The families of planters, overseers, slave-dealers, tradespeople, and professional men dwelt side by side, in peace if not in harmony. By common consent a narrow passageway was kept always open beside the tentlike dormitories, and in the main cave a central space was set apart as common meeting-ground. Here children played while their mothers sewed by candle-light or gossiped, and men fresh from trench or hospital gave news of the troubled outside world to spellbound listeners. Public prayer also was here daily offered for a swift deliverance from the perils of the siege. My father's duties as both chaplain and rector required him to leave the cave each morning and to be gone all day, and we only knew him to be safe when he returned at night.

To me, at first, before the novelty of it all wore off, this gnomelike life was the *Arabian Nights* made real. Ali Baba's forty thieves and the *genii* of the ring and lamp lurked in the unexplored regions of the dimly lighted caves; and the sound of a guitar here, a hymn there, and a negro melody somewhere else, all coming to us from among swaying Oriental draperies, sent me off at night to fairyland on the magic rug of Bagdad which is a part of every well-trained boy's dream equipment. But squalling infants, family quarrels, and the noise of general discord were heard at intervals with equal distinctness.

These discomforts, supplemented by the odor of stale food in the heavy, earth-laden atmosphere of the overcrowded caves, so offended my mother's sensibilities that, persuaded by her, my father caused a private cave for the exclusive use of his own family to be constructed in one of the hills behind the Military Hospital. Here, under the shadow of the yellow hospital flag which, antedating that of the Red Cross Society, was held sacred by all gunners in modern warfare, it was believed we should be comparatively safe. ☆ ☆ ☆

But the flag "did not fully meet the expectation," the cave's occupants sadly discovered.

☆ ☆ ☆ . . . whether it was because shells could be thrown into our little valley without endangering the hospital I do not know; but I am certain that if as many shells fell in and around the hospital grounds as fell above and around the cave, the hospital was far from being a place of safety.

Fortunately, a majority of these shells were of the smaller sort, with their force fairly spent before they reached us. If one of the huge bombshells from the mortar boats had fallen and exploded on the summit of our little hill, it would probably have put an end both to our cave-dwelling and to ourselves.

As it was, two of these iron monsters fell in a neighboring field about half a mile distant. Then, exploding almost simultaneously and only a few feet apart, they seemed to shake the very foundations of the earth. My mother, with my youngest sister, then about four years old, witnessed this double explosion. It tore a great hole in the earth, into which a team of oxen might readily have been driven, and filled the air with flames, smoke, and dust. Although horror-stricken herself, my mother said to her frightened child:

"Don't cry, my darling. God will protect us."

"But, mamma," sobbed the little girl, "I's so 'fraid God's killed, too!" ☆ ☆ ☆

This was, postscripted his sister, Lida, "the coziest cave in all Vicksburg and the pride of our hearts...."

☆ ☆ ☆ There was, first, an open walk, with parapet six feet high cut into the hillside. In one wall of this was a low and narrow opening overhung by creeping vines and shaded by papaw-trees. This was our side door. Here the rector smoked his coconut pipe, and the children made mud-pies and played with paper dolls cut from a few picture-papers and magazines that happened somehow to be among our belongings.

This cave ran about twenty feet underground, and communicated at right angles with a wing which opened on the front of the hill, giving us a free circulation of air. At the door was an arbor of branches, in which, on a pine table, we dined when the shelling permitted. Near it were a dug-out fireplace and an open-air kitchen, with table, pans, etc. In the wall of the cave were a small closet for provisions and some niches for candles, books, and flowers. We always kept in tin cups bunches of wild flowers, berries, or bright leaves which the children gathered in their walks. Our cave was strongly boarded at the entrances, and we had procured some mattresses which made comfortable beds. For a time we slept in the tent, and only used the cave for a shelter....

It was curious to see how well-trained the little ones were. At night, when the bombs began to fly like pigeons over our heads, they would be waked out of sound sleep, would slip on their shoes, and run, without a word, like rabbits to their burrows. In the daytime they climbed the trees, gathered papaws, and sometimes went blackberrying up the road, but never far, for the first sound of cannonading sent them scampering home.

We took into Vicksburg with us, besides bedding and clothing, a barrel of flour, a barrel of white sugar, some corn-meal, a few sides of bacon, coffee (Rio and ground chicory), tea, butter, and eggs. Of the sugar we made many a platefull of taffy to the music of minié balls and Parrott shells; the rest of the provisions fed the eleven during most of the siege. At the last we would really have suffered for food but for the kindness of a friend who furnished us facilities for buying absolute necessaries from the army stores.

While we had no actual communication with our friends, we heard through the officers and the rector a great deal that was going on in the town. Many of the citizens lived in caves, going to their homes as often as they dared. One young lady, spending a sultry night in her own bedroom, could not sleep, but got up and sat by the window; and while she was there a spent ball went right through her bed, crushing a bonnet-box and bonnet under it.

A mother, rushing to save her child from a bursting shell, had her arm taken off by a fragment. Another mother had her baby killed on her breast.* My own little brother, stooping to pick up a minié ball, barely escaped being cut in two before our eyes, a Parrott shell passing over his back so close that it scorched his jacket. There were many other narrow escapes and some frightful casualties; but, taking the siege as a whole, there was among the citizens a surprisingly small loss of life. ☆ ☆ ☆

Everyone in and around Vicksburg, friend and foe, seemed to be living a mole's existence. Colonel Bevier spoke of the Union troops who were:

☆ ☆ ☆ . . . approaching, like moles, through the ground, in parallels, pushing their sharpshooters to the front, who ensconced themselves in innumerable rifle-pits, and behind every stump and tree, and from the land-side kept up a constant discharge of hot shot, shrapnel, shell and grape, while "Porter's Bombs," from over the river, with hideous screeches, cleaved the upper air.

No safe place in all the corporation could be found except behind some of the parapets where the soldiers lay, and in the deep holes which the citizens burrowed in the sandy soil and occupied as residences; even some of these were invaded by unwelcome messengers, scattering death and destruction all around.

When we were "off duty" and gathered by our camp fires, the danger was as great, possibly greater, than in the trenches. On one occasion, Major Waddell and myself were sitting on the ground engaged at dinner. I leaned back for the purpose of extracting a toothpick from my pocket, just as a baby shrapnel came dancing over the hill and glanced slightly against the Major's temple, but strong enough, for all that, to send him to a hospital-couch for a month. The little piece of "gray goose quill," occupied as it was in a different mission

*Probably rumor, unsubstantiated.

107

from that which Cowper contemplated, saved my life, for the ball pierced the place where my head, but for that, would have been.

My brave comrade, however, when I visited him, humorously congratulated himself on getting into drier quarters and among quieter sleepers.

On the day before, as a matter of both safety and comfort, the Major and myself had constructed by excavation a joint bed, and this, filled with leaves and covered with blankets, enabled us to slumber like kings.

Towards morning a heavy rain submerged us, of which I was totally unaware until vigorously punched by his elbow, with—

"Dang it all, lay still, won't you! Every time you turn over you let in cold water." ☆ ☆ ☆

JUNE 6

The Twentieth Day

"The firing was kept up all of Monday. . . .
General Grant's numbers and position will
be absolutely impregnable in a few days.
Particulars cannot be given but they are of
the most cheering."
                    —WASHINGTON *Intelligencer*

"We learn that Grant's army is very short
of provisions and if this communication
can be cut the tables will turn on the
starving game."

                    JACKSON *Mississippian*

The morning "dawned quite clear," Will Tunnard observed.

☆ ☆ ☆ A few summer clouds floated lazily across the azure sky, and
the day eventually became one of the hottest yet experienced. The
city was rife with rumors, among which was the report of Johnston
approaching with succor. The story almost gained full credence by
the report of cannon being heard toward Big Black. The welcome
sounds were received with shouts along the whole line. Long, anxiously,
eagerly had the men been listening for the welcome signal, and now
felt as if relief had assuredly come.

There was much stir among the enemy's troops, and large numbers
began to move toward their rear, plainly indicating that danger menaced them at some point. The Federals appeared in numbers on the
opposite side of the river, firing into the city with long-range rifles
and also with several Parrott guns planted behind the levee. This addition to the means of annoyance by the enemy made it a very dangerous
undertaking for the pedestrian to travel along the streets.

Our river batteries immediately opened on the foe, shelling in turn
the woods and embankment on the opposite side, everywhere in range
of the guns. The Yankees were thus compelled to become very wary
in exposing themselves. The artillerymen armed themselves with Enfield rifles and repairing to the river bank, kept up a sharp fight
with them across the turbid waters of the stream. There were no
casualties resulting from this harmless long-range amusement. ☆ ☆ ☆

109

While across the lines, in his protected ravine, where he had set up his hospital tent, Dr. Tompkins was giving his "Dearest Mollie" the progress of the siege:

☆ ☆ ☆ ... we kill more sheep, cattle, mules and horses than anything else. After dark we went up still closer to their forts. We had one man wounded, severe flesh wound of the foot by our own shell; as usual, none hurt by the Rebs. Our artillery continues to shell the Rebs once a day for an hour or sometimes only half an hour and it must be a dreaded time to the Rebs. I suppose they have their holes in the ground to get into but someone must stand guard and picket. ...

The mortars shell the town at night. The day we were on picket after dusk I went up to the point where I could see the shells from the mortars. It was a splendid sight. First we would see the flash of the mortars, then the shell, like a star, would mount up like a rocket, only several times higher.

Ten seconds after the flash of the mortar we would hear the report. At about the same time the shell would begin to descend and increasing in velocity as it descends; just about as it reaches the ground it bursts. The explosion of the shell is louder than the report of a 32-pounder gun. The effect of the explosion on the inhabitants of the town can easily be imagined.

Every time a shell bursts the dogs in turn set up a terrible howling. They must be well supplied with dogs from the noise they make. ... ☆ ☆ ☆

Far to the north, where it was also a hot summer, Mollie herself was writing: "I do wish I could see you. If you were not quite so far off I'd make you a visit soon as school is out."

Another member of the Illinois medical delegation, Mrs. A. H. Hoge (the former Jane Currie) of the Chicago office of the Philadelphia Sanitary Commission, was herself becoming a familiar, heavy-set figure inside the Union hospital tents as well as in the trenches. This rather grim-faced woman wrote:

☆ ☆ ☆ The game of life was played on a great scale. Men lived and died with locomotive speed. The rattling of musketry, the crash of artillery and the thunder of continuous trains of army wagons, miles in length, made fit music for this war-life and pressed men forward without time or wish at look at "things behind."

The elements of nature harmonized with the scenes of this great drama. Here rains were torrents and left rivers and ravines in their wake. The shimmering rays of the tropical sun melted, blistered, and licked up the moisture of the valleys and hillsides, as did Heaven's descending fire the water in the trenches of Baal's altar. Winds were tornadoes, snapping the trunks of lofty pines and cedars as stems of pipe-clay.

Animal and vegetable nature seemed to partake, in a measure, of this intense type of existence. Evergreens grew to the dignity of forest-trees; even the scathed trunks of the sylvan monarchs were robed with graceful vines and mosses that trailed to the ground from their lofty branches. . . .

At Vicksburg, I was an unwilling witness of a southern tornado. At 5 P.M. I left the tent for the Landing to remain till the following day, as the threatening of the rebel outbreak was so serious that it was considered impracticable for a woman to remain in the encampment during that night.

The day had been clear, the sun scorching—its oblique rays were graceful as I entered the ambulance. In accordance with orders, the drivers took a back and thickly wooded road to avoid the wagon trains coming from the Landing. Within twenty minutes after I left, I observed a cloud of inky blackness just above the horizon. As it rose and spread impetuously, its rim was exquisitely bordered with a pure white fringe that floated in graceful beauty from the edge of the towering masses of cloud that soon veiled the canopy with darkness. The artillery of heaven blazed and crashed till my heart almost ceased to beat.

Even the stolid mules betrayed fear, brayed, plunged and swayed from side to side, threatening to overturn the ambulance. Suddenly, after a terrific peal of thunder, a deep moan, as from a lion's lair, swept through the forest. In an instant, huge trees cracked, twisted and were uprooted as though a mighty, but unseen hand, was plucking them for titanic warfare whose artillery was playing around us. We were on a rude bridge flanked by huge forest tree. Retreat was not possible, and an advance extremely difficult.

At this juncture I perceived a monster pine, slowly but surely bending towards us. Escape seemed impossible. Breathless and speechless, I covered my face with the blanket and bade farewell to earth. With the energy of desperation, the drivers lashed the brutes into a fearful leap that carried the ambulance its length ahead, and as the forest king stretched his great trunk across the spot we had just passed, he grazed the rear part of the vehicle sufficiently to teach us gratitude to God for this signal deliverance.

Three miles of timber were traversed on that terrific night before we reached the Landing. Although the tornado lasted but a few minutes, the tottering trees and broken branches continued to fall and made this ride one of the shuddering memories of my life. The soldiers who drove the ambulance, though terrified at the time, forgot it as soon as passed, and did not consider it worth repeating the next day when we returned to the tent—they were so inured to horrors. They had toiled up the bluffs of Vicksburg, in the face of cannon and rifles, with no protection but God's shield, and thought not of what was behind but pressed forward.

On a bright June day I visited the field-hospitals at Vicksburg, and was rejoiced to find them so clean, comfortable and well supplied. They were situated on a clearing, on a pleasant green bluff, with sufficient trees for shade. There were three long rows of new hospital tents abreast with accommodations for several hundred men, provided with comfortable cots, mattresses, soft pillows, clean sheets and pillow-slips—even mosquito-bars admirably arranged on uprights.

The refreshing air that rustled through the tents kept the atmosphere pure and fanned the patients with their welcome breezes. Experience had taught that hospital tents were more favorable to the health of sick and wounded men than even well-built and furnished barracks, houses or transports. Cleanliness, purity, abundance of fresh air, suitable and nourishing food were the best medicines for the army; and in proportion to their prevalence, the percentum of deaths was diminished.

In passing through those inviting hospitals, I noticed a swarthy-visaged man, with an intellectual face, sitting upright in his cot. He was a German, and in answer to my inquiries, informed me that he had been a Lutheran minister of the gospel. From motives of patriotism and religion, he had enlisted to do his adopted country service, and influence his comrades, many of whom had been the sheep of his flock. I asked him if, after two years' experience, he felt satisfied as to the wisdom of his course. He replied, "Entirely so."

He said he believed he had done more for the souls of men than he could have done in his home pulpit; that his example had raised a company for a regiment, and that he had done some good fighting for a glorious cause, and was not so badly wounded but that he hoped and expected to do more. He had the spirit of Luther, as well as his name, ecclesiastically. He added, if God should spare his life through the war, he meant to spend a year in travelling through the length and breadth of the land to tell what God and the Commissions had done for the army. . . .

Many weary days and nights I watched in this tent. They seem in the distance like ghostly dreams, and come back at midnight to haunt me. There was intense isolation, but no loneliness in that tent at the Chickasaw Bayou.

The muttering of delirium, in which sharp, quick orders were given, companies called out, men cheered and led to battle, grated painfully on a strained ear and aching heart. Huge insects, stinging and whirling round the single candle that flickered in the night air, green-eyed lizards, slimy serpents, hooting owls and flitting bats were companions as cheery and as welcome as Macbeth's witches on the midnight heath.

The trains of army wagons lumbering over the road all night long, within a few hundred yards; the neighing and braying of the horses and mules at an adjoining "coral," the crack of the rifle, sometimes of platoons of musketry, suggesting the rebels might at any moment, in desperation, cut their way through our army lines and sweep over the spot where our tent stood, the crash of artillery and screaming of shells as they poured into the doomed city forbade all silence, made night hideous and crazed the wounded patient's brain.

As I sat shivering and melting by turns, now wet with cold dew that pierced my vitals and anon steamed by the protecting blanket, veering from Scylla to Charybdis in vain efforts to be comfortable, I could but follow those deadly missiles in their fiery flight, from Parrotts, howitzers and mortars. My heart ached as I fancied the flight of the men, women and children who had refused to abandon the city when warned by General Grant before the siege. ☆ ☆ ☆

At this time there existed two principal types of hospitals within the Confederate lines: those for the sick and those for the wounded. The typical hospital was a converted residence, although almost everyone's home—Dr. Balfour's, for example—served as a ward or clinic for at least one or two ailing defenders.

Capt. Charles A. Brusle, with the 3d Louisiana, estimated a Vicksburg hospital population in early June of eight hundred, although he probably was conservative. He also believed that the death rate was soaring to twenty or more daily. Visiting one of these hospitals, Brusle saw: " . . . men with both legs off; some with an eye out, others without arms and, again, some who could boast of manly beauty and personal attraction rendered hideous by the loss of a nose or a portion of the face so as to be unrecognizable by their nearest and dearest kindred."

Still more graphic was the description of the wounded and the dying by William Lovelace Foster, Chaplain of the 35th Regiment, Mississippi Infantry, in a letter to his wife, Sarah Mildred, who lived in Starkville, in the eastern part of the state.

☆ ☆ ☆ I visited the Brigade Hospital where most of our wounded were carried, and since my business was now with the wounded and dying, I thought I could do more good there than by remaining at our regimental hospital, for as soon as the wounds were dressed they were removed to some brigade hospital.

The wounded were in this hospital which was called No. 1 and situated about a quarter of a mile behind our lines. The building where the sick remained and where the cooking was done for all was situated on a high hill, a beautiful residence.

The wounded were placed in tents on either side in deep hollows. As I entered one of these valleys, a most horrid spectacle greeted my eyes. Every tent was filled with the wounded and dying. There they lay, poor, helpless sufferers; some groaning from excessive pain, others pale and silent through weakness and the loss of blood.

As I approached the surgeon's tent, my eyes fell upon the bloody table where the amputations were performed. Upon it had just been laid a suffering victim—a man from our regiment whose knee had been shattered by a piece of shell. They were applying chloroform to his mouth and nose. He now becomes insensible and seems to rest in sweet sleep.

The surgeon, whose duty it is to perform the bloody job, rolls up his sleeves and takes a drink of brandy to strengthen his nerves. A tight cord is passed around the leg—then the gleaming knife cuts through the flesh all around—a flap of skin and muscle is turned back—then with a strong stroke the knife cuts down to the bone and next the saw with a quick stroke completes the job and the leg is removed. The artery having been tied with a small cord, the flap is then turned down over the stump and a few stitches complete the job.

The leg is thrown on the ground, where lay other limbs, hands, fingers, etc. All this time the poor soldier lies sleeping, unconscious of his loss or pain. He is then borne off to his bunk, where he must lie for weeks upon weeks, unless, indeed, he be carried to his grave—which was the case with more than half upon whom this operation was performed. This was the first case of amputation that I witnessed, and it made a vivid impression upon my mind. The poor boy did not get over the influence of the chloroform for that day; in fact, he was stupid and drowsy as long as he lived. He survived for seven or eight days and died.

On passing through the hospital what a heart-rending spectacle greets the eyes! Here we see the horrors of dreadful war! . . . The first sight that greeted my eyes was most appalling. There lay a man with the most frightful countenance, scarcely human so much disfigured he was. His hair, eyebrows and eyelashes singed off and his face blackened and burned to a crisp with powder. . . . He belonged to some battery—the caisson had exploded, scattering death and ruin all around. His groans were pitiful and low and plaintive. He can only lie upon his back. There he lies and there he must lie for weeks unless death comes to his relief.

Passing along still further on, without mentioning common wounds, I beheld a youth, not more than seventeen, with his eyes and face most uncommonly swollen. A ball has passed just under the eye, entering his face and lodging there in the bone, which could not be removed. Both of his eyes were closed—not a groan escaped his lips. With difficulty could he eat or drink—in fact he could subsist only on soup and fluids—he could not chew solid foods. There he lay day after day, week after week, so meek and resigned, while not a murmur escaped his lips. He could not change his position.

Still further along my attention was arrested by a strong, athletic, noble-looking young man who was wounded by a minié ball passing clear through his mighty chest. His chest was heaving and his heart palpitating so as to shake his whole body and his whole frame agitated by this fatal wound. What can manly strength and muscular power avail against such missiles of death? The strong as well as the weak fall helpless victims.

There lies another, shot through the jaw. His mouth lies open and his tongue is tied back. Here is another scalped on the head—his jaws are locked and he soon dies with convulsions. Another is wounded in a peculiar way—the ball enters his ear, passes but goes down through his shoulder, lodging in the vital parts of his body. . . . Here are several with their arms out. There is one with his whole underjaw torn off and his shoulder mutilated with a shell—he soon expires. Here is one with his arm and leg both amputated. What would life be to him if he could survive?

Why should I proceed any further? Every part of the body is pierced. All conceivable wounds are inflicted. The heart sickens at the sight. . . .

The weather is excessively hot and the flies swarm around the wounded—more numerous where the wound is severest. In a few days the wounds begin to be offensive and horrid. . . . Nor can this be avoided unless a nurse were detailed for every man—but there is only one allowed for every eight men. Those that can hold a brush in one hand must use it constantly and those that are helpless must suffer.

Never before did I have such an idea of the cruelty and the barbarism of war.

On Saturday there was a shower of rain. I was curious to know whether the enemy would cease firing during the rain. Instead of that they rather increased it, no doubt getting a view of our men as they would arise to adjust their blankets. The harder it rained, the more frequent their fire.

Now it is Saturday morning. On account of a severe cold and sore throat and general weakness through dysentery, I could not preach. But there is no Sabbath quiet here. War knows no Sabbath. I thought of the quiet Sabbaths at home and contrasted them with the noise and din of war that was now raging all around us. I thought, will I ever see those peaceful days again?

Here we were shut in by a powerful foe—prisoners. There was no rest for our brave men, nor did the enemy take any. It was a day of no spiritual comfort to any soul. How unnatural is war. ☆ ☆ ☆

Winchester Hall still languished through the cricketing heat in a third type of convalescent place—a rooming house in which he could be attended by his own family. Other Confederate soldiers, with injuries not mortal, also rented quarters and were nursed by friends or servants while they healed.

Colonel Hall continued to "suffer from the wound" he had sustained in the savage assaults of May:

☆ ☆ ☆ . . . for three weeks the pain was acute and unceasing. It was necessary to keep down the inflammation, and as ice was not to

be had Mrs. Hall had a frame made over and attached to the bed-
stead, from which she suspended a bucket, with a small hole in the
bottom filled with candle wick, so that when the bucket was filled
with water, it would drip on the injured limb. There was not an
hour day or night in which she did not examine and regulate the
drip, as the wick sometimes clogged.

There was no way of taking off the surplus water, so that it saturated the part of the mattress covered by the limb, and the limb, as
it could not be moved prudently, rested for some three weeks on this
wet surface, until the bone was knit.

Members of the regiment called frequently—Colonels H. A. Clinch,
D. Betzhoover, and Edward Higgins called also from time to time. I
read several novels while lying on my back, which Colonel Betzhoover
kindly loaned to me.

Our domestic life went on as usual. Shelling did not affect the appetite of the little ones, and Mrs. Hall managed to give them three
meals a day of camp fare, and every afternoon send them out for
a walk, during which, as a pastime, they gathered some of the metal
that a liberal enemy had scattered broadcast.

Twenty-one different specimens of shot and shell was the result of
their labors. One of my sons made a specialty of collecting minié balls,
of which he had two or three pounds, besides a spent one which
struck him, but without serious injury.

It would be an idle task to attempt to describe the horrid engineery
used against us day and night. Bloodier inventions could have come
only from the confines of the damned. The batteries on water and
land commanded the entire area within the fortifications. No spot
within the city and suburbs was safe or knowingly spared. Women,
children, and the wounded were exposed more than the soldiers in
the trenches. There were lulls in the storm of shot and shell, only
because the besieger required rest to gain renewed strength for his
diabolical mission.

The shelling usually was fiercest at dawn, one battery and another
and another would open, until every gun and mortar seemed on
duty—vicious and unrelenting as artillery covering an assault. The incessant fire of small arms about the same time led one readily to
imagine an assault was really made. This matinee was kept up with
rare intermission; while throughout the night, as well as day, there
was, at one point or another, more or less firing, with small arms
and artillery.

Sometimes, in the dead of night, just as an unusual stillness might be remarked, a sudden sharp discharge of small arms would be heard for a few moments, when the great guns would join until we were ready to exclaim:—"Hell is empty and all the devils here."

There was on the grounds, about the dwelling, a cave, which was a protection, perhaps, from fragments of shell, and here Mrs. Hall would repair with the children when the shelling seemed, as insurers say, extra-hazardous. The usual heavy firing at dawn would awaken me, but no one else in my little camp. I would arouse Mrs. Hall. She and a servant would dress the children with a deliberation that invited admonition on my part before they started, and they would remain in the cave until there was a lull in the shelling.

Twenty-first Day

"The works of the enemy are progressing
rapidly and begin to assume a formidable
appearance."
                              —PEMBERTON IN HIS DIARY

This Sunday was "very hot and clear," and as Sergeant Tunnard noted, "the mortars after several hours' silence, opened fire again, very lively. This Sabbath-day finished the third week of the siege, and still no hopes of relief. The men did not lose heart, but still kept in fine spirits. The members of the regiment fought today with renewed vigor, and a reckless exposure of their persons, killing and wounding a large number of the enemy. Heavy firing was heard west of the Mississippi, afterward ascertained to have been an attack on the Yankee forces at Milliken's Bend [and Young's Point] by the troops of the Trans-Mississippi Department."

The shelling was also impressive by the measure of Pvt. Stephen C. Beck, with the 124th Illinois Volunteer Infantry: "The continuous roar of artillery cannot be described. There were 300 field pieces on General Grant's line of works besides some heavy siege guns. There were two 84-pounders planted near General Logan's headquarters that were very active, playing on the rebel forts. . . .

"General Grant would visit us in the trenches every few days and would talk encouraging words to the boys such as 'we have got them right where we want them,' or 'it is only a question of time, they must surrender soon or starve. It is impossible for them to obtain commissary supplies. The time must come when the last meal would be eaten.' "

Not all of those, however, who came under the fury of the Federal army were actually in Vicksburg. Families were caught outside of the city by this huge, encompassing behemoth and kept there—those who were not as fortunate, perhaps, as the Lords or McRaes, who at least made it back to their homes, short hours ahead of the attackers.

"My father's home," recalled a young girl, Ida Barlow (Trotter), originally from Winona, Mississippi, "was not in the city but was in the Yankee lines. Being overage for active service, he was at home with my stepmother and the three smaller children—my oldest brother, Captain James Arthur Barlow having joined Lee's Army in Virginia and gave up his life at the battle of Malvern Hill."

She continued:

☆ ☆ ☆ Our home was surrounded by Yankees both day and night, as the headquarters of General Grant was only about a mile from our home. We were utterly in their power and in a constant state of uneasiness for fear we would be killed.

One morning a company, commanded by a Captain Chambers, halted at our gate, and asked if we had seen any "rebs." My father had seen none, so the march proceeded on toward the town. A few yards from the house they were encountered by a volley of shot from a company of our men who were in ambush in some gullies on the outskirts of the town.

The Captain was killed and many men were wounded. As a result— they were brought into the house, until ambulances could be sent for to carry them to the hospital. The Yankees were so enraged with my father, saying he had known the Rebs were hiding under the hill, which he did not, that they at once put the torch to our home and told my father that if he was on the premises at sundown they would hang him.

Leaving our home a mass of smouldering ashes, we went bareheaded with nothing except what we had on—my father even being without a coat—to our grandfather's.

All the provisions they could find, all the stock and fowls and the gardens were taken, orchards and growing fields had been turned into pastures for their horses. We drew our rations just like the soldiers did (and awful living it was too) fat pickled pork, hardtack so old it had bugs in it, a little flour and coffee.

My grandmother soaked the hardtack in water overnight to soften it, then fried it in the grease that came out of the meat and drank the coffee without sugar.

Inside the city it was worse a thousand times. The soldiers who were fighting night and day and the inhabitants who were packed away in the caves like rats in a hole made no murmur—the brave creatures were so intent upon subduing the enemy that they made no complaint, every man, woman and child giving aid to rout the destroyers of their life, home, peace and liberty. So they were exposed to burning suns, drenching rains, fogs, dews, in fact were at the complete mercy of the elements.

They were cut off from all help as the city was surrounded on all sides by the enemy, but even if it had not been there was nothing [of supplies] in the surrounding country to send to them.

Hunger and starvation was the inevitable, as everything had been eaten that would sustain life. Fowls, cattle, horses, mules, dogs, cats, frogs, or any living thing in reach, except the gaunt human creatures who stared at one another with bloodshot eyes and parched lips.

During all these days and nights, we in our homes were in mortal dread, and it would take a book instead of the few pages I am permitted to write to tell of our varied experiences. We were in the Yankee lines outside the city, but day after day the flare and boom of cannon and the whizzing balls were our constant companion.

One day the advance guard came up and ordered us to vacate the house as the line of battle would be formed through our yard. My grandmother and father refused to go, and my dear grandmother took her knitting, sat on the front gallery, and said, "Come on gentlemen—I will die where I have lived."

The line of battle was, however, placed just below our garden, and we sat in the house and saw the trees cut into shreds, and cannonballs cut through the tops of the houses. We heard the bellowing of the great guns, and heard the screams of the frantic and wounded men.

After the battle was over and our home was filled with the wounded, right busy was every member of the family obeying orders from the surgeon and administering to the needs of the suffering. My grandmother had hid everything in the house and storerooms that she could possibly hide, and curious were the places in which she secreted them.

She had a few shingles taken from the roof, and had many things put in on the ceiling. She had all the silver and jewelry buried in boxes under the house, and to keep some meat where we could get it to eat, she put two mattresses on a bed and placed a layer of bacon and hams between them.

She had my aunt, a Mrs. Hall (who was fond of lying down and reading) to undress and feign sickness, and it was my duty to take the great peafowl fly brush used in the dining room and keep the flies from off the make-believe patient—who spent her time patiently reading novels.

My cousin, Miss Elizabeth Read, was, however, not so patient, and spent her time doing all she could to aggravate the Yankees and kept the older members of the family in a constant state of uneasiness for fear they would kill us or burn the house as a result of our cousin's attacks upon the enemy with her tongue.

One night a little servant girl came in and said "Miss Bettie, dem dar Yankees is a sleeping on your piano," whereupon she bounced in the parlor and demanded them to dismount. Several fellows had stretched themselves upon the great square piano for a comfortable nap.

A young officer got up and said, "We will get down if you will come and play for us."

She said, "I will not play for you, but I will play for these Confederate prisoners I see you have here."

So, while she was playing, the handsome fellow came and turned the music for her. She noticed that he wore a beautiful diamond ring, and told him she knew he had stolen it from some Southern girl. He held out his finger and said, "You can have it if you can get it off my finger."

She said, "Give me your knife." He did so, and she whacked it with the knife and the blood flew.

He said, "Why I believe you would kill me if you could."

She told him no, and he unbuckled his belt, handed her his pistol and said, "Now you have the chance." But just then my aunt passed the door and screamed when she saw the pistol. ☆ ☆ ☆

JUNE 8

Twenty-second Day

> "Vicksburg is closely invested. . . . I will make
> a waste of all the country I can between
> the two rivers [the Big Black and the
> Yazoo].
>
> — GRANT TO HALLECK

"Truly," observed Henry Ginder, a civilian construction engineer employed by Pemberton's army, "we are surrounded by a wall of fire. The atmosphere is smoky and filled with the sulphurous smell of gunpowder." He continued, to his wife in New Orleans:

☆ ☆ ☆ Three weeks this day since we were shut up in this place. I should never have believed that we would have been left so long without assistance. I do not blame your outsiders (I don't believe it's your fault, my darling), for I believe that the powers that be have a clear idea of the importance of holding this place, indeed I think this very knowledge is what makes Johnston act so slowly; he wishes to run no risks but makes a sure thing of it by making all due preparations.

Our poor men have now been lying three weeks in the trenches without relief, day and night, the iron hail falling on them by day and night; and every day some are killed or wounded. Nor have they much to eat, our cornmeal is nearly out. We have plenty of beans and rice, and an attempt was made to make bread of these three articles mentioned, but the soldiers could not eat the mixture. I sat on the front porch of our house last night and observed the bright flash of the mortars as they vomited forth their dreadful progeny which rose and burned through the air like a firefly, until a more vivid flash and a louder report told that the fuse had communicated with the powder inside the shell and which was given "to stand from under." Then I sat on the back gallery and observed the flashes round the horizon, sometimes a shell whizzing past looking like a meteor.

They are plowing up the land with their deadly missiles and sowing it with gunpowder. Sometimes the powder falls around us, and sounds like a shower of rain among the trees. We are lulled to sleep by a lullaby of roaring cannon and bursting shells, and in the morning the same sounds take the place to our ears of birds singing and chanticleer's clear ring.

We have had no couriers for many days but we hear that the Yankees have captured many, each one having at least 10,000 caps, from which they know we are short of that important article. I may have mentioned this in a previous letter for I never have read one ever since it was written. I write without painstaking for I may be writing for the Yankees. (I meet but a few acquaintances here; yesterday I saw and spoke to Capt. Bredow, and also to Symon Berry who is a member of Wilkins' Battery).

Four of my magazines are finished and many hundreds of thousands of cartridges removed into them for which I am right glad, for hitherto they have been in a wooden house, through which two shells passed knocking the powder right and left. If they had exploded the loss would have been alarming, if not fatal.

The weather is growing so hot it fairly makes one dizzy to remain in the sun long, particularly on these dusty, white-looking sands where I breathe nothing but dust which fills my ears, eyes, nose, hair, everything. I got me two pairs of drawers but could obtain no undershirts and my old ones are all to pieces.

But I am hoping to see you soon, my darling, which consoles me for all discomforts. I wonder if you are feeling easy, trusting in our Heavenly Father. I myself have been too busy to feel as miserable as I have been. Do you write to me as I do to you? You are not very prolific in describing your feelings afterwards, and if you have not written I shall never know very clearly how you have felt.

Give my love to Cousin Mary, her husband, their family, also to Aunt Sally, their family and all other friends.

Your loving husband. ☆ ☆ ☆

And another lonely married man, Dr. Tompkins, was back at his portfolio, following a brief, illegal meeting with the enemy "halfway" in no-man's-land:

☆ ☆ ☆ . . . they said we had them penned in but they still had hope as strong as the first day they went in there that they would raise the siege after awhile and that we would not get Vicksburg. They say they have a hard time in Vicksburg. The shells from the mortars, when they strike the ground without bursting, go in 15 feet. If they strike a two-story house—6 by 25—they demolish it completely.

Today a deserter came out and he says Jeff Davis is in Vicksburg. He says we may keep him under guard and when we go into Vicksburg if Jeff is not there we may shoot him—the prisoner. Only a few believe the story, however.

It has been awful hot here the last three or four days. I never saw it so hot before any place as it was in the pits yesterday. ☆ ☆ ☆

"The struggle," continued Will Tunnard, "raged with unabated fury. The enemy's lines were slowly but surely approaching nearer to our own breastworks, and the struggle was daily becoming more fierce and deadly. The Federals procured a car-frame, which they placed on wheels, loading it with cotton-bales. They pushed this along the Jackson Road in front of the breastworks held by our Third Regiment. Protected by this novel, movable shelter, they constructed their works with impunity, and with almost the certainty of eventually reaching our entrenchments. Rifles had no effect on the cotton-bales, and there was not a single piece of artillery to batter them down. They were not a hundred yards from the regiment, and the men could only quietly watch their operations, and anxiously await the approaching hand-to-hand struggle."

Sergeant Tunnard continued:

☆ ☆ ☆ There was no shrinking or quailing. Danger had long since ceased to cause any fear, and fighting was a recreation and pastime with the majority of the men. Exploding shells and whistling bullets attracted but little notice. Even death had become so familiar that the fall of a comrade was looked upon with almost stoical indifference; eliciting, perhaps, a monosyllabic expression of pity, and most generally the remark, "I wonder who will be the next one."

Men are not naturally indifferent to danger, nor do their hearts usually exhibit such stoical indifference to human agony and suffering; yet the occurrence of daily scenes of horror and bloodshed, through which they passed, the shadow of the angel of death constantly hovering over them, made them undisturbed spectators of every occurrence; making the most of to-day, heedless of the morrow.

Though constantly threatened with death, they pursued with eagerness limited occasions for amusement. The song and jest went around, fun actually being coined from the danger which some comrade escaped, or attempted to nimbly dodge. ☆ ☆ ☆

The children were quite "nimble" themselves, as Willie Lord wrote:

☆ ☆ ☆ We soon became familiar with the sound of those shells that

125

gave warning of their approach, and expert in seeking the shelter of the cave when we heard them coming through the air. The cone-shaped Parrott shell, our most frequent visitor, fortunately could be heard a long distance off, and so gave time for flight to our underground home.

Rifle-bullets made of lead and shaped like miniature beehives occasionally found their way into our valley among the larger shot and shell. These little messengers of death were called "Minié balls," and as they whistled past made a peculiar beelike sound, strangely in keeping with their beehive form, and ending with a thud as they struck the hillside or a tree. The sound, as I recall it, was, *b-z-z-z-z-z-z-z-ip*; and of nothing were we more afraid, for when we heard it the bullet was beyond all question close at hand. One of these "Minié balls" struck and wounded, but not dangerously, a young girl as she was sitting with her parents on the piazza of her home, which, sheltered by a hill at the rear of the hospital, was considered safe. The bullet was at once located and extracted, and a clever convalescent soldier at the hospital transformed it later into a set of Lilliputian knives and forks, to the girl's infinite pride and delight.

A short time before this I myself had narrowly escaped death from a spent shell which passed so near the top of my head as to stir my hair, and fell close behind me. So far had the force of propulsion left this shell that my mother, standing not far distant, distinctly saw the missile just escape hitting my head. I had, fortunately, stooped for the moment to gather something from the ground. The unexploded shell, after the charge had been carefully withdrawn by my friends the Missourians, was added to my juvenile war collection.

It is only fair to say, however, that we were very much safer in our valley cave, and had more open air freedom, than when we were in the city proper. ☆ ☆ ☆

His mother, Margaret Lord, who like her sisterwomen of Vicksburg had not "undressed" and changed clothing for several weeks, was also remarking on the dexterity and stoicism of the children, who "bear themselves like little heroes.

"At night when the balls begin to fly like pigeons over our tent and I call them to run to the cave, they spring up, even to little Ponlie, like soldiers, slip on their shoes without a word and run up the hill to the cave."

And adding to the description of the new cave which her husband had helped build "with his own reverend hands," Mrs. Lord continued:

☆ ☆ ☆ Imagine to yourself in the first place a good-sized parapet, about 6 feet high, a path cut through and then the entrance to the cave—this is secured strongly with boards, it is dug the height of a man and about 40 feet under the hill.

It communicates with the other cave which is about the same length opening out on the other side of the hill—this gives us a good circulation of air. In this cave we sleep and live literally under ground. I have a little closet dug for provisions, and niches for flowers, lights and books —inside. Just by the little walk is our eating table with an arbor over it, and back of that our fireplace and kitchen with table.

In the valley beneath is our tent, and back of it the tents of the generals. This is quite picturesque and attractive to look at but Oh! how wearisome to live! ☆ ☆ ☆

Twenty-third Day

"Murfreesboro, June 9—A lady from
Shelbyville, arrived today, says that a report
of the surrender of Vicksburg was prevalent
in the rebel camp. A later arrival confirms
the existence of the rumor and the same
person states that the rebel papers had
published the particulars of the
capitulation."
—CINCINNATI *Gazette*

"Last night," General Shoup dictated for his official daily report, "the enemy fired into our working party on the left, wounding two men.

"We are constructing a rough stockade at that point, to prevent a dash from the enemy's works, now not more than 75 yards distant. We work under great difficulties; want axes and entrenchment tools.

"On the right we are strengthening ourselves steadily and surely; are making in the ditch and in front of the redan trough stockades with brush and wire entanglements."

To Sergeant Tunnard it seemed that the firing was kept up "all night long," and:

☆ ☆ ☆ The movable breastwork in front of the entrenchments of the Third Louisiana became a perfect annoyance to the regiment, and various plans were proposed for its destruction, only to be declared unavailable. Some of the men actually proposed to make a raid on it, and set it on fire, a plan which would have been the height of madness.

Finally, a happy invention suggested itself to the mind of Lieutenant W. M. Washburn, of Company B. He thought that if he could fill the cavity in the butt of the Enfield rifle balls with some inflammable material which would ignite by being fired from the rifle, the great *desideratum* would be obtained. Thus, procuring turpentine and cotton, he filled the ball with the latter, thoroughly saturated with the former. A rifle was loaded, and, amid the utmost curiosity and interest, fired at the hated object.

The sharp report was followed by the glittering ball, as it sped from the breastworks straight to the dark mass of cotton-bales, like the rapid flight of a firefly. Another and another blazing missile was sent on the mission of destruction, with apparently no satisfactory results, and the attempt was abandoned amid a general disappointment. The men, save those on guard, sought repose, and all the line became comparatively quiet.

Suddenly someone exclaimed, "I'll be d——d if that thing isn't on fire!" The whole regiment was soon stirring about, like a hive of disturbed bees. Sure enough, smoke was seen issuing from the dark mass. The inventive genius of Lieutenant Washburn had proved a complete success, and the fire, which had smouldered in the dense mass of cotton, was about bursting forth.

The men seized their rifles and five companies were immediately detailed to keep up a constant and rapid fire over the top and at each end of the blazing mass to prevent the enemy from extinguishing the flames. They discovered the destruction which threatened their shelter, and made impotent attempts to extinguish the fire with dirt and water. But as the light increased, the least exposure of their persons made the unwary foe the target for a dozen rifles, hand-led by skillful marksmen.

The regiment was in darkness, while the blazing pile brought into bold outline every man of the enemy who thoughtlessly exposed himself within the radius of the light.

The rifles of the regiment sang a merry tune as the brave boys poured a constant shower of bullets above and around the great point of attraction, which was soon reduced to ashes and a mass of smouldering embers. How the men cheered and taunted the foe can better be imagined than described.

The achievement was a source of general satisfaction and rejoicing. The Yankees could not understand how their movable breastwork was thus given to destruction, under their very eyes. ☆ ☆ ☆

"This is the 23rd day of the siege," recorded Dr. Alison, "and no relief yet. Surely Johnston could have reached here in this time. Our situation is becoming desperate. No place of safety. If you stand still there is danger from the pieces of shell that fill the air, and if you move the danger becomes greater. The whole town is enfiladed."

☆ ☆ ☆ The wounded are killed in the hospitals, surgeons wounded while attending to their duties.

129

Two days since Major [F. W.] Hoadley was killed in camp within 20 feet of where I was dressing a wound. Our hospitals are crowded with wounded. Some poor fellows are compelled to lay out in the open air and get attention from any doctor who happens to pass that way. Sick lists are very large, the men having lain in the trenches for three weeks with no protection from the sun.

They can't stand up without having a dozen bullets whistling around their heads, and to attempt to walk around is certain death. Our troops have behaved nobly, but nature can't stand it much longer. Night is almost as bad as day. The air is filled with missiles of destruction.

I have read of besieged cities and the suffering of the inhabitants but always thought the picture too highly painted. But now I have witnessed one and can believe all that is written on the subject. Rations, though short, are still enough, and we have good water most of the time, so do not as yet suffer from that source.

But the stench from dead mules and horses (killed by shells) is intolerable. ☆ ☆ ☆

Vicksburg's young girls joined with the defenders in their sadness and disbelief at the loss of Maj. F. W. Hoadley, a prominent Arkansas political figure who was with the 1st Tennessee Heavy Artillery. Hoadley, "one of the handsomest officers in the army," as Lida Lord thought, was struck by shrapnel originating from the direction of Sherman's batteries, and he "fell with his face to the foe," according to Colonel Higgins, his commander.

He was mourned by the *Citizen* as "a man of fine intelligence and untiring industry and zeal in the cause, kind to the men under him and a gentleman in every sense." The dashing young officer was also "a great favorite with the girls," lamented Lida, who continued:

☆ ☆ ☆ The loss in the trenches was heavy. The men suffered terribly. The hot sun burned and blistered them, while the freshly dug earth poisoned them with malaria.* They were half-starved, shaking with ague, and many of them afflicted with low fevers and dysenteric complaints. Many succumbed and had to be taken to the hospital, where kind ladies tended them as best they could.

If the men suffered, the officers had compensation; they were absolute

---

*No one suspected then that malaria was carried by mosquitoes, which abounded in the vast Yazoo delta.

heroes in the eyes of some of the prettiest girls in the South, who knitted their socks and hemmed their handkerchiefs, put blossoms in their buttonholes when they started for the batteries, and welcomed them back to an evening in the caves, where home-made candies, flowers, songs, flirtations and whist combined to wring some festivity even out of those gloomy hours. And when the officers could not leave their posts, the girls, fearless as they were fair, made up riding-parties to the forts and trenches, going in the twilight so that they could see and dodge the fuses of the shells.

Speaking of fuses, the rector told us one day a very funny thing he had seen during one of his trips to town. Every day, as long as the siege continued, he crossed that hospital ridge and passed over the most exposed streets on his way to the church, always carrying with him his pocket communion-service, apparently standing an even chance of burying the dead, comforting the dying, or being himself brought home maimed, or cold in death. His leaving was a daily anguish to those who watched him vanish over the brow of the hill.

One evening, coming back in the dusk, he saw a burly wagoner slip off his horse and get under it in a hurry. His head appeared, bobbing out first from one side, then from the other. Above him in the air, bobbing too, and with a quick, uneasy motion, was a luminous spark. After a full minute spent in vigorous dodging, the man came out to prospect. The supposed fuse was still there, burning brilliantly.

"Darn the thing!" he grunted. "Why don't it bust?"

He had been playing hide-and-seek for sixty seconds with a fine specimen of our southern lightning-bug, or firefly! . . .

Service was held daily in the Episcopal Church, and was always well-attended by citizens, ladies, and soldiers off duty. No one seemed to be deterred by fear of casualties, though the church was pretty badly riddled by fragments of shell and cannon balls. However, it was struck only once during prayers, and then there was no excitement or damage. A great deal of the beautiful ivy that had covered it for years had been torn, scorched and killed, and every pane of glass was broken; but no drop of blood ever stained its sacred floor.

That daily church service was very impressive. The responses were often drowned by the rattle of musketry and the roar of bombs. The gold buttons of the rector, who was also a chaplain, gleamed under his surplice, and many of the women were in deepest black; for Bull Run and Manassas, Fort Donelson and Chickasaw Bayou had already desolated Mississippi homes. ☆ ☆ ☆

JUNE 10

Twenty-fourth Day

"New York—Rumors of disaster at Vicksburg
and Port Hudson have been afloat today, but
we are unable to obtain any information in
the absence of which they may be set down as
canards."
—WASHINGTON *Evening Star*

"Jackson Cavalry*—Through mistake, a report
which was nothing more than street talk,
crept into our edition yesterday, stating
that a large force of Confederate cavalry
had entered Vicksburg."
—JACKSON *Mississippian*

"The weather," wrote Hugh Moss this Wednesday, "has been exceedingly dry and sultry, and the dust was almost untenable on our lines, but today the heavens have poured forth a bountiful rain, refreshing vegetation and animals. Late in the evening the heavens began to frown and the lightning darted rapidly through the elements, dark and heavy clouds arose in frightening magnitude and the rumbling thunder—all combined to produce a sublime scene. Eight o'clock came and the rain fell in torrents. I was on guard and the lightning was so vivid that it seemed that the very atmosphere would turn to electricity. The rain has been a blessing to us, filling the cisterns with water."

A bedraggled Sergeant Tunnard reported the same storm at somewhat more length:

☆ ☆ ☆ Ere the gray dawn it began to rain, and soon poured down in torrents. There was no cessation of the rapid and heavy firing around the lines. Sunshine and storm were alike impotent to stay the progress of the fight, or prevent the hail of deadly missiles from being poured upon the heroic defenders of the besieged city. All day long the rain

*The newspaper was not referring to the famed Gen. Thomas J. "Stonewall" Jackson, who had been killed a month before at Chancellorsville. William Hick Jackson commanded a division of cavalry which had joined Johnston's growing army on June 3. This Jackson unit came from Middle Tennessee and was standing by for orders to to help lift the siege of Vicksburg.

fell, filling the trenches with water, and thoroughly wetting the exposed, unsheltered troops.

The scenes at the breastworks beggared description. In the mud and water the men fought on, as if Heaven did not add to their sufferings the inconvenience and horrors of their situation. As usual, they made sport of each other's sufferings. At night the storm culminated into a terrific and concentrated fury.

The long weeks of heat and the constant and heavy cannonading had impregnated the whole atmosphere with electricity, which now burst forth with tenfold fury. Lightning, with its jagged edges and forked tongues, darted from the dark masses of clouds upon the city, followed by the deep, sullen and heavy roll of Heaven's sublime artillery, mingling its volume of sound with the scarcely less voluminous and heavy thunder which rolled its incessant waves around the fortifications.

A scene of such sublime and soul-stirring grandeur, linking together man's fierce passions and Heaven's dark frowns, could scarcely be imagined, much less described. The Yankees added to the many rumors afloat, by shouting to our men the following information, "You had to get England to assist you after all!"

The mouth of the Mississippi is blockaded and Price is in possession of Helena, Ark. We have enough men at Milliken's Bend to keep Kirby Smith in check, and after we capture Vicksburg, we will soon drive Price out of his comfortable quarters. The men only hoped that half of the information was correct, while they defiantly scoffed at the idea of Vicksburg ever surrendering, as thus proclaimed so confidently by the enemy.

A number of the regiment visited Vicksburg and the camps, to obtain stove pipes and tin gutters to sharpshoot through, by planting them in the entrenchments. ☆ ☆ ☆

"The heat of the sun," echoed Osborn Oldroyd, "increased, and we must improve our quarters. Accordingly a part of the day has been spent in cutting cane and building bunks with it on the side of the hill. Such improvements protect us better from the sun." He continued:

☆ ☆ ☆ Last night I sat on the top of a hill awhile, watching the mortar shells flying into the city from the river. High into the air they leaped and, like falling stars, dropped, exploding among the houses and shaking even the very hills. The lighted fuse of each shell could be seen as it went up and came down, and occasionally I have seen as many as three of them in the air at once. The fuse is so gauged as to explode the shell within a few feet of the ground. The destruction being thus wrought in the city must be very great.

We learn from prisoners that the inhabitants are now living in caves dug out of the sides of the hills. Alas! for the women, children and aged in the city, for they must suffer, indeed and, should the siege continue several months, many deaths from sickness as well as from our shells must occur. I am sure Grant has given Pemberton a chance to remove from Vicksburg all who could not be expected to take part in the fearful struggle.

We have been looking for rain to cool the air and lay the dust, and this afternoon we were gratified by a heavy shower. ☆ ☆ ☆

And just as Oldroyd suspected, the inhabitants were "suffering" more and more. Mary Loughborough wrote:

☆ ☆ ☆ Our policy in building had been to face directly away from the river. All caves were prepared, as near as possible, in this manner. As the fragments of shells continued with the same impetus after the explosion, in but one direction, onward, they were not likely to reach us, fronting in this manner with their course.

But this was unexpected—guns throwing shells from the battle field directly at the entrance of our caves. Really, was there to be no mental rest for the women of Vicksburg?

The cave we inhabited was about five squares from the levee. A great many had been made in a hill immediately beyond us; and near this hill we could see most of the shells fall. Caves were the fashion—the rage—over besieged Vicksburg. Negroes, who understood their business, hired themselves out to dig them, at from thirty to fifty dollars, according to the size. Many persons, considering different localities unsafe, would sell them to others, who had been less fortunate, or less provident: and so great was the demand for cave workmen, that a new branch of industry sprang up and became popular—particularly as the personal safety of the workmen was secured, and money withal.

It was about four o'clock one Wednesday evening—the shelling during the day had gone on about as usual—I was reading in safety, I imagined, when the unmistakable whirring of Parrott shells told us that the battery we so much feared had opened from the entrenchments. I ran to the entrance to call the servants in; and immediately after they entered, a shell struck the earth a few feet from the entrance, burying itself without exploding. I ran to the little dressing room, and could hear them striking around us on all sides. I crouched closely against the wall, for I did not know at what moment one might strike within the cave.

A man came in much frightened, and asked to remain until the danger was over. The servants stood in the little niche by the bed, and the man took refuge in the small ell where I was stationed. He had been there but a short time, standing in front of me and near the wall, when a Parrott shell came whirling in at the entrance, and fell in the center of the cave before us all, lying there smoking. Our eyes were fastened upon it, while we expected every moment the terrific explosion would ensue. I pressed my child closer to my heart, and drew nearer to the wall.

Our fate seemed almost certain. The poor man who had sought refuge within was most exposed of all. With a sudden impulse, I seized a large double blanket that lay near, and gave it to him for the purpose of shielding him from the fragments; and thus we remained for a moment, with our eyes fixed in terror on the missile of death, when George, the servant boy, rushed forward, seized the shell, and threw it into the street, running swiftly in the opposite direction. Fortunately, the fuse had become nearly extinguished, and the shell fell harmless— remaining near the mouth of the cave, as a trophy of the fearlessness of the servant and our remarkable escape.

Very thankful was I for our preservation, which was the theme of conversation for a day among our cave neighbors. The incident of the blanket was also related; and all laughed heartily at my wise supposition that the blanket could be any protection from the heavy fragments of shells.

And so the weary days went on—the long, weary days—when we could not tell in what terrible form death might come to us before the sun went down. Another fear that troubled M—— was that our provisions might not last us during the siege. He would frequently urge me to husband all that I had, for troublesome times were probably in store for us; told me of the soldiers in the entrenchments who would have gladly eaten the bread that was left from our meals, for they were suffering every privation, and that our servants lived far better than these men who were defending the city. Soon the pea meal became an article of food for us also, and a very unpalatable article it proved. To make it of proper consistency, we were obliged to mix some corn meal with it, which cooked so much faster than the pea meal, that it burned before the bread was half done. The taste was peculiar and disagreeable.

However, it soon proved unwholesome, for the soldiers were again allowed to draw rations of the remaining corn meal, with the peas in the kernel to be boiled with meat. We were, indeed, experiencing the rigors and hardships of a siege, for we ate nothing now but meat and bread.

Still, we had nothing to complain of in comparison with the soldiers; many of them were sick and wounded in a hospital in the most exposed parts of the city, with shells falling and exploding all around them. One shell went completely through a hospital in the center of the city, without exploding or injuring anyone, save by the severe shock to the invalids: a fragment afterward came through the side of the same house, severely fracturing the hip of a soldier, who was lying already wounded; one or two wounded men were, also, killed by fragments of shell while in the hospital.

Even the very animals seemed to share the general fear of a sudden and frightful death. The dogs would be seen in the midst of the noise to gallop up the street, and then to return, as if fear had maddened them. On hearing the descent of a shell, they would dart aside—then, as it exploded, sit down and howl in the most pitiful manner. There were many walking the street, apparently without homes. George carried on a continual warfare with them, as they came about the fire where our meals were cooking.

In the midst of other miserable thoughts, it came into my mind one day that these dogs through hunger might become as much to be dreaded as wolves. Groundless was this anxiety, for in the course of a week or two they had almost disappeared. [And Dr. Tompkins would perhaps hear them no more.]

The horses, belonging to the officers and fastened to the trees near the tents, would frequently strain the halter to its full length, rearing high in the air, with a loud snort of terror, as a shell would explode near. I could hear them in the night cry out in the midst of the uproar, ending in a low, plaintive whinny of fear.

The poor creatures subsisted entirely on cane tops and mulberry leaves. Many of the mules and horses had been driven outside of the lines, by order of General Pemberton, for subsistence. Only mules enough were left, belonging to the Confederacy, to allow three full teams to a regiment. Private property was not interfered with.

Sitting in the cave, one evening, I heard the most heartrending screams and moans. I was told that a mother had taken a child into a cave about a hundred yards from us; and having laid it on its little bed, as the poor woman believed, in safety, she took her seat near the entrance of the cave. A mortar shell came rushing through the air, and fell with much force, entering the earth above the sleeping child—cutting through into the cave—oh! most horrible sight to the mother—crushing in the upper part of the little sleeping head, and taking away the young innocent life without a look or word of passing love to be treasured in the mother's heart.

I sat near the square of moonlight, silent and sorrowful, hearing the sobs and cries—hearing the moans of a mother for her dead child—the child that a few moments since lived to caress and love—speaking the tender words that endear so much the tie of mother and child. Oh, the little lonely grave! so far distant, yet so ever present with me; the sunny, auburn head that I laid there six months after this terrible war began!

I could not hear those sobs and cries without thinking of the night—that last night—though so suddenly stricken and so scared, she would still live to bless my life. And the terrible awakening!—to find that, lying in my arms all my own, as I believed, she was going swiftly—going into the far unknown eternity! Sliding from my embrace, the precious life was called by One so mighty—so all-powerful—yet so merciful, that I bowed my head in silence.

Still the moans from the bereaved mother came borne on the pleasant air, floating through the silvery moonlit scene—saddening hearts that had never known sorrow, and awakening chords of sympathy in hearts that before had thrilled and suffered. Yet, "it is better to have loved and lost than never to have loved at all." Yes, better the tender memory of a hidden life that glows in our hearts forever; better, all will say who have known the light and consolation given from on high, when we throw ourselves before His Throne in utter wretchedness, and arise strong—strong in the strength that never faileth—the Lord's strength.

How very sad this life in Vicksburg!—how little security can we feel, with so many around us seeing the morning light that will never more see the night! I could not sit quietly within hearing of so much grief; and, leaving my seat, I paced backward and forward before the low entrance of my house. The courthouse bell tolled twelve. ☆ ☆ ☆

In extreme duress, man, as always, still could pray—and that is what some of the defenders of Vicksburg were doing.

The Soldiers Christian Association of the 42d Georgia Regiment dramatized its own entreaties by inserting an ad in the *Citizen*, "Resolved—[to] set apart all or a portion of the hour between sundown and dark of each day to supplicate Almighty God that He will pardon our sins, receive us graciously and deliver us from the hands of our cruel enemies, and that we solicit all Christians and soldiers throughout this beleaguered army to enter with us in prayer at that time."

PART 2 FROM
DEATH
TO
MORNING

JUNE 11

Twenty-fifth Day

> "Murfreesboro—A lady who came within our
> lines states that the rebels are in receipt of
> very depressing news from Vicksburg and that
> well-known rebels in Chattanooga and
> Shelbyville are selling off their goods and
> property to noncombatants at great sacrifices,
> in anticipation of our speedy occupation of
> those places...."
>
> —PHILADELPHIA *Bulletin*

To General Shoup the night had proven a soggy encore of "more rain." However: "No unusual movement on the part of the enemy. He has not been at work since the rain began. He is running a regular zigzag, using gabions and sap-roller in front of redan. The relief of the redan is so great that we cannot bring a gun to bear on his sap-roller.

"The sharpshooters are extremely vigilant, and are within 60 or 70 yards, excellently covered. In front of the center of my position the enemy is constructing approaches to gain the point in front of [the 27th Louisiana] lunette. The 26th Louisiana is securing its front against a dash by means of a picket with brush entanglements. Have directed that my entire line should be protected by brush; it is progressing rapidly."

One Confederate insisted that his foe was closer than the sixty-some yards noted by Shoup, observing laconically, "night after night . . . we furnished details to dig in the rifle pits until our lines of pits got so close to the enemy's that the dirt we cast out with our spades was mingled with that cast out of their pits."

After the night's drenching, the morning "dawned cloudy." Sergeant Tunnard continued:

☆ ☆ ☆ The day cleared off cool and pleasant. Below the city two gunboats floated lazily at anchor, while above not a vessel was in sight. In front of the Third Louisiana the enemy planted two ten-inch Columbiads,* scarcely a hundred yards distant from the lines. These terrible missiles, with their heavy scream and tremendous explosion, somewhat

*Actually eight-inch Dahlgrens.

startled the boys, being a new and unexpected feature in the siege, and necessarily increasing the already accumulated dangers of their situation. After knocking the breastworks to pieces, and exhibiting their force and power, the enemy commenced a systematic method of practice so as to make the shells deadly missiles of destruction.

So skillful and expert did they soon become in handling these huge siege-pieces that they loaded them with powder, producing force sufficient to only propel the shells over the breastworks, and they rolled among the men, producing a general scramble to escape the force and danger of their explosion. Frequently they rolled some distance down the hill-side ere exploding. One of these shells entered one of the shelters excavated in the hill side, where a group was assembled. Ere the party could escape, the terrible missile exploded.

Strange as it may appear, but one of the party was killed outright, while all the remainder were wounded and bruised with but one single exception. Several were severely burned by the large grains of powder with which the shell was loaded, making torturing but not dangerous wounds. The mere idea of forcing powder into a fresh burn will afford some conception of the agonizing, excruciating pain of this species of wounds. . . .

No prospects of assistance, and provisions were becoming very scarce. Fresh beef had long since been used up and, also, a large number of sheep, and the troops were now living on rations of bacon. The labor of keeping the works repaired was increased by the tremendous power and destructive force of the shot from the siege guns. Yet the brave men did not despair or give way in spirit under these trying circumstances. . . .

We give the following synopsis of rumors daily circulated as a fair specimen of the means used to buoy up the spirits of those inclined to despair in the midst of the gloom, horrors and hardships of the siege: Generals Forrest and Featherston destroy nine transports in the river loaded with provisions; General Price captures two gunboats above, three transports, and had crossed the Mississippi River; General Johnston was at Clinton, Miss., with 25,000 troops and positively asserted that he was approaching to succor the garrison. Such were the reports constantly circulated, and usually received with a large margin of allowance for their falsity.

Our mortar opened on the Yankees late in the evening. As the shell marked its graceful curve in the air and suddenly fell into the enemy's lines, the troops cheered most vociferously. They enjoyed, to the fullest extent, the astonishment and consternation of the Yankees. But a few shells, however, were fired ere the enemy concentrated upon the point whence came the dangerous missiles, the fire of every gun within easy range pouring such a storm of shell upon the offending mortar as caused its speedy abandonment.

It was almost certain death to remain in its vicinity. This mortar was used only a short time, and then the attempt to render it effective given up. A heavy siege-gun, planted near the extreme point of the peninsula, above the mortar fleet, opened fire on Vicksburg, but with inaccurate range, rendering its missiles harmless visitors. ☆ ☆ ☆

Mrs. Hoge, meanwhile, continued her busy and not infrequently outspoken peregrinations about the battlefield. The Sanitary Commission worker, who happened to be the mother of Col. George B. Hoge of the 113th Illinois Infantry, entered the encampment and assembled all soldiers not on duty for "a stirring speech." Capt. J. J. Kellogg of Company B, who previously had reported on the storming operations of May, recalled:

☆ ☆ ☆ Among other things she said, "Before you left Chicago we ladies presented your regiment with a flag, and your colonel when he received that flag pledged himself that it should ever be defended and sustained with honor. What has become of that flag? I desire to see how well you have kept that promise."

The color sergeant brought it to her.

Said she, "There are suspicious-looking holes and rents in this flag. How is that?"

"That flag," said the color bearer proudly, "has been many times carried in the front when we went across the edge of battle, and those marks were made by bullets and fragments of shell, and madam, two men who carried it before me, fell with it in their hands, and both are dead from the effects of their wounds."

"Enough," said the old lady. "You have redeemed your pledge, and I will tell the women of Chicago who presented that flag to you, when I go back, how nobly your pledge has been redeemed."

Then she asked some of us who knew the song to come forward and sing with her "The Star Spangled Banner." I was one who with others thus volunteered, and amid the thunder of artillery firing and the click of minié bullets over our heads we sang that song with Mrs. Hoge, as she held the flag in her arms.

One day when we had our men out in the rifle pits at the extreme front we saw a Union flag lying in a slight ravine a little ways in front of our rifle pits, which had been abandoned by some regiment in one of the charges. At the risk of his life one of our boys crawled out and brought in the flag.

It proved to be the regimental colors of the 4th West Virginia, and when we were relieved from duty we marched up to the colonel's tent of the 4th West Virginia and called him out. I with a few simple, and I thought well-chosen remarks, restored the lost colors of his regiment to him and wound up by saying, "Take back your flag, colonel, and next time when you are in battle hang on to it."

He took the flag spitefully from me, turning very red in the face, said nothing about setting up the cigars or drinks and without thanking us even, vanished into the bowels of his tent. We boys were all mad, and if we had known how he was going to act we would have left the flag out there on the battlefield where they had abandoned it. I thought afterwards that perhaps my presentation speech wasn't just to his taste. ☆ ☆ ☆

Mrs. Hoge possessed ample reason to circulate within the Federal lines. But there were increasing numbers whose presence was dubiously justified, if at all. It was not difficult to secure river transportation if a person knew "someone" in Washington, Nashville, or even southern Illinois, home eyrie of the politically influential Maj. Gen. John A. Logan, 3d Division commander in McPherson's 17th Corps.

"Floods of visitors began to pour in," observed General Grant. "Some came to gratify curiosity; some to see sons or brothers who had passed through the terrible ordeal; members of the Christian and Sanitary Commission came to minister to the wants of the sick and wounded. Often those coming to see a son or brother would bring a dozen or two of poultry. They did not know how little the gift would be appreciated; many soldiers had lived so much on chickens, ducks, and turkeys, without bread, during the march, that the sight of poultry, if they could get bacon, almost took away their appetite.

"But the intention was good."

Good or not, from the standpoint of motivation, the Sunday-visiting atmosphere was most incongruous on the field of battle.

JUNE 12

Twenty-sixth Day

Walnut Hills, Vicksburg—". . . everything has
settled down into that dull, dreary monotony
which was at once the curse and death of many
during the siege of Vicksburg last summer. The
weather is dreadfully hot and its enervating
effects are already seen in the faces and forms
of the stoutest men."

—WASHINGTON *Intelligencer*

On this Friday an impatient General Halleck, in Washington, telegraphed the communication-head at Cairo, Illinois, for relay via riverboat to Grant at Vicksburg:

"Hope you fully appreciate the importance of time in the reduction
of Vicksburg. The large reinforcements sent to you have opened Missouri and Kentucky to rebel raids. The siege should be pushed night
and day with all possible dispatch."

Grant replied with a note of optimism, but at his leisure: "Everything progresses well here. Johnston's forces are at Yazoo City, Benton,
Brownsville, and Clinton. I am fortifying Haynes Bluff to make my
position certain, but I believe I could go out with force enough to
drive the rebels from between the two rivers. Deserters come out daily.
All report rations short. We scarcely ever lose a man now. Health and
condition of troops most excellent."

Although Grant's telegraphic network ultimately was stretched more
than forty miles to link all corps and division headquarters, there were
gaps from this southern military theater to Washington and all of the
North. They could be bridged only by the slow method of steamer to
Memphis or Cairo.

Conditions were none too good for Signal Corps communicators and
military telegraphists, whose very prerogatives and duties in their different commands often clashed. So close were many stations to the
lines of battle that General Sherman's operators sometimes had to tap
away with their heads inside cracker boxes. "Old Tecumseh," the aggressive 15th Corps commander, was, as a matter of fact, rather a pa-
tron of telegraphy. He would introduce the first mobile power source
for his telegraphists, on whom he placed unusual reliance. These power

sources were wagons that carried "blue vitriol" acid batteries, cumbersome but effective.

Few telegraphists worked in such a poor environment as the youthful Marsden K. Booth. He succumbed to malaria at his post on the Yazoo "whose motionless, slimy green and tepid waters exhaled miasma that was usually poisonous in July and August, when the waters are low, stagnant and warm and full of decaying vegetation."

Captain Kellogg, on the other hand, was rather impressed by the "beauty" of the Yazoo, if not necessarily its therapeutic qualities. He wrote, after his regiment was moved to the river's mouth by the Chickasaw Bayou:

☆ ☆ ☆ We established our new camp at that point, little thinking at the time what an unfortunate move it was for us. In the formation of these new quarters my tent position came down close to the waters of the stagnant bayou, and when I was driving stakes for my new home, a great green-headed alligator poked his nozzle above the surface of the bayou waters and smiled at me.

Upon examination of the ground along the bayou shore, I discovered alligator tracks where they had waltzed around under the beautiful light of the moon upon a very recent occasion, so I built my bunk high enough to enable me to roost out of reach of those hideous creatures at night.

Though I had built high enough to escape the prowling alligators I had not built high enough to get above the deadly malaria distilled by that cantankerous bayou. We soon learned what a loss we had sustained in exchanging the pure cold springs of the Walnut hills for the poisonous waters of our new vicinity.

At first the blue waters of the Yazoo fooled us. It was as blue and clear as lake water and we drank copiously of it, but felt badly afterwards. We didn't know we were drinking poisoned water until an old colored citizen one day warned us. Then we looked the matter up and found that the interpretation of the word "Yazoo" was "the river of death" and that its beautiful blue waters were the drainings of vast swamps and swales. ☆ ☆ ☆

Others also bore witness to exceptions in General Grant's unqualified claims as to the health of his command. Capt. Thomas H. Parker, with the 51st Regiment of Pennsylvania Volunteers, encamped on Snyder's Bluff nine miles above Vicksburg, was himself made aware of health dangers following the posting of sanitary orders:

☆ ☆ ☆ . . . to all the regiments for cautionary measures against that scourge of all sickness: the yellow fever. It warns us not to expose ourselves unnecessarily to the scorching rays of the sun in daytime or to the damp and chilly night air; also to use no water for drinking or culinary purposes other than that obtained from wells and springs, in which barrels or boxes must be sunk for the purpose of guarding them against any uncleanly matter finding its way into the water, which undoubtedly would be the case in the event of rain, for the current of water which necessarily must flow down the deep gullies and ravines would wash or carry down in its rushing career the carcasses of dead mules and other filth that accumulates from one rain 'till another. We are recommended to bathe our persons at least twice a week.

. . . this is the greatest country that we have been in yet for insects of all descriptions. Here is where you can find your fine, plump mosquitoes, sandflies, beetles, bugs, ants, worms of all kinds, ticks and in fact anything in the insect line. ☆ ☆ ☆

At that, Parker was more fortunate than a soldier from the 17th Michigan Volunteers whose right arm was badly mangled by an alligator when he went swimming in the Yazoo. His life was barely saved by two of his buddies, who waded in to fight off the reptile.

Not swamp water or bugs but food shortages and the insistent shelling, together with flooding and other damage to caves and storehouses, occupied a forefront in Henry Ginder's concerns. The Confederate engineer wrote home:

☆ ☆ ☆ A courier from Johnston came in last night, brought papers as late as the 6th, but I don't expect to see them. News about Lee's victory in Virginia contradicted. Port Hudson said to be invested. He brought 20,000 caps, quite an acquisition. Things here are pretty much in status quo. Firing going on as usual, from night till morn, from morn to dewy eve. Mortars more active than ever.

Not a day passed but in riding back and forth the shells burst around my path and minié balls whiz past my ears. Last night I was on foot returning from the scene of my labors, I heard a 13-inch shell coming, but couldn't see it; it came nearer and nearer until I thought it would light on my head, when splosh! it went a few yards into the earth a few feet to my left, throwing the dirt into my face with such force as to sting me for some time afterwards. The Lord kept it from exploding before it reached the earth, otherwise it would have singed the hair off my head and blown me to pieces into the bargain.

I was obliged to condemn another of my magazines on account of cavings. Moreover, there was a general cave of 50 feet off the side of the hill which would have buried me and my negroes if we hadn't been working somewhere else at the time. It buried two of my magazines entirely and filled up the road.

I was ordered to repair to the scene of the avalanche and work day and night to open the road, but that night a most terrible thunderstorm came up with an incessant display of lightning and roars of thunder, pouring of rain. I retired with the hands to a neighborhood building where we stretched ourselves on the floor and slept until morning.

. . . the breakfast of the negroes consisted of a small piece of cornbread, as much as you, my darling, could eat at an ordinary breakfast— for dinner they had a similar piece and a very small piece of bacon. On such food I cannot have heart to push them.

Perhaps you think that I too am suffering for want of food. We are economical, take only two meals a day, at 8 A.M. and 4 P.M., but at these times we have enough and more variety than you would suppose for we live with a man who has a vegetable garden and keeps our table pretty well supplied.

Tadeus, my carpenter, was struck by lightning the night of the storm but not seriously hurt.

Most of the ammunition had been removed into my magazines when the explosion took place in the wooden buildings where it had been for so long a time, and we might have lost the whole of it had it been there still.

I pitied our poor soldiers the night of the rainstorm, lying in it all night and unable to do anything else the next morning for fear of Yankee sharpshooters, who expend more ammunition in one day than we have on hand. If they don't get this place, it will have been a most unprofitably costly job to them; if they do get it, it will be a very cheap bargain.

The other night they were approaching our lines behind a wagonload of cotton bales but by means of hand grenades we set them on fire and they were obliged to "dust." We have also made two or three sorties to drive them out of their saps which were coming too close. We have got some "thunderballs" ready to roll down on them when they make another assault. They are powder barrels full of shells and fuses; the barrel will first be blown to pieces and then the shells will explode among the Yankees. ☆ ☆ ☆

JUNE 13

Twenty-seventh Day

"The enemy's mortar batteries on the opposite
side of the river have been studiously pouring
their bursting shells into a certain part of the
city the past 25 days. So far, in proportion to the
immense mass of destructive missiles hurled in
our midst, very little damage has been done, save
in our hospitals. Towards these buildings, now
the majority in the city, the enemy directs his
special attention; and wherever a yellow flag—
the emblem of the sick and wounded and
suffering—is visible, there the humane Yankee
directs his one-sided, dastardly warfare. We
cannot point to an instance of savage-like,
barbarian, cowardly assault as these mortar
batteries exhibit. Knowing as the enemy must
that our city is inhabited solely by helpless
women and children, sick, wounded and dying,
still he exhibits an ultra-inhuman persistence
and butcher-thugism . . . how long, how long,
oh Lord! shall we witness these acts of the
barbarian?"

—VICKSBURG *Citizen*

"I consider saving Vicksburg hopeless."
—JOHNSTON TO CONFEDERATE
SECRETARY OF JAMES A. SEDDON

Capt. Lyman Jackman, with the 6th New Hampshire Infantry, arriving from Memphis aboard the transport *General Anderson*, witnessed
his first display of "butcher-thugism." He wrote: "The boom, boom of
the mortar fleet every two minutes, the splash of the water against
the sides of the boat and the shrill saw-file notes of the myriads of insects
on the shores kept one's eyes and ears open, so that sleep was impossible. The writer, with some others, sat on the bow of the boat till a
late hour watching the shells as they fell on Vicksburg. We timed the
shells as they left the mortars on their aerial flight and found that it
took about 18 seconds for them to land in the city."

Osborn Oldroyd was himself convinced that "the siege continues with increased fury, and the boom of cannon announced the sacrifice of more lives." He added:

☆ ☆ ☆ Instead of any cessation, the artillery plays upon the city almost every moment throughout the day. The variety of the projectiles becomes greater. The shrapnel, I think, must be most formidable to the enemy. It is a shell filled with 80 small balls, which, when the shell is exploded, scatter in every direction.

It makes a fearful buzzing sound as it flies—a warning to seek cover, if such can be found.

Besides this, there are the Parrott, canister, grape and solid shot. The canister and grape are also cases wherein are enclosed a number of small balls. But the least fragment from an exploded shell is sufficient to wound or kill. . . .

The rebs have succeeded in planting a [ten-inch] mortar, which has sent a few big shells into our quarters. This sort of practice did not last long, for a hundred guns around our line soon roared the mortar to silence. But one shell dropped near my tent, buried itself in the earth, and exploded, scattering dirt for yards around and leaving a hole big enough to bury a horse. Another fell on top of the hill and rolled down, crashing through a tent. The occupants not being at home, it failed to find a welcome.

These shells are visitors we do not care to see in camp, for their movements are so clumsy they are apt to break things as they go. However, they are rather rare, while the bullets are so frequent that we have almost ceased to notice them. Their flights remind us of the dropping of leaves and twigs from the trees around us. The balls of lead as they fall are found bent and flattened in every conceivable shape. A friend from the 96th Ohio, on a visit to me, as he walked over, met a rebel bullet which took a piece out of his arm.

I have a great curiosity to see the court house at Vicksburg. It stands on a hill, and seems to be the target for many cannon. There is a Confederate flag waving from it defiantly. A proud day it will be when we haul it down and raise in its stead the Stars and Stripes, never to be displaced again. The buildings in the city must, by this time, be pretty well-riddled with shot and shell.

The women, it seems, did not all leave the city before the bombardment began, and I suppose they have determined to brave it out. Their sacrifices and privations are worthy of a better cause, and were they but on our side, how we would worship them.

It is rumored in camp that Grant is getting reinforcements from the eastern army. I have a great desire to see them, for while we have always thought them to be no less brave, they are said to be better clothed and equipped than the western boys. In fact, from the eastern army, during the last year, the standing report among western boys has been merely such catch phrases as "Bull Run," "Burnside crossing the Rappahannock," "All quiet on the Potomac."

Perhaps such reports of their substance will continue to fill the headlines of news from those departments until Lincoln commissions Grant commander of the whole army. Should that occur, one grand move forward will be made and the Southern Confederacy will be crushed forever. ☆ ☆ ☆

A shell "burst just over the roof" of Dora Miller's cave "this morning. Pieces tore through both floors down into the dining room. The entire ceiling of that room fell in a mass. We had just left it. Every piece of crockery on the table was smashed. . . . The *Daily Citizen* today is a foot and a half long and six inches wide."

Yet with all their destructive power, the shells continued to fascinate the objective-minded, such as young Ephraim Anderson, who observed:

☆ ☆ ☆ The shelling of these mortars at night presented a grand and beautiful display of fireworks—luminous and brilliant as can possibly be conceived. Thrown from a distance of four miles, and at an angle of probably forty-five degrees, the fuses being on fire, sparks could be seen falling and trailing their bright lines along, as the iron monsters rose higher and higher on their aerial flight, and finally bursting, seemingly at times among the stars, exhibited dazzling coruscations of unsurpassed beauty, brilliancy and splendor. At first it was a pleasure to look upon the bombardments at night, but they finally lost much of their interest in the constant rush, incessant occupation and increasing dangers that surrounded us.

Although the lines were so closely invested, letters reached the command from Missouri, brought in by an underground line—a regular rebel mail carrier, who had originally belonged to the brigade—his name was Louden; but I received no letter, and had heard nothing from home since before the battle of Elkhorn [or Pea Ridge]—and what would I not have given at the time for only one line, saying "All's well!"

General Bowen received his commission as major-general by this mail line, and Pemberton got dispatches from Johnston. Whereupon, it was

stated that we had only to hold out a few days longer, when we would
be relieved. Glorious anticipation!

It was the custom every night, a little after dark, to throw out pickets
beyond the works to guard against surprise, and to keep the enemy
from approaching under cover of the darkness and fortifying nearer
to our lines—an enterprise our active foe was constantly attempting.
The fortifications nearest our works were, with few exceptions, covered
with a thick coat of earth thrown upon something of sufficient strength
to bear it up. There were portholes about two and a half inches in
diameter and two feet apart from which they fired, while to the rear
and at their backs was an open space at the top, probably a foot wide,
which admitted plenty of air.

Their works were decidedly better than ours, having the advantage
of this earth covering and portholes, while those constructed by us
were without either, with the exception of the position occupied by
Green's brigade. It had been stationed about two hundred yards to
the left of the Jackson Road, and had constructed portholes similar to
those of the Federals, through which they could fire with comparative
security.

One night, at dark, Lieutenant Stockton of our regiment was on duty
to station the guard outside the works in front of the regiment. The
posts had been visited about forty yards out, and seeing nothing of
an enemy, he proceeded on his round with the guard and had got
through with every post except the last, when, as he was in the act of
placing his men here, several Federals rose up from their ambush in
the cane, within ten feet, presented their pieces and demanded his
surrender. The lieutenant was taken by surprise and in front of his
men, and the result was, he and two of the men were captured, while
two fell back and made a successful retreat.

The two men who came in reported the capture of Stockton and
part of the picket, and that the post was in the hands of the Federals. Lieutenant Alford of our company was then ordered to go out
with a detachment of ten men and dislodge the enemy. He proceeded
with his squad, and a revolver in each hand to execute the order. Having
been on duty out there before, he knew the situation of the picket
posts, and approached this one very guardedly. When within six steps,
he was ordered to halt and surrender. Leveling a pistol in each hand,
he commenced firing into the ambuscade. The enemy, not expecting
such a result, returned the fire in a very random manner, and Alford
still continued to pour double shots, in rapid succession, upon the as-

tonished Federals, and succeeded in routing them and clearing the post.

Upon turning to his men, he found that all had run except Tip Marders, who still remained by his side. Returning to the regiment he got the guard that had just retreated, and posted it at the disputed position. He was not aware that any of his men had left until the firing was over, and he called for the guard to come forward, and his mortification was equal to his surprise, on finding that they had deserted him at so critical a moment.

Alford's gallant conduct on the occasion showed the true and genuine stuff of which he was made—a better soldier or braver man never lived. Supported by a single man, by his rapid fire and undaunted courage, he drove and put to flight a force at least six times his number, and continued master of the field. He received the applause of the regiment and the thanks of Colonel Cockrell for his soldierly bearing.

There were ten thousand stand of new arms in Vicksburg which were on their way to the trans-Mississippi department, and now blocked up by the siege; they were fine guns, of British manufacture, and were issued to our and other commands, and a good many troops in the ditches still retained their old guns also, and had two shots in readiness for emergency. ☆ ☆ ☆

Twenty-eighth Day

"Major General S. G. Gholson has issued an order
revoking all furloughs and leaves of absence
granted to officers and men in the State Militia.
Absentees are required to join their commands
immediately. . . .
"Our latest advices from Vicksburg are highly
encouraging. No fears are entertained of the
fall of that heroic city."
— JACKSON *Mississippian*

"All that we can attempt is to save you and your
garrison. To do this, exact cooperation is
indispensable. By fighting the enemy
simultaneously at the same point of his line,
you may be extricated. Our joint forces cannot
raise the siege of Vicksburg."
— JOHNSTON TO PEMBERTON

"Ho! for Johnston!" wrote Editor Swords, of the Vicksburg *Citizen*.
"The most agreeable news now-a-days is to hear from General Johnston. But we have nothing to record of his movements except that we may look at any hour for his approach. We may repose the utmost confidence in his appearance within a few days. We have to say to our friends and the noble army here that relief is close at hand.

"Hold out a few days longer and our lines will be opened, the enemy driven away, the siege raised and Vicksburg again in communication with the balance of the Confederacy."

Sergeant Tunnard observed that the "cannonading and musketry continued unabated." And also:

☆ ☆ ☆ Another courier reached the city with a large supply of percussion-caps. The enemy were daily reinforcing their already tremendous army, thus increasing their available strength, while every man disabled inside of the lines added to the weakness of the defenders. General Grant's facilities for prosecuting the siege to a successful termination were thus increased to an almost certainty, and he could afford to prolong the contest, and accomplish by starvation and a lengthened attack what he could not obtain by either stratagem, skill, or brute force.

A successful general he certainly was; yet the accomplishment of his plans was purely the result of having at his command all the available means and strength of the most powerful nation on the face of the globe. Not a circumstance transpired within our lines that the foe did not know, and they were informed of the true condition of affairs, knowing full well, and confidently expecting that the gaunt skeleton of famine, then seizing the besieged forces, would ultimately prove the conqueror. They needed but to wait, while they kept up, with unabated fury, their daily and nightly attack on the place. All around the city the firing was very lively and continuous, even from the sharpshooters on the opposite side of the river.

Thus closed the twenty-eighth day of the siege, adding to our list of wounded and killed the names of William McGuinness, Company A; S. W. Sanders, Company B; and W. Burns, Company H.

Our upper river batteries exhibited some excellent skill in firing on the wreck of the *Cincinnati,* to prevent the enemy from working on it and moving the guns, which they were attempting to accomplish.

W. McGuinness, mentioned among the wounded to-day, was shot through the right eye as he was looking through one of the pipes planted in the earthworks to observe the effects of his shooting. He was seen by one of the enemy, who fired at him with deadly aim. This incident is given to show how close the combatants were to each other, and with what certainty each party used their rifles upon the smallest-sized object exposed to their aim. McGuinness recovered, but lost his eyesight and a piece of the bone from the side of his face. The escape from death was miraculous. ☆ ☆ ☆

This was Sunday, but Oldroyd heard "no bells to ring us to church," adding:

☆ ☆ ☆ I wish we had one day in seven for rest and freedom from care; but there is no such thing now for the soldier. It is shoot, shoot, dodge, dodge, from morning to night, without cessation, except when we are asleep. When the time comes, we can lie down and sleep soundly all night, right under our cannon, firing over us all the time, without disturbing us in the least. But let the long roll be sounded—every man is up at the first tap—for that sound we know means business for us.

Occasionally the rebs plant a mortar in some out of the way spot and drop a shell or two into our midst; but a few well directed shots from our big guns at the rear soon settle them. These rebels obey very well.

We have several large siege guns, lately planted in the rear of our division, which it took ten yoke of oxen to haul, one at a time to their places. I had been told that the balls from these guns could be seen on their journey, and could not believe it until I put myself in range of the monsters, just behind them, when I found I could see the balls distinctly, as they flew across the hills towards Vicksburg. These guns are nine-inch calibre and they are about twelve feet long. They are monsters, and their voices are very loud.

Sunday is general inspection day, and the officers passed through our quarters at 10 A.M., finding our guns and accoutrements bright and clean. If any young lady at the North needs a good housekeeper, she can easily be accommodated by making a requisition on the 20th Ohio. In fact we can all do patchwork, sew on buttons, make beds and sweep; but I do not think many of us will follow the business after the war is done, for the "relief" always so anxiously looked for by the soldiers must then come.

I heard one of our boys—a high private in the rear rank—lament that he was—

> "Only a private, and who will care
> When I shall pass away?"

Poor lad, he was in a sad way! But it was mere homesickness that ailed him. If dissatisfied with his position as a private, let him wait, for if he survives the war, he will, no doubt, have a chance to be captain of an *infant-ry* company.

We are now so close to the Third Louisiana redan that a hardtack was tossed into it by one of our boys, and then held up on a bayonet there to satisfy us of its safe arrival. Some of the boys have become reckless about the rifle-pits, and are frequently hit by rebel bullets. Familiarity breeds a contempt of danger.

Some of the boys wounded at Raymond have got back to us, and are now ready again to do their part. They are, however, more timid than we who have been at the front so long. It is fun to see these newcomers dodge the balls as they zip along. But they, too, will soon become accustomed to flying lead.

Several of the boys have been hit, but not hurt badly, as the balls were pretty nearly spent before reaching them. Those returning from Raymond say they have marked the graves there, but I fear it will not be long before the last vestige of the resting places of our late comrades will be lost. ☆ ☆ ☆

Chaplain Foster, of the 35th Mississippi, proved his poet's affinities even under siege conditions: "The Sabbath again spreads its sweet, soft light over the earth. All nature is calm and serene. The birds sing sweetly, the soft and gentle breeze rustles through the green leaves, the blooming spring has now merged into the gay and cheerful summer. But while all nature is quiet and beautiful and refreshing, wicked men have made this a place of torment and evil. On this holy Sabbath there is no rest, but war, with all its horrors, is desecrating its peaceful hours. . . ." There had been, however, a momentary lull in the shelling.

☆ ☆ ☆ . . . the people of the town, the wounded at the hospitals and all the attendants felt great relief.

The caves were deserted in town and women and children came out with joy and entered again their pleasant rooms. The streets were filled with citizens. The whole town seemed to breathe freer. Now one could see ladies walking the streets at their leisure—not with the hurried, uneasy step that marked their gait during the bombardment. What a blessing to walk the pretty streets of this city of hills without hearing the rushing of shells or the singing of flying fragments.

But, alas! This quiet did not last long. Afar off in the distance, from the same fatal spot across the peninsula, a cloud of white smoke rises up. Then the dull, heavy sound is heard—a sound too familiar to our ears. Now comes the rushing shell, high up in the air it explodes and sends its whirling pieces all around. Before this unwelcome noise had died out in the distance, another cloud arises and here comes another unwelcome visitor, and then another follows in quick succession.

The mortar boats, after a silence of one or two days, have again opened upon the devoted city. What a bustle among the people— what a confusion in the streets. Mothers send for their children. They prepare to leave their comfortable houses. Everyone walks with a quick and hurried step. The courier puts spurs to his horse and flies with speed upon his errand. The teamsters put their horses into a quick trot and seek refuge behind the steep hills.

The streets are soon cleared. The same feeling of dread and suspense settles upon the mind. I happened to be in the town when the firing began and was deeply impressed with the change that came over the city. All our hopes were dissipated—the mortars had not left, neither had they been silenced. They had only ceased for want of ammunition. Now they had a new supply. ☆ ☆ ☆

The Reverend Foster would have been heartened and probably surprised as well at the compassion that some Union soldiers evinced toward their enemy, especially for "the women and children as well as soldiers." Pvt. Hosea R. Rood of the 12th Wisconsin Infantry Regiment continued:

☆ ☆ ☆ There was no safety in any house in Vicksburg and, in order to escape destruction from the iron hail, the people of the city who could do so dug great holes in the hillsides and moved into them. It is said that some of those dugouts were made quite homelike. But, for all their precautions, I do not suppose many days passed when some citizens were not killed. Someone was one day looking into the city with a strong glass. He saw a lady walking down a street and leading a little girl. A shell, or a piece of one, struck the child killing her instantly. Poor people! they were learning by sad experience something of the horrors of war.

While Gen. Pemberton was holding out as well as he could, Joseph E. Johnston was hoping to do something either to raise the siege or help Pemberton tear himself out of the clutches of Gen. Grant. Johnston hovered about on the east side of the Big Black River but he hardly dared cross for fear of failing to get back again. His being in our rear made it necessary for us to maintain a strong picket line in that direction as well as fight in front.

Pemberton and Johnston managed to keep up some communication by sending couriers through the thickets and swamps along the Yazoo, yet they could not form any plan by which they could hope to save either Vicksburg or Pemberton. But there is no doubt that Pemberton, in order to induce both soldiers and citizens to hold out as long as possible, gave encouragement that Johnston would yet do something to help them.

In the meantime the people inside were getting hungry, and their larders had come to be much like "Old Mother Hubbard's." Mule-meat came to be considered a luxury. In fact, starvation stared many of the citizens in the face.

Flour was held at $1,000 per barrel, meal at $140 per bushel, molasses at $10 per gallon, and beef at $2.50 per pound. For people who had little or no money, the prospect was not very encouraging. The army was also very poorly fed and they could not have held out from day to day with very good courage. This was about the condition of things with the enemy, but so far as our army was concerned it was well-fed and in good condition, and was improving in fighting ability every day. ☆ ☆ ☆

JUNE 15

Twenty-ninth Day

"Flagship *Black Hawk*—The situation of affairs
has altered very little. We are still closing on
the enemy. General Grant's position is a safe
one though he should have all the troops that
can possibly be sent to him. We have mounted
six heavy Navy guns in the rear of Vicksburg
and can give the army as many as they want.
I think that the town cannot hold out longer
than 22d of June. The gunboats and mortars
keep up a continual fire."

—ADMIRAL PORTER TO SECRETARY WELLES

"Our forage is all gone. The men are on 1/4
rations. The ammunition is nearly exhausted.
We can hold out 10 days. . . ."

—NEW YORK *World*, PRINTING A PURPORTED
DISPATCH FROM PEMBERTON TO JOHNSTON
AS CONVEYED BY A SUPERINTENDENT
IN MEMPHIS OF THE ADAMS EXPRESS CO.

"The day was cloudy," wrote Sergeant Tunnard, "and threatened rain.
The firing was very rapid, and shot and shells flew into and over the
place in every direction. The enemy seemed to feel in a particularly
lively humor. . . ."

Chaplain Foster was once more writing his wife, this Monday, noting
that the rations "were now greatly shortened, in fact they were reduced
to one-fourth. Still they bore it cheerfully but complained of great weakness. Their rations were cooked by a detail and sent up to them in the
trenches. Day and night they must lie cramped up in the ditches—
drenched at times with rain, remaining wet until dried by the sun;
then exposed to the hot rays of a burning sun." He went on:

☆ ☆ ☆ Towards the end of this week such hardships and exposure
and the scanty diet began to tell upon our garrison. The cheeks became thin, the eyes hollow and the flesh began to disappear from the
body and limbs and the whole appearance was haggard and careworn.

Yet they were cheerful and did not complain. A few of them at a time were allowed to retire in the valley behind the lines and rest a while, but it was but poor resting, for the shells and minié balls were as dangerous here as in the trenches. Many of them preferred lying in their places in the ditches. Some would read their testaments, others would sleep half the day.

Thus would they quietly pass their time while the storm of war was raging over their heads and about them. Now the monotony of the scene would be rudely broken by the sudden death of one of their comrades, or a fearful wound inflicted by a bursting shell.

They were restrained from firing, and the enemy daily drew nearer our lines. ☆ ☆ ☆

The "rebs," however, had company enough in their misery.

"Tired! Tired! Tired!" lamented Pvt. George Crooke, with the 21st Iowa Infantry Regiment, continuing:

☆ ☆ ☆ The weather is getting hotter every day, and that, with our constant toil, is constantly reducing our number. We scarcely know when one day ends and another begins, and as for a solid night of sleep that is now past hoping for. Last night I had the privilege of doing it if I could, but "heaven's dread artillery" put ours to shame. The rain fell in torrents, and having nothing overhead but a few branches, thrown across poles, my attention was fully occupied in making a very narrow, scant rubber cover [across] as large a portion of my sacred person as possible.

We are now nightly in expectation that the rebels will make a break and endeavor to cut their way through our lines at some point or other, since Johnston fails to arrive to their aid, and they are just as likely to do it in our direction as any other.

The siege progresses slowly. We gain a little every day. The doomed city is completely invested. Reinforcements can't get in, and those who are in can't get out. Deserters tell us they are now on quarter rations and short of ammunition. We have taken several men lately trying to get in with packages of gun-caps. They are remarkably quiet in their riflepits and forts. We do pretty much all the firing. Sometimes, however, when we get too bold, they open on us a lively little turn.

We are considerably annoyed by the spent or falling balls from their sharpshooters when they fire at our artillerymen. Our regiment lies right behind the battery under the brow of the hill, completely sheltered from a direct range, but the bullets fired at the artillerymen, having expended their propelling force, fall over our camp, wounding one or more men almost every day. Yesterday a poor fellow in Company E was killed and several wounded by them. It is impossible to guard against them, and the wonder is that not more of our men are hit.

The weather is very hot, regularly and persistently so. In spite of the heat, worry and work, our boys manage to get some fun out of the situation. The other night, when one of them was on picket, one of the rebel pickets a few rods off called out and asked him how we liked their "Sunny South."

"Oh, bully!" was the reply. "We wear our overcoats all day."

By the bye, it is sometimes very amusing to hear the sharp things said by the pickets to one another. You must know that the pickets very seldom fire at each other. Ours are instructed not to fire, unless they are fired upon or advanced upon, and I presume the rebels get instructions of the same import, for we can, and do, walk in full view of them, not more than twenty rods off, with the bright, full moon shining over our heads, making it almost as light as day. The other night I was going along the lines and sat down on the brow of the hill to take a good look at their fortifications—for we cannot get near as close to them in the daytime.

While sitting there, I heard one of their men call to one of ours and ask him if we had any more Enfield rifles we wanted to get rid of—being a sneer at the unsuccessful charge we made, and alluding to the 500 or 600 muskets they picked up on the battlefield. But he got his answer, and quickly:

"Yes," replied the Fed., "we've got lots of 'em, and we're anxious to trade them for batteries; if you have got any more howitzers over there that you want to trade, bring them along." This was cruel, and the rebel felt it, for he held his peace. . . .

Cannon cannot wake us any more. We sleep while batteries close by are bellowing their thunders but, strangely enough, a volley of musketry or even a single musket shot, although far off, will wake us instantly. I suppose the condition of the mind when one goes to sleep has something to do with it, and that is now a condition of expectancy all the time, a condition of *qui vive*, looking for a break-out of rebels, a sudden attack in the night. ☆ ☆ ☆

"The excessive heat," added Lewis Crater, an adjutant with the 50th Pennsylvania Volunteers, "the malaria that settled like a pall of death around the camps upon the Yazoo River, the scarcity of water and its bad quality and the forced marches told fearfully upon all . . . the hardships which all were obliged to endure were excessive. Water, which the horses refused to drink, the men were obliged to use in making coffee. Fevers, congestive chills and other diseases attacked the troops. Many sank down upon the roadside and died from sunstroke and sheer exhaustion."

One of the defenders, Capt. William H. Claiborne, acting assistant adjutant to Col. Alexander W. Reynolds, briefly summed up the situation from his perspective: "Things look very dark!"

Formerly with the Crescent Rifles of Baton Rouge, the twenty-nine-year-old Claiborne, like so many in Pemberton's army, was serving beside a close relative. He was Capt. Ferdinand Osman Claiborne, commanding the 3d Maryland Battery of General Stevenson's Division. Colonel Reynolds—known familiarly, however, as "general"—was Stevenson's 4th Brigade commander.

"Ferd," a cousin, "nearer" to Bill Claiborne than "a brother," was doing his best to ease the rationing. He "got hold of a fine turkey, the last rose of summer beyond a doubt. They invited me to join in his dissection—the feast was spread in Ferd's tent at 3 P.M. and we dined luxuriously to the music of minié balls and Parrott shells."

Food, as the siege ended its fourth long week, continued to dominate the thoughts of all within Vicksburg. Although blackberries were growing in profusion outside of the city, to delight the Federal soldiers, nothing was harvested inside the noose that was the Confederate lines except the hardshell, tasteless peas. The daily ration, according to Sergeant Tunnard, was: "Flour, one-quarter of a pound; rice flour, one-quarter of a pound; peas, one-quarter of a pound; rice, sugar and salt, in equally small portions. Tobacco and bacon, one-quarter of a pound. It was a small allowance for men to sustain life with, exposed to the horrors of the siege, and almost constantly occupied. Yet the troops were unusually healthy."

Mule meat remained a staple. "Tom-cat wienerwurst" flourished as a current jest but without proven basis in fact, as did the sly insinuation, "What's become of Fido?"

Even so, many people clung strangely to a bitter sense of humor, fragmented and tenuous as its threads necessarily were. One resident— and there was dispute as to his true identity—wrote this spurious bill of fare of an equally fictitious hotel:

Mule at the Hotel de Vicksburg

BILL OF FARE

SOUP

Mule Tail

BOILED

Mule Bacon with Poke Greens
Mule Ham Canvassed

ROASTS

Mule Sirloin
Mule Rump Stuffed with Rice

VEGETABLES

Peas and Rice

ENTREES

Mule Head Stuffed A La Mode
Mule Beef Jerked A La Mexicana
Mule Ears Fricasseed A La Gotch
Mule Hide Stewed New Style Laid on
Mule Spare Ribs Plain
Mule Liver Hashed

SIDE DISHES

Mule Salad
Mule Hoof Soused
Mule Brains A La Omelette
Mule Kidney Stuffed with Peas
Mule Tripe Fried in Pea Meal Batter
Mule Tongue Cold A La Bray

JELLIES

Mule Foot

PASTRY
Pea Meal Pudding Blackberry Sause [sic]
Cotton Seed Pies
China Berry Tarts

DES[S]ERT

White Oak Acorns
Beech Nuts
Blackberry Leaf Tea
Genuine Confederate Coffee

LIQUORS

Mississippi Water Vintage 1492 Superior	$3.00
Lime Stone Water Late Importation Very Fine	2.75
Spring Water Vicksburg Brand	1.50
Waul Legion Well Very Pure	5.00

Meals at all hours, gentlemen to wait upon themselves, any inattention on the part of servants will be promptly reported at the office.

Jeff Davis & Co.
PROPRI[E]TORS

The proprietors of the justly Celebrated Hotel De Vicksburg having enlarged and refitted the Same are now prepared to accommodate all who may favor them with a Call. Parties arriving by the River or Grant's inland rout[e] will find Grape Canister & Cos Carriages at the landing or any Depot on the line of entrenchments. Buck Ball & Co take Charge of all bag[g]age. No effort will be spared to make the Visit of all as interesting as possible

E. S. B., *Clerk*

If the menu were wildly exaggerated, its spirit nonetheless made all too much sense to the people of the unhappy river port—Alexander Abrams, for one. He wrote now of the deterioration within the city:

☆ ☆ ☆ By the middle of June, Vicksburg was in a deplorable condition. There was scarcely a building but what had been struck by the enemy's shells, while many of them were entirely demolished. The city had the appearance of a half-ruined pile of buildings, and on every street unmistakable signs of the fearful bombardment it had undergone presented themselves to the observer.

Many families of wealth had eaten the last mouthful of food in their possession, and the poor class of non-combatants were on the verge of starvation. The situation of the latter was indeed terrible; for while the former class of population were able to buy what little food remained in the hands of the heartless speculators, at such prices as they— money-grasping and unpatriotic creatures—would demand, the poor people were without money, and consequently their sufferings were terrible.

It is true there was not much provision in the city; in fact there was scarcely any. At the same time, the prices charged for what was there were such as to make a man wonder whether the sellers had the slightest touch of pity in them. Shut up as they were in our lines, with a knowledge that at any moment one of the hundreds of shells falling around them might end their existence, their thirst for money remained unabated, and the holders of what food there was actually asked and received the following prices: Flour, $5 per pound, or nearly $1,000 per barrel; meal, $140 per bushel; molasses, $10 and $12 per gallon; and beef (very often oxen killed by the enemy's shells, and picked up by the butchers) at $2 and $2.50 per pound.* As we are unacquainted with the names of these infamous parties, we are unable to publish them to world, to receive the scorn their conduct merits.

The military authorities assisted these poor unfortunates as much as they possibly could, and Lieutenant General Pemberton gave them the privilege to grind all the corn they could get at the government mills; but this assistance went but a small way to relieve their wants, and they would undoubtedly have perished but for the benevolent and generous conduct of the wealthier classes of citizens, who set to work for the purpose of averting the horrors which threatened them. Among those who aided with their time and means in this highly meritorious work, we take great pleasure in giving the names of W. H. Stevens, Rev. Rutherford of the Methodist Church, Victor F. Wilson, and a German by the name of J. Kaiser. This last named gentleman acted nobly. He had several hundred bushels of corn at his residence, which he handed over to a committee appointed for the purpose, reserving for himself *just enough* to last his family during the siege. We make particular mention of his conduct, because it was an act of char-

---

*Prices that agreed to the dollar with those quoted by the Wisconsin soldier, Hosea Rood.

ity rarely met with in his nation and the exception on his part deserves more than a passing notice. . . .

As might be expected, several of the women and children were killed or wounded during the siege; among those who were unfortunately struck by the balls and shells, we only recollect the following as killed: Miss Holly, Mrs. Cescie, and a Miss Jones. Among those who were wounded are a Mrs. Hazzard, Mrs. C. W. Peters, Mrs. W. H. Clements, Mrs. Major T. B. Read, Miss Lucy Rawlings, Miss Margaret Cook, and a Miss Hassley. These are only a portion of those who got injured, the remaining names we were unable to procure.

Notwithstanding the heavy list of casualties among the women and children, their spirit remained unbroken, and the same desire was expressed among them, that the city should be successfully defended. Even those who were wounded half forgot their pains in the height of their patriotism, and suffering as they were from their wounds, their unanimous desire was that the city should be held until relief should come, even if they had to die for it.

The conduct of these heroic women should be remembered long after the independence of the South is achieved. . . . ☆ ☆ ☆

One of these women, Mary Loughborough, was sitting near the entrance to her cave, and:

☆ ☆ ☆ . . . thinking of the pleasant change—oh, bless me!—that tomorrow would bring, when the bombardment commenced more furiously than usual, the shells falling thickly around us, causing vast columns of earth to fly upward, mingled with smoke. As usual, I was uncertain whether to remain within or run out. As the rocking and trembling of the earth was very distinctly felt, and the explosions alarmingly near, I stood within the mouth of the cave ready to make my escape, should one chance to fall above our domicile. In my anxiety I was startled by the shouts of the servants and a most fearful jar and rocking of the earth, followed by a deafening explosion, such as I had never heard before.

The cave filled instantly with powder, smoke and dust. I stood with a tingling, prickling sensation in my head, hands and feet, and with a confused brain. Yet alive!—was the first glad thought that came to me;—child, servants, all here, and saved!—from some great danger, I felt. I stepped out, to find a group of persons before my cave, looking anxiously for me; and lying all around, freshly torn, rose bushes, arbor-vitæ trees, large clods of earth, splinters, pieces of plank, wood, etc.

A mortar shell had struck the corner of the cave, fortunately so near the brow of the hill, that it had gone obliquely into the earth, exploding as it went, breaking large masses from the side of the hill—tearing away the fence, the shrubbery and flowers—sweeping all, like an avalanche, down near the entrance of my good refuge.

I stood dismayed, and surveyed the havoc that had been made around me, while our little family under it all had been mercifully preserved. Though many of the neighboring servants had been standing near at the time, no one had been injured in the slightest degree; yet, pieces of plank, fragments of earth, and splinters had fallen in all directions. A portion of earth from the roof of my cave had been dislodged and fallen. Saving this, it remained intact. . . .

Some friends sat with me: one took up my guitar and played some pretty little airs for us; yet, the noise of the shells threw a discord among the harmonies. To me it seemed like the crushing and bitter spirit of hate near the light and grace of happiness. How could we sing and laugh amid our suffering fellow beings—amid the shriek of death itself?

This, only breaking the daily monotony of our lives!—this thrilling knowledge of sudden and horrible death occurring near us, told tonight and forgotten in tomorrow's renewal!—this sad news of a Vicksburg day! A little negro child, playing in the yard, had found a shell; in rolling and turning it, had innocently pounded the fuse; the terrible explosion followed, showing, as the white cloud of smoke floated away, the mangled remains of a life that to the mother's heart had possessed all of beauty and joy.

A young girl, becoming weary in the confinement of the cave, hastily ran to the house in the interval that elapsed between the slowly falling shells. On returning, an explosion sounded near her—one wild scream, and she ran into her mother's presence, sinking like a wounded dove, the life blood flowing over the light summer dress in crimson ripples from a death-wound in her side, caused by the shell fragment.

A fragment had also struck and broken the arm of a little boy playing near the mouth of his mother's cave. This was one day's account.

I told of my little girl's great distress when the shells fell thickly near us—how she ran to me breathless, hiding her head in my dress without a word; then cautiously looking out, with her anxious face questioning, would say: "Oh! mamma, was it a mortar tell?" Poor children, that their little hearts should suffer and quail amid these daily horrors of war!

About four o'clock, M——'s dear face appeared. He told us that he had heard of all the danger through which we had passed, and was extremely anxious to have us out of reach of the mortar shells, and near him; he also thought we would find our new home on the battlefield far superior to this; he wished us to go out as soon as possible. As at this hour in the evening, for the last week, the Federal guns had been quiet until almost sundown, he urged me to be ready in the shortest time possible; so I hastened our arrangements, and we soon were in the ambulance, driving with great speed toward the riflepits.

O the beautiful sunlight and the fresh evening air! How glowing and delightful it all seemed after my incarceration under the earth! I turned to look again and again at the setting sun and the brilliant crimson glow that suffused the atmosphere. All seemed glad and radiant: the sky—the flowers and trees along our drive—the cool and fragrant breeze—all, save now and then the sullen boom of the mortar, as it slowly cast its death-dealing shell over the life we were leaving behind us.

Were it not for the poor souls still within, I could have clapped my hands in a glad, defiant jubilee as I heard the reports, for I thought I was leaving my greatest fear of our old enemy in the desolate cave of which I had taken my last contemptuous glance; yet, the fear returned forcibly to me afterward. ☆ ☆ ☆

Also at sunset this Monday, Pemberton dispatched to Johnston: "His [the enemy's] fire is almost continuous. Our men have no relief; are becoming much fatigued, but are still in pretty good spirits. We are living on greatly reduced rations, but I think sufficient for 20 days yet."

JUNE 16

Thirtieth Day

"Officers who have lately left the garrison at
Vicksburg concur in representing the troops
in the very best of spirits. The idea of
surrendering never enters the head of any
of them, from General Pemberton to the
lowest private."
—JACKSON *Mississippian*

"Headquarters, Vicksburg—Deserters coming
into our lines today report that the men and
line officers are discontented and are only
prevented from deserting in more numbers
by the hope that they may be honorably
surrendered in a few days."
—*National Intelligencer*

"Dawned pleasant," wrote Sergeant Tunnard, "light summer clouds
floating gently across the empyrean. The firing had continued all night,
and there was no diminution in its rapidity and volume. The place,
as usual, was full of rumors of succor. The rations furnished the men
were still good; sufficient to keep away actual starvation, but not to
satisfy the voracious appetites of the troops.

"How the other troops felt, we know not, but the boys of the Third
Regiment were *always hungry*. They had always possessed somewhat
fastidious tastes and were quite epicurean in their appetites, which
they had heretofore indulged to their fullest extent. Imagine, then,
the deprivation which they suffered, the great self-denial practiced by
them in thus receiving the scant rations daily dealt out to them, without murmuring over their condition. True, there was yearning after
the forbidden flesh-pots of 'Egypt,' but no possibility or probability
of their desire after forbidden meats being satisfied."

Activity this mid-June appeared to be on the increase along the
Federal-held far banks of the Mississippi.

"Nine transports loaded with troops," reported the Vicksburg *Citizen*,
"came down Thursday evening and landed at the old Yankee landing
just above the head of the canal. Yesterday morning the sick and
wounded were brought down the Yazoo from Grant's besieging army

and landed at the same place. Tents for a large number of men were visible at and above Grove's place during the day."

The same issue also revealed: "Yankees seem to be erecting a negro encampment at Town's place, beside the mouth of the canal. Large numbers of negro men, women and children can be seen plainly with a spy-glass moving to and fro in Town's field. Yesterday morning the transport *Forrest Queen* came up with a load of negroes which were landed at the above-mentioned place."

In the editorial column, a letter signed "by An Old Citizen" discussed "the crisis and General Pemberton":

☆ ☆ ☆ In this our day of peril a word to our soldiers and citizens we trust will not be out of place. How much have we at stake in the pending contest? Don't commence figuring to solve the question, figures will not do!

It is liberty or slavery! It is happiness or misery! It is order or anarchy! It is prosperity or adversity! It is constitution and law or tyranny and despotism! It is peace and joy or wretchedness and woe! It is food and nourishment or starvation and nakedness! It is honor or dishonor! In short it is life or death!

Then what is our duty? To citizens *first*:—let every man capable of bearing arms who is subject to enrollment by law go voluntarily and take his place in the ranks and aid in driving back the vandal foe.

Secondly—let every man who is able to bear arms of any age enroll himself in some volunteer company for home defense.

Thirdly—let the speculator quit his occupation and aid in achieving our independence. For if we lose he is a lost man with a lost country. Not worth a dollar, not even as well off as Judas Iscariot with his thirty pieces.

Fourthly—let the citizens bring out their surplus grain and meat and vegetables and sell it to the government at a fair price to feed the army.

Pardon me for mentioning names. Lieutenant General Pemberton has of late been the subject of much harsh criticism. . . . General Pemberton is not equal to our Lee for he is without a peer! But he is a soldier by profession and education, is well and favorably known to our President. All admit his untiring vigilance in the cause. . . .

He has as game officers under him . . . as ever drew a sword! Nerve your arms for the conflict . . . we will be free.

Fifthly—sustain and encourage our generals and soldiers in the tented field. If our generals do not come up to the standard of greatness let us bear with them, give them "aid and comfort" instead of contumely and reproach. We cannot afford to stop now and erase the claims of our generals to the entire confidence of everybody! We have too much at stake. We need all their energies, all their talents, all their skill and all their time. ☆ ☆ ☆

Meanwhile, Union miners had bored a tunnel to within forty feet of the Confederate lines even as Southern diggers ran their counter-sap as close as six feet to the invaders' tunnels. It was an underground race against time, a weird and deadly contest between human moles. The winner?—the side that detonated the first mine. The men worked in a dark, dank, subterranean world, constantly menaced by cave-ins, always anticipating the flash that would herald eternity.

"On discovering that the enemy were engaged in mining our works," wrote Abrams, "and seeing our inability to prevent the prosecution of their work, measures were immediately taken to countermine and blow up the working parties of the enemy. These attempts, however, were not successful, as the inadequate means at our command, and the position of the hills on which our works were erected, rendered any undertaking of this nature very difficult. On one portion of the line occupied by Major General M. L. Smith, the countermining was partially successful, several of the enemy having been killed when it was blown up; even this we cannot vouch for, not having been present at the explosion, although the information was received from a very good source." Abrams continued:

☆ ☆ ☆ The enemy, by means of their sappers and miners, had gradually approached until they had erected powerful works within thirty yards of some portions of our line. On the left of the Jackson Road they had occupied the hill mentioned previously and erected a large fort on it. This hill was on the immediate left of the road, about thirty yards distant from the line of fortifications occupied by the Third Louisiana, of Hebert's brigade.

It was a very high and strategic position, entirely overlooking our works, and which Brigadier General Hebert desired to hold on the Monday his troops were placed in position, being apprehensive of the enemy taking possession of it, which would have enabled them to have kept up a destructive fire on the 3rd Louisiana, and also enfilade the road held by the consolidated 21st and 23rd Louisiana regiments. His desire not being granted, the hill was left to the enemy, who quickly perceived the advantageous position they had gained, and put it to good use accordingly. ☆ ☆ ☆

Henry Ginder was aware of a mine being excavated toward Lee's sector of General Stevenson's division:

☆ ☆ ☆ . . . but he would not allow it. By means of sharpshooters prevented them from working during the day; at night his pickets walk right up to the enemy's pickets and are halted; they agree not to fire on each other, but our pickets tell them they will not allow any work to go on. The firing has been unusually brisk for a day or two past.

Two carriers came in 2 days ago, bringing 200,000 caps, quite an acquisition; evidently we are expected to hold out some time longer, but it is dangerous to depend on it. God alone can enable us to do so, and principally by keeping back the enemy. They have established a battery of two 10-inch Columbiads on shore opposite the city to help their mortars, so the iron hail is increasing. There is no house or yard where people cannot gather all sorts and sizes and shapes of missiles; some use them for ornaments to their gateposts. My suggestion is that, if we are successful, a monument be raised, composed entirely of these missiles; I am sure a lofty one could be erected. One of their 9-inch guns in our rear tears away more dirt during the day than we can replace at night. We are tearing up our tents to make sandbags, which are very useful in making repairs and to protect our men against sharpshooters.

A paper was issued here on Sunday, purporting to make extracts from some that had run the blockade, but it contained no news at all, only some Yankee lies, such as that their losses from Grand Gulf to this place were some 50,000.

We know they were not more than $\frac{1}{3}$ that number. The paper was printed on wall paper. Our vegetables are disappearing fast, being stolen by our soldiers. The worst of it is, that, as they come at night, they cannot tell whether anything is ripe and they take them away green; so they do no good to them or us. (Since the rain the weather has not been so intolerably warm as it was before.) We hear that [General Nathaniel] Banks has been defeated at Port Hudson, but we don't believe a word of it.

We have frequent displays of lightning at night all round our horizon, so that it is sometimes difficult to tell whether a gun has fired or a cloud has discharged its superabundant electricity.

I was obliged today to have some large needles to sew up some bagging for sandbags. I took a paper file, such as one you may remember, as I stuck my receipts on at home, cut it in two, doubled up one end for the eye, and ground the other end on a grindstone to make a point; such are the shifts we resort to.

It is 9½ P.M., yet the cannonading in the rear is tremendous, while an occasional mortar shell from the river gives notice to the Yankees on shore that their friends are alive and kicking.

"Thou must save, and thou alone." ☆ ☆ ☆

Sergeant Tunnard himself was reporting one of the vegetable raids which Ginder had mentioned:

☆ ☆ ☆ . . . two of the non-commissioned staff of the regiment were returning to camp from the entrenchments when the following colloquy occurred:

"Sergeant," says one to the other, "wouldn't you like some vegetables, especially some good cabbage?"

"Major," was the reply, "as a Yankee would say, I rather reckon as how I would. Vegetables! What a luxury! Where can they be found, and what do you mean?"

"Aisy, now, as the Irishman would say. I have been reconnoitering lately, and have found a large garden of cabbages; but the owner of the place is very watchful, and swears that he will shoot the first soldier he catches in his garden. I have discovered a picket loose at the bottom. It is on our route, and suppose we make a raid and 'cabbage' a mess of something green."

"Agreed, with all my heart. But, Major, what shall be the *modus operandi*?"

"Well, you watch at the opening in the fence, and I will go inside. If anything suspicious should happen, whistle and I will know what it means."

The two plotters were soon arrived at the scene of operations. It was a large garden, extending eastward down a gentle slope to a small rivulet, or rather ditch, running north and south. The opening was soon found. Major instantly entered, and proceeded on a course directly westward, and then his form disappeared in the murky gloom of the night. Sergeant sat down by the fence, and, thrusting his head into the opening made by shoving aside the bottom of the picket, became all ears and eyes in his watchfulness. Out toward the breastworks came the sound of the sharpshooters' rifle shots, with the occasional roar of a piece of artillery. Lights glimmered in some of the houses.

Mortar shells, with blazing fuses, described graceful curves through the air in their flight into the besieged city. The atmosphere was calm, the stars looking out from the clear sky overhead as if angel eyes gazing upon the din, uproar and carnage of battle below. What wonder that the soldier fell into a reverie, and lived once more amid scenes far away.

What wonder that ———. Phiz! Zip! What was it? Only a stray minié ball that made a close passage to his scalp, cutting the hair from his head. A rude awakening from his pleasant thoughts; yet still he changed not his position.

He was on guard, and could not desert his post. The minutes seemed ages. What could Major be doing? Assuredly not going to carry off the whole cabbage bed! Yet he was gone sufficiently long to accomplish such an undertaking. He's be hanged if ———. The shrill scream of an approaching shell from a rifled gun this time cut short his new train of thought. Knowing, from the peculiar sound, that he was nearly in range, he looked in vain for some sheltering protection.

The ground was smooth and level, not a single indenture to protect the smallest object. Action must be instantaneous, and he threw himself close alongside of the bottom board of the fence.

With an exultant scream the shell tipped the pickets above his prostrate form and descended into the garden in the exact direction taken by Major. The sergeant jumped to his feet, and a shrill whistle broke upon the air. Breathlessly, intently, he listened. No answering signal penetrated the darkness and disturbed the reigning silence. Again and again the signal was given. Still no response. Running rapidly along the fence a few yards, he was about to climb over when Major came hastily to the spot, a mountain of perambulating cabbage.

The tension to which the nerves of the sergeant had been strung relaxed in invectives.

"Why in the devil, Major, didn't you answer my signal? I thought that shell had killed you, and one of the Third Regiment would be found dead in a citizen's garden, slain in the very act of stealing. What a disgrace for a veteran to be caught stealing! People would have proclaimed 'retributive justice,' and 'served him right.' "

"By the way what were you doing when that last customer so unceremoniously and uninvited visited us?"

"Well, you see, sergeant, the ground is very hard, and the cabbage strong-rooted, and I was stooping down, with a good hold on the stalk with both hands. You can imagine the position: about to give it a 'strong pull, a long pull, and a pull altogether,' when I heard that —— shell coming, and immediately threw myself upon the ground."

"How close did it strike, Major?"

"It went into the ground about a foot from my head, and nearly buried me alive."

"I should judge so, from your personal appearance, covered as you are with dirt, from your head to your heels. Why, you look like an Irish grave-digger. Let's leave this place, as the Lord has warned us both that 'thou shalt not steal,' more forcibly than pleasantly."

The two men traveled off at a "double-quick," carrying their "greens" with them. Arriving in camp, they soon forgot their narrow escape, as they laughed and talked over a huge dish of boiled cabbage, which was consumed with a voraciousness and keen relish commensurate with the danger braved in procuring it. ☆ ☆ ☆

JUNE 17

Thirty-first Day

"Within the past few days the rebels are nerved
to desperation or have acquired more courage—
it is a question which—and manifest quite a
disposition to return our artillery fire."
—*National Intelligencer*

"The streets were full of exciting rumors
yesterday but many of them bore so much
improbability upon their faces that we do
not think proper to cumber our columns
with them."
—JACKSON *Mississippian*

The *Mississippian* also wrote editorially:

☆ ☆ ☆ All eyes are now turned eagerly towards Vicksburg. Tremendous firing has been heard there for the last two days and intelligence as to the result of it is looked for with intense anxiety. Our people, however, evince the most perfect confidence in the valor and endurance of our brave garrison. When all the circumstances of the various sieges and bombardment of Vicksburg are weighed it will be conceded that the annals of war scarcely furnish a parallel to the stubborn resistance and unflinching heroism which she has displayed.

Let her still hold out and those who have participated in her defense will deserve and receive the proudest laurels which adorn the Southern hero's chapter. The gratitude of a nation will be theirs. And she will hold out.

We are confident that she is invincible. A few more repulses of the enemy—the loss of a few more of his tens of thousands, and Vicksburg will rise from the ordeal nobly defiant and wreathed in perennial glory. ☆ ☆ ☆

Newspapering at best was a touch-and-go affair. The invading armies had smashed the Hinds County *Gazette* office at Raymond as well as that of the *Mississippian* at Jackson, although the latter was able to patch up the wreckage and start again. Editor Swords thus concluded that "the Yankees . . . have no good will towards the Confederate press."

This belief was borne out anew as the same editor reported on a narrow escape: "As we were working on our edition on Tuesday afternoon a 13-inch bombshell made a dash into our office, striking a short distance from the press and going through the floor and into the lower room, thence into the ground where it exploded, and sending its fragments upward again bulged up the floor and filled the office with dust, smoke and a suffocating stench of powder. There were at the time perhaps 50 persons in the office and not one was injured in the slightest degree.

"The Yankees have no better sense than to throw bombshells at the printers while they are trying to circulate truth and intelligence among the people."

Even a few hundred yards in the rear of Vicksburg proper, inhabitants such as Dr. Lord's family were experiencing a surprising sense of detachment. They had burrowed deeply into the sheltering embankments. Willie Lord continued his chronicle:

☆ ☆ ☆ Only faint echoes reached us of the suffering and calamity brought upon Vicksburg by the constant rain of deadly projectiles. Bombshells in the form of huge iron spheres weighing nearly three hundred pounds and filled with gunpowder flew through the air, their burning fuses leaving a trail of smoke by day and of fire by night. A peculiar hissing, screaming noise accompanied their flight and, exploding with tremendous violence, they wrecked houses and streets "like small earthquakes."

Fireshells containing tow saturated with oil kept the fire brigade constantly busy in extinguishing the flames of burning houses. Chainshot, cannonballs linked in deadly union by iron chains, swept the streets from wall to curb. Canisters, like big vegetable cans, but filled with grapeshot, which were solid iron balls about the size of hickory nuts, say a hundred or more to the canister, scattered their contents far and wide. All these, together with shells filled with scrap iron, links of chain, rusty nails and even bits of tin, were among the many kinds of missiles thrown into the city.

When we think of this iron hail, estimated at 60,000 shells every twenty-four hours, descending upon the town by night and by day, the mortality among the citizens, even considering the protection of the caves, was wonderfully small. But while comparatively few non-combatants were killed, all lived in a state of terror.

Several attempts were made to find water in the vicinity of our cave, but as the well-holes brought forth only mud we were at last compelled to buy our drinking water of a woman who lived upon a farm near by, on which there was an unfailing well of good water. This woman's husband was a soldier in the trenches.

Returning home on furlough, because of some temporary disability, he learned of his wife's inhospitable thrift and whipped her soundly. The ill-earned money had long since been squandered, but with many apologies and the information that he had "walloped her good for her meanness," he gave camp and cave the freedom of his well.

My father, in his daily walks between the cave and the city, never met with a mishap, and saw disaster overtake only one unfortunate upon the road. The circumstances of this tragedy are so peculiar as to seem well worth relating, showing as they do that often when a man seeks most to avoid danger he places himself most directly in its path.

My father had intended to take the direct road to the city, as usual, but was overtaken by an acquaintance and persuaded by him to take a more circuitous but supposedly "safer road." They had proceeded only a short distance when they heard a Parrott shell coming toward them.

"Stand still!" said my father, himself standing firm, as he always did when away from shelter in such an emergency. But his companion either did not hear or failed to understand the advice. Mad with excitement, with body bent low and face white with terror, he started down the road on a run. He had run only a few yards when the shell exploded directly in his path, leaving him a mangled corpse by the roadside, while my father stood unharmed where he had called to his friend to stop.

The church of which my father was rector was the only church in Vicksburg—with the exception of the Roman Catholic cathedral—where services were held throughout the siege. Daily, in the absence of sexton and vestry, the rector opened the church, rang the bell, robed himself in priestly garb, and took his place behind the chancel rail. Then, with the deep boom of cannon taking the place of organ notes and the shells of the besieging fleet bursting around the sacred edifice, he preached the gospel of eternal peace to an assemblage of powder-grimed and often bloodstained soldiery, than whom, I have heard him say, there never were more devout or attentive auditors.

[Lucy McRae, however, observed that although the Reverend Lord "rang his church bell every Sunday morning and tried to have services, people could not venture outside of the caves for very long. Still, the church bell reminded us that it was the Sabbath day."]

And this I know, that while destruction and desolation lay all around and about the church and its shell-strewn grounds, not even sparing the adjacent rectory, the ivy-clad tower, although a conspicuous landmark and therefore desirable as a target for Porter's gunners, was never struck by shot or shell.

Soon after we took possession of our valley cave an amusing incident occurred. The hill which partly walled in our little valley shut out from our view the hospital buildings, but not the yellow hospital flag, which floated from a lofty flagstaff upon the summit of the hill itself. This spot was most readily reached from the public road by a narrow footpath, which ran along the top of a high embankment.

A Sister of Charity from one of the city convents, guided by a negro boy and returning from an errand of mercy among the wounded soldiers, met midway on this narrow path a convalescent corporal, who gallantly saluted and stood at attention to let the Sister pass. As she was about to do so a shell of the smaller kind, with a slowly burning fuse, fell in the pathway at his feet. This proved too much for the corporal's equanimity and equilibrium. For a moment he stood a statue of horrified surprise; then, falling backward, he rolled down the sloping side of the embankment to pusillanimous safety. Hardly had he disappeared when the negro boy stooped, seized the smouldering shell, and pitched it far out from the other side of the embankment, where it harmlessly exploded in mid-air before it could reach the ground. . . .

My father witnessed the death of a man killed by a cannonball in Vicksburg; and, strange to say, an investigation showed that the shot came from a gun of one of the city batteries fired wantonly and at random toward the town itself. The victim was an orderly, and stood holding an officer's horse on the main street of the city. Even as my father watched him, admiring his erect and soldierly bearing, the ball struck the orderly's head from his shoulders and left the headless trunk, still holding the reins of the horse and standing as erect and soldierlike as when alive. The noiseless cannonball had so quietly done its deadly work that the horse took no alarm, but stood as still as the corpse that held it. In a moment the men on the street rushed to the spot, and the horse then reared in affright and the body fell to the pavement.

To my father it seemed an almost interminable length of time that the dead soldier held the living horse, whereas in reality it was the matter of a few seconds; but it was long enough for the horror of it all to become an ineffaceable memory.

The newspapers, which now appeared printed on the blank side of wallpapers of varied colors and designs, the supply of white paper having become exhausted without the possibility of replenishment, at last unwillingly admitted that the city was threatened with famine. Fabulous' prices were asked and paid for all kinds of food. Our own supply of provisions was reduced to a half-barrel of meal and about the same quantity of sugar; so that, like everyone else, we began to look forward with anxiety to what might await us in the near future. That the army's commissariat was also at a low ebb was demonstrated by the single "hardtack," or army cracker, and small bit of salt pork issued as a ration to the soldiers in the ranks, together with the general order that all government mules be butchered and served to the men as an extra ration to prevent scurvy and starvation. As it was, wounds and sickness had brought to the hospital six thousand of the less than thirty thousand defenders of the city. ☆ ☆ ☆

Chaplain Foster, as though using the medium of correspondence for sermoning to his "dear Mildred," continued to depict the macabre horror inside the city's many sick houses:

☆ ☆ ☆ Here comes the sad ambulance. Within, one heard doleful groans—the bottom is bloody with newly shed blood. With great pain to the sufferers their mangled bodies are borne along to the tent prepared for them. Another ambulance approaches—more wounded.

We look with anxiety to see if any of our friends are in the number. Thus it was during nearly every day our hospital was filled. How our men suffer in those rough ambulances. Some of them were simply small wagons without any springs . . . just to think of a wounded man with broken limbs and mangled body being borne on such a rough, jolting vehicle as this. Every step is filled with pain and agony to the poor sufferer. No wonder they groan under such circumstances. It is a wonder that they are as patient as they are.

During this week a great many of our wounded in this hospital died. The first 10 days generally decides whether the wound will prove fatal or not. The weather was so warm that many died who might otherwise have recovered.

More than one-half of the cases in which a leg was amputated proved fatal. In nearly every case where a leg was broken by a shell, death was the result.

The case which I have described, whose limb I saw severed from his body, survived several days. Every day I would carry to him a cup of buttermilk and he would express such gratitude, for he could not do anything, and he subsisted on what I brought him and a little loaf of bread.

He never seemed to recover from the effects of the chloroform. His eyes ever have a sleepy, drowsy expression. He was as patient as a lamb, for he was a child of God. Day after day he lay on his back, troubled and perplexed by the swarming flies—disturbed by the bursting shells. Gradually he sank, growing weaker and paler, until he found relief from all his pain in the sweet sleep of death. I have described this case because it represents the condition of hundreds and their sad end.

Poor Captain Cropwood, his end is drawing nigh. Ever since he received his awful wound he has been willing to converse upon the subject of religion. I talked with him freely and he seemed desirous to place his thoughts on the future and endeavor to make some preparation; but his pain was so great, his body so restless and his mind so confused that he often complained that he could not collect his thoughts and place them upon our subject.

I exhorted him to look up to Christ and trust in Him. Said he: "Parson, my mind is too weak." What a poor chance has the unpardoned sinner to make his peace with God when death is staring him in the face? His mind is confused, he is filled with terror—there is so much to do and so little time remaining that the mind shrinks back from the task. How few ever make their peace with God in their dying moments?

As yet the captain had entertained some hope of recovering. One morning I called in to see him and saw a great change had come over his face. His pulse was fluttering fast. Mortification had begun and was progressing rapidly. He felt the change; he called me close to his side and told me his fears and requested me to ask his doctor if there was any chance for him.

I did so and was told there was no hope in his case. I went back to the Captain with sad heart, afraid almost to tell what was the opinion of the physician—but upon his request I informed him that he must die, and watched his countenance closely.

He was not surprised, for he had already felt the approach of death. Oh, what a moment that must be when the truth flashes across the sinner's mind that he must soon stand before his God!

During all this day and the coming night he was sinking rapidly.

The next morning when I came around to see him he was suffering intensely. He said to me: "I am passing away." He would use the same expression to his friends around, "I am passing away."

He then pointed to his servant, who had been faithfully watching by his bedside day and night. I turned around and the tears were running from the boy's eyes, running down upon his cheeks and falling to the ground. He sobbed like a child. No doubt he loved his master. The Captain said he hoped that his sins were forgiven. He now said, "Oh, that I could now go," and a few minutes after he shut his eyes in death. . . .

Ah, the sufferings of the wounded! The whole air in the tents was contaminated. It sickened the heart and the body to pass among them. There lies one who has been mortally wounded, shot through the middle of his body. His wound is awfully offensive. There is no hope for him and his wounds are not dressed. At last death comes to his relief. He was a Catholic and said that all his trust was in Christ. . . .

Pen can never tell the misery and agony of the wounded soldiers in these cheerless hospitals . . . besides all this, the mortar shells were bursting all around them, sometimes pieces flying so near them as to unstring their nerves. . . .

At night they have no rest, for the air above them is almost always filled with a rushing, exploding bomb. If they should happen to fall asleep, they are soon aroused by the crashing sound. Sweet sleep is kept far from their eyes. In the morning we wake from such disturbed slumbers, unrefreshed and feverish, to spend a restless day amidst the heat and swarming flies. In the morning their prayer is, "Would to God it were evening," and when evening comes, "Would to God it were morning. . . ."

During this week our wounded men died rapidly—four or five every day at the hospital. Wrapped up in their blankets and placed in very inferior boxes, they would be placed in shallow graves in the adjoining hollow. Sometimes the name would be marked—sometimes only a rude board and a small mound of earth would tell the spot where the unknown dead lie. ☆ ☆ ☆

Sergeant Tunnard, too, spoke of a soldier's burial, in noting the death of "J. Lee of Company B," who was "carried down the hillside and laid upon the ground, near the spring where the men came for water. Comrades were passing to and from the lines, laughing, talking and joking with each other, all unmindful of the dying soldier. Bullets whistled by, and huge shells screamed his requiem, or thundered his dirge in their fearful explosions, as his spirit departed amid the din of the fierce conflict.

"Yet, such a scene was a common occurrence, and men whose souls once thrilled with all the finer sensibilities of the human nature, looked on with stolid, stoical indifference. With a blanket for a winding-sheet, and in his soiled and battle-stained garments, the brave soldier was placed in the hastily-dug grave, and left to rest in peace."

Fallen Confederates were customarily interred in trenches fifty feet long and three feet wide—six bodies to a trench. Then, as a mourner had observed, they were "lowered into the cold earth which was hastily heaped above the mortal remains."

Thirty-second Day

"We are much gratified to learn that nearly
all our wounded soldiers in the hospitals are
impoving very rapidly and many of them
again able to go on duty."
— VICKSBURG *Citizen*

"Grant's position, naturally very strong, is
entrenched and protected by powerful
artillery, and the roads obstructed. The
Big Black covers him from attack and would
cut off our retreat if defeated."
— JOHNSTON TO PEMBERTON

"Cloudy and very warm," Tunnard commenced his Thursday entry. "The Vicksburg *Whig* published an extra, containing a few items concerning the siege of Port Hudson. This paper, published at intervals, was printed on one side of wallpaper, taken from the sides of rooms. It was very small, and a great curiosity in the way of a relic. It was decidedly an 'illustrated' sheet, not exactly after the style of *Frank Leslie* and *Harper* pictorials." He continued:

☆ ☆ ☆ The river began to rise, and the boats below had disappeared. At this time the enemy became imbued with the mania for setting fire to the city, and, as the shells exploded, a stream of liquid fire descended from them. At night they presented a beautiful spectacle, notwithstanding their destructive mission. No serious consequences resulted from this new species of warfare. . . .

Cannonading brisk and very rapid, in fact, terrific in the afternoon. The day was unusually sultry. Another Columbiad opened on the regiment at close range, and the enemy's lines were now so near that scraps of paper could be thrown by the combatants into each other's ranks. Thus, a Yankee threw a hardtack biscuit among the men of the regiment, having written on it "starvation." The visitor was immediately returned, indorsed as follows, "Forty days rations, and no thanks to you."

Despair held no rule in the brave spirits who defended this portion of the work, and the tremendous mass of iron poured upon them no terrors for their unflinching souls. Another building was destroyed by fire, caused by the explosion of a shell.

Editor Swords of the *Citizen* wished to praise these defenders of Vicksburg, as he wrote: "Great encomiums have been pasted upon the Confederate armies in Virginia and Tennessee, and truly do these veteran troops deserve a full measure of credit for the trials and hardships they have gone through. But in point of patriotic determination, bravery, endurance of fatigue, hunger, the heat of the sun, the pelting rain and an abiding faith in their prowess there is no army in the Confederacy to compare to that which now interposes its living breastworks in defense of Vicksburg. Such heroism, such determination and such stoical indifference, mingled with patience and fortitude as is exhibited by these troops, is truly wonderful."

The civilians, too, were meriting their own "encomiums." Mary Loughborough, one of their more communicative number, was en route to her new *cul de sac*:

☆ ☆ ☆ The road we were travelling was graded out through the hills; and on every side we could see, thickly strewn among the earthy cliffs, the never-to-be-lost sight of caves—large caves and little caves, some cut out substantially, roomy, and comfortable, with braces and props throughout, many only large enough for one man to take refuge in, standing. Again, at a low place in the earth was a seat for a passerby in case of danger.

Driving on rapidly, we reached the suburbs of the city, where the road became shady and pleasant—still with caves at every large road excavation, reminding one very much of the numberless holes that swallows make in summer; for both the mortar and Parrott shells disputed this district; and a cave, front in whatever direction it might, was not secure from fragments. M—— impatiently urged on the driver, fearing that when the firing recommenced we would still be on the road. Suddenly, a turn of the drive brought in sight two large forts on the hills above us, and passing down a ravine near one of these, the ambulance stopped. Here we saw two or three of the little shell and bombproof houses in the earth, covered with logs and turf. We were hastily taken out and started for our home, when I heard a cutting of the air—the most expressive term I can use for that peculiar sound—above my head; and the balls dropped thickly around me, bringing leaves and small twigs from the trees with them.

I felt a sudden rush to my heart; but the soldiers were camped near and many stood cautiously watching the effect of the sudden fall of metal around me. I would not for the world have shown fear. So, braced by my pride, I walked with a firm and steady pace, notwithstanding the treacherous suggestions of my heart that beat a loud "Run, run." M——, fearing every moment that I might fall by his side hurried me anxiously along. Within a short distance was the adjutant's office, where we took refuge until the firing became less heavy. Here we found friends and sat chatting some time.

The "office" was a square excavation made in the side of the hill, covered over with logs and earth, seemingly quite cool and comfortable. I had been confined for so long a time in a narrow space of earth that daylight, green trees and ample room became a new pleasure to me. At sundown there was a cessation in the rapid fall of balls and shells and we again started for our home. I was taken up a little footpath that led from the ravine up under a careless, graceful arch of wild grapevines, whose swinging branchlets were drawn aside; and a low, long room, cut into the hillside and shaded by the growth of forest trees around, was presented to my view as our future home.

What a pleasant place, after the close little cave in the city!—large enough for two rooms—the back and sides solid walls of earth, the sloping of the hill bringing down the wall to about four feet at the entrance, leaving the spaces above, between the wall and roof, for light; the side, looking out on the road through the ravine, was entirely open, yet shaded from view by the clustering vines over the pathway.

I took possession delightedly. A blanket, hung across the centre, made us two good-sized rooms: the front room, with a piece of carpet laid down to protect us from the dampness of the floor, and two or three chairs, formed our little parlor; and the back room, quiet and retired, the bedroom. Over the top of the earth, or our house, held up by huge forked props, were the trunks of small trees laid closely across together; over that, brush, limbs, and leaves, and covering all this the thickness of two or three feet of earth beaten down compactly, and thought perfectly safe from minié balls and Parrott or shrapnel shells.

We had our tent fly drawn over the front, making a very pleasant veranda; for a narrow terrace had been made along the entrance, from which the hill sloped abruptly down to the road in the ravine opposite the dwelling; in the rear the hill rose steeply above us. All was quiet tonight, as it usually is, I was told, when the moon is not brightly shining.

The Federal commanders fear that the Confederates will strive to improve their defenses by the moonlight, which is certainly done, firing or not, for the fortifications need constant strengthening, being frequently badly torn by the Parrott shells.

The next morning at four o'clock, I was awakened by a perfect tumult in the air: the explosion of shrapnel and the rattling of shrapnel balls around us reminded me that my dangers and cares were not yet over. How rapidly and thickly the shells and minié balls fell—Parrott of various sizes—canister and solid shot, until I was almost deafened by the noise and explosions! I lay and thought of the poor soldiers down below in the ravine, with only their tents over their heads; and it seemed in this storm of missiles that all must be killed. How strange so few casualties occur during these projectile storms!

Our little home stood the test nobly. We were in the first line of hills back of the heights that were fortified; and, of course, we felt the full force of the very energetic firing that was constantly kept up; and being so near, many that passed over the first line of hills would fall directly around us.

How dewy and pleasant the morning! I stood looking out from the little terrace, breathing the fresh air, and learning the new surroundings, so far as my eye went, for it was not safe to venture out from the covering of the cave—the ravine fronting me, shady, dark, and cool—the sun just rising over the hilltop and lighting the upper limbs of the large trees. Up the ravine, the Headquarters' horses were tethered, lazily rising and shaking their coats after the night's rest on the ground—shaking off their drowsiness to begin the breakfast of mulberry leaves. Amidst the constant falling of rifle balls, the birds sang as sweetly, and flew as gayly from tree to tree, as if there were peace and plenty in the land. ☆ ☆ ☆

And one of her increasingly numerous Federal foes, Osborn Oldroyd, was himself smitten by beauty in war's continuing paradoxes:

☆ ☆ ☆ I do not often go star-gazing, but last night I saw and watched the beauty above. Daytime is glorious, but when night unfurls her banner over care-worn thousands among these hills, and the stars come out from their hiding places, our thoughts seek loftier levels. It was just as though one day had died, and another was born to take its place. Not a breeze stirred the foliage, except as fanned by the whirling shells.

My thoughts were of home and of the dear sister there, bedridden, with but little hope of health again. Her dearest wish, I know, is to see her only brother once more before she passes away to that heavenly peace for which she is destined. Through these terrible two years past, thoughts of home and a safe return to an unbroken family circle have been my constant guiding star.

If what they say is true, the garrison over there is already familiar with mule meat and scanty meal rations. If they have had to eat mules such as we have killed in the trenches, I pity them, for they are on a tough job. Several cows which I suppose had served families there with milk we had to kill for browsing too close to our lines. ☆ ☆ ☆

JUNE 19

Thirty-third Day

"The siege of Vicksburg progresses slowly but,
we are told, favorably. Persons in official
circles looked for the assault and capture of
the city before this. General Grant's approaches
were within a few yards of the rebel works at
the latest dates. Our advices from Grant's army
are to the 19th at noon. At that time heavy
firing was going on from both sides."
    —*Harper's Weekly*

Dana, the heavily bearded, conscientious emissary, was again filing a report to Secretary Stanton:

☆ ☆ ☆ All indications point to the speedy surrender of this place. Deserters who came out yesterday say that the Tennessee and Georgia regiments have determined to stack their arms within three days and refuse to continue the defense on the ground that it is useless, and that it is impossible to fight on the rations they receive. All the deserters are worn out and hungry, and say the whole garrison are in the same condition; besides, the defense has for several days been conducted with extraordinary feebleness, which must be due either to the deficiency of ammunition, or exhaustion and depression in the garrison, or to their retirement to an inner line of defense. The first and third of these causes no doubt operate to some extent, but the second we suppose to be the most influential.

These deserters also say that fully one-third of the garrison are in hospital, and that officers, as well as men, have begun to despair of relief from Johnston. The troops of [Major] General [Francis J.] Herron [division commander] got into position yesterday.

The advance of the Ninth Army Corps is also believed by General Grant to have arrived at Young's Point, though he has no positive report, and does not expect one till it has its place as a part of the besieging force on the south of the city, whither he has sent orders for it to proceed. After the arrival there of this corps, General Herron is to move to the right of General [Jacob] Lauman, and occupy that portion of the lines which is now held by [Alvin P.] Hovey's division, which McClernand will then station as a reserve to support the other divisions of his corps.

All of W. S. Smith's division are now at Haynes' Bluff, where I saw them yesterday working upon the entrenchments with admirable zeal. The fortifications there for an army of 25,000 troops will be in a condition for practical use by the 16th instant. It is a stronger defensive position even than Vicksburg. . . . ☆ ☆ ☆

"A strange stillness pervades our hitherto noisy and tumultous camp," wrote Pvt. David Lane of the 17th Michigan Volunteers. "The men are scattered in every direction, lounging listlessly in the shade, not caring even to play cards, so oppressive is the heat. I am sitting in the shade of a mulberry tree . . . we alternately write or lounge as the mood takes us. Most assuredly I never felt the heat in Michigan as I feel it here."

Oldroyd agreed:

☆ ☆ ☆ The weather is getting altogether too hot for comfort. A few sunstrokes have occurred, but without proving fatal so far. One poor fellow even dropped at midnight, when I presume the surgeon's diagnosis must have been—moonstruck. There are more ways than one of shirking a battle, for which purpose some are even willing to part with a finger or toe.

If the rebels are short of provisions, their ammunition seems to hold out, for they are quite liberal in their distribution of it. But when Sherman begins firing from the east, McClernand from the west, McPherson from the rear, and the mortars from the north, then look out for big fireworks. The cannon are all pointed towards the town, but some of the shells fall far short of it. When these burst in mid-air, we can see a small round cloud of smoke left behind, and then there is a sharp lookout for fragments to be scattered in every direction. Our artillerymen have had such good practice during the siege that they can generally drop a shell wherever they want to.

Boys at the front have time for sport which is not to be interrupted even by stray shells. I noticed four of our boys playing euchre, when a shell from the enemy came careering just above their heads; but they treated it with entire indifference. Another group I saw playing "seven-up" under a blanket caught at the four corners in the hammers of muskets stuck in the ground, and thereby forming a very good shelter from the sun. A shell burst right over this group, scattering its fragments all around, but even this failed to disturb the game, further than to call forth the timely comment, "Johnny passes." ☆ ☆ ☆

The shells were no respecter of soldier or civilian, man, woman, or child, as the Reverend Foster already well knew. He was standing

☆ ☆ ☆ . . . on the portico of the second story of the hospital building, watching the firing around the lines and enjoying the beautiful scenery that was spread out before me, for it was a high commanding point and overlooked the whole city, as well as part of our lines, and while I was thus employed, enjoying the wide extended view and the cool refreshing breeze, one of those mortar shells exploded in front of me, high up in the air, and sent large fragments with singing, silvery sound right towards the building.

It descended close to the porch on which I was standing and struck the ground near the steps with great force, tearing up the yard at a fearful rate and filling the second floor with dirt and sand. One of the sick men, a pale, slender fellow, was just going out to get a drink of water. He was knocked prostrate upon the ground, almost covered up in dirt and we thought he was torn all to pieces. No doubt he thought the same for he lay there for some time.

Feeling no pain, he at last concluded that he could rise up. He stood upon his feet, shook the earth from his clothes, surveyed his whole person and then proceeded on quietly to the well, where he had started to get a drink of water, as if nothing had happened to him. This incident disturbed my pleasant reverie and I preferred not to remain any longer on that porch—as beautiful as the scenery and as refreshing as was the breeze.

Again, Lieutenant Brock and myself were reclining on the side of the hill watching those mortar shells. Here comes one making its path directly towards us—it explodes in a dangerous position. We got as near as possible to a large apple tree near us and awaited the result. Here comes one of those fragments. It threatens to fall upon our defenseless heads but the shield of God warded it off and it falls to our side, but two or three steps from us, and throws all the dirt over us. The piece would weigh 20 pounds, tearing up a large hole and burying itself more than two feet in the earth. This shocked our nerves considerably; we felt thankful for our deliverance. . . .

On the lines there is no change. The firing continues incessant. . . .

How long shall the endurance of our men be tested? Who ever

heard of men lying in ditches day and night, exposed to the burning sun and drenching rains for a period of 30 days, and that, too, under continual fire and on quarter rations?

Their limbs become stiff—their strength is frittered away—their flesh leaves their limbs and their muscles relax and their eyes become hollow and their cheeks sunken. Their clothes are covered with dirt and, Oh, horrible! Their bodies are occupied by filthy vermin. The detestable "body guards." Thus were men of refinement and polish, in the habit of preserving great external decency, subjected to this deep and severe humiliation.

Nor could this be avoided, for the ditches were alive with these crawling pests and to escape was impossible. This was not the least of the many vexations with which the brave defenders of our country were afflicted.

Our men began to show signs of discouragement. They have waited for Johnston so long that hope deferred makes the heart sick. Often they imagine that they can hear his cannon in the rear. News is brought in that he has crossed the Big Black; that they had an engagement with the enemy and defeated them. But so many false reports have been circulated that our men are slow to credit any.

It is now the middle of June and no relief. The sanguine still hope, while the desponding give up all hope. ☆ ☆ ☆

In the evening darkness Col. Rawlins was writing Grant's morning orders for all divisions: "At 4 A.M. on the 20th instant a general cannonading will be commenced from all parts of the line on the city of Vicksburg. Firing will continue until 10 A.M. . . . Care must be taken to retain for emergency at least 100 rounds each for all the field artillery and 20 rounds per gun for the siege guns. . . . Troops will be held under arms from 6:30 A.M. ready to take advantage of any signs the enemy may show of weakness, or to repel an attack should one be made.

"It is not designed to assault the enemy's works but to be prepared."

JUNE 20

Thirty-fourth Day

> "Yesterday afternoon, the enemy on the peninsula
> endulged in what they considered would be
> pleasant amusement annoying our batteries from
> a couple of Parrott guns planted on the east side of
> that neck of land. Forebearance ceasing to be a
> virtue, two of our guns responded to the challenge,
> when the Yanks found it convenient to hunt holes
> to dodge the missiles that were hurled at them,
> with great precision. . . . About half past four
> o'clock this morning the enemy opened one of the
> heaviest shellings of our rear with artillery. . . ."
>   —VICKSBURG *Citizen*

Sergeant Tunnard wrote:

☆ ☆ ☆ At early dawn every gun along the line suddenly opened, keeping up a rapid and continuous fire. All concurred in the opinion that such a tremendous cannonading had never been equalled in their experience, and the volume of sound surpassed anything yet heard. It seemed as if heaven and earth were meeting in a fearful shock, and the earth trembled under the heavy concussions.

The gunboats approached from below, but ere reaching the range of our batteries, retired with their flags at half-mast, causing much speculation as to the meaning of this manœuvre. The cannonading was kept up steadily all day. The men were in unusually fine humor. They seemed to care little that a powerful enemy was within arms-length of them, and that their flag was flaunting its folds in their very faces.

A glance over the breastworks would exhibit a panoramic view of a large portion of the adjacent works, the puffs of smoke curling upward from the guns, used with such dexterous skill, or the light, vapory cloud arising from the discharged rifles of the sharpshooters. Such a glance must be taken very hastily, as the whiz of a minié ball, or the shrill scream of a shell, admonished the spectator that he was seen and already made a target of. The view, under such circumstances, was perhaps more pleasant to the eye than comfortable to the other senses.

193

During the day, one of the enemy climbed up to the parapet of the Third Louisiana works, and boldly looked over, no doubt with the very laudable intention of having a good view of affairs within the forbidden ground. He paid a fearful forfeit for his temerity, being shot and instantly killed by one of the regiment standing near the spot where he exposed himself.

The attempt was considered an unusually bold and foolhardy one. The combatants watched for each other with the keen-sightedness of an eagle, and the ferocity and vigilance of a tiger seeking prey. Consequently, the least exposure was instantly discovered, and as quickly brought a bullet to the spot. ☆ ☆ ☆

As Oldroyd reported the barrage: "This morning our whole line of artillery—seven miles long—opened on the doomed city and fortifications at six o'clock, and kept up the firing for four hours, during which time the smoke was so thick we could see nothing but the flash of the guns. No fog could have so completely hid from view objects around, both close and familiar.

"Had the rebs made a dash for liberty then, they could not have been discovered until they were right upon us. But they did not do it. Our infantry was all called out in line of battle, and we stacked arms till the firing ceased. Oh, what a calm after that terrific bellowing. There was every variety of tone today from the dogs of war—from the squeak of a little fiste to the roar of a bulldog. The sound of some brass pieces was so loud as to drown the reverberations of the larger guns, and not a return shot was fired."

Lucy McRae's family had been warned of the approaching barrage. She wrote:

☆ ☆ ☆ One evening it was currently reported that the enemy would open fire all around the lines early the next morning, and an officer had persuaded Miss Lightcap, a young lady friend and neighbor, who was in the cave with us, that they would be safer nearer the lines under the cover of the hills. Mother consented to go, so up came the tent, a large basket was quickly packed with the meager stock of provisions, and away we went across Glass Bayou bridge, climbing the hill on the other side of the bridge late in the evening, and traveling the road just behind our batteries, where all along were dug trenches for our soldiers to fight behind. This was a very dangerous route by daylight, but under cover of night we felt safe.

The mortars were silent, resting, as all thought, for the next day's work. When the command was given to stop, the tent was pitched in a kind of ravine near the lines. Several tents were pitched there occupied by families living near by. Mother and Miss Lightcap spread down comforts, and we all huddled in the tent for sleep.

Just about daylight we were aroused by the belching cannon, and before we could think where we were, a cannonball that had spent its force on the side of the hill came rolling into the tent. The young lady screamed as it rolled upon her, and in less time than it takes to tell it we were all up and out of the tent. Balls were whizzing, cannon booming from the rear, mortars replying in rapid succession from the front.

Mother's quick perception soon told her we would be in the midst of a battle if she remained longer; so with alarm she cried, "Rice, take that tent up and let us go to town!"

Rice replied, "Yes, ma'am, let us go 'way from dis place before us all is killed." He was soon at work, as well as the rest of them, putting things together while the shot were falling around. An officer whom mother knew rushed up and cried, "Mrs. McRae, keep close under the bank, and don't take the road until you are obliged to." He afterward said he never expected us to reach town.

On we came, jumping behind trees, fences, or into trenches, shells exploding above us, scattering their pieces around us. We children were crying, mother praying, and all running between the shells, as we thought, and trying to reach Glass Bayou bridge, which was on the edge of town. Rice had dropped his tent, and Mary Ann had no lunch-basket, and as we came to the bridge a mortar shell exploded at the other end. We all fell to the ground, and when we got on our feet again not a word was spoken except "run," and we did run. Mother had me by the hand pulling me, while my brothers were close by us. When we reached the cave we were glad enough to get to it, for somehow we always felt safer under the shadow of the houses.

Our house was struck several times by shell, but father was never hurt, although a minié ball passed through his whiskers as he sat in the hall and lodged in the rocker of an old chair near him. The Parrott gun was dreaded because, as soon as you heard the report of the gun, the ball was on you. One lady standing in a cave door had her arm taken off. Many narrow escapes were made when minié balls would whiz by. ☆ ☆ ☆

Chaplain Foster had felt his way down to the "river's edge to bathe before broad daylight" when caught in the bombardment. He noted:

☆ ☆ ☆ While I was thus enjoying myself in the cool refreshing waters of the mighty river, a tremendous cannonading opened along the whole line. It was certainly the heaviest that occurred during the siege, for the enemy had been mounting new guns all the time. They had received and planted some heavy pieces and they opened upon us with all their might this morning as soon as they could see to shoot. Some of their shot came clear across the whole town and fell half way across the river. They make a peculiar sound when they strike the water, sounding more like they came in contact with a rock than with yielding element. . . . The gunboats below also joined in the revelry. . . .

Now, no place is secure in the town—houses are no protection against these mighty monsters of death.

Now there is confusion and bustle among the citizens of Vicksburg. There is hurrying to and fro with the women and innocent children. They must leave their comfortable homes and go to their dark, gloomy caves. Better to live in a cave than be slain in a fine house. ☆ ☆ ☆

"More news from Johnston," wrote Hugh Moss. "Two men couriers arrived last night and state that he was 25 miles from here when they started and on his way with 75-100 thousand men, his advance guard then skirmishing with the enemy. May he arrive here in due time, for we are now living on almost nothing. We live on peas mostly. The blockade here raised and my communications home again renewed, I would feel new blood course through my veins."

General Grant, vaguely apprehensive that Johnston might try a bold sally toward Vicksburg, had established a defensive line of batteries and entrenchments to the east of his main offensive works. Pemberton, however, racked with doubts and spurred by the late bombardment, summoned a staffer this Saturday, Capt. George D. Wise, for "duty surrounded with difficulties and danger."

It soo became apparent that the General wished Captain Wise to pass through enemy lines and convey to Johnston, verbally, "the urgent necessity for speedy action!"

So far as the young Virginia lawyer knew, Vicksburg's commander had not fully confided in his generals that he was dispatching a personal emissary to Jackson. So concerned was Pemberton that he would not commit his thoughts or instructions to paper, "not even in cypher."

The General assured the Captain, however, that he had checked "all departments" and had become convinced that his men were "already enfeebled by their long service in the trenches without relief and without adequate food and reduced rations."

Pemberton said he did not believe Vicksburg's defenders could hold out longer than July 10, nor did he consider them able to "endure the fatigue of a march." While "there might be sufficient ammunition to meet the emergency of an assault," the General "could not permit the men to reply to the continuous fire upon them."

After talking for almost an hour, Pemberton told the Captain to suggest to Johnston that he lead his troops in by the Graveyard Road, while he himself would attempt to escape with his own forces via the Hall's Ferry Road, a mile to the south.

It should have seemed to Wise, if it did not, a very curious bit of thinking on Pemberton's part. Should the rather frantic maneuver actually succeed, then the only change in Vicksburg's situation would be a new trapped army. There would result a "new team," a switch in defenders, but just as outnumbered as before.

JUNE 21

Thirty-fifth Day

"Although the city of Vicksburg has been in a
state of siege and our inveterate enemy has been
bombarding us incessantly for more than a month,
we are still able to say that this is the age of
improvement. Cut off from all outside resources,
we are enabled to bring into play our own
native genius . . . we have succeeded in making our
paper a pictorial sheet . . . citizens will please
save these illustrated papers until the war is over
when they can ornament the walls of their
rooms. . . ."

—VICKSBURG *Citizen*

In witness, Dora Miller wrote, "the *Citizen* is printed on wallpaper; therefore has grown a little in size. . . . The gentlemen who took our cave came yesterday to invite us to come to it, because, he said, 'It's going to be very bad today.' I don't know why he thought so. We went, and found his own and another family in it; sat outside and watched the shells till we concluded the cellar was as good a place as that hillside. I fear the want of good food is breaking down H. I know from my own feelings of weakness, but mine is not an American constitution and has a recuperative power that his has not. . . .

"I had gone upstairs during the interregnum to enjoy a rest on my bed and read the reliable items in the *Citizen* when a shell burst right outside the window in front of me. Pieces flew in, striking all round me, tearing down masses of plaster that came tumbling over me.

"When H. rushed in I was crawling out of the plaster, digging it out of my eyes and hair. When he picked up beside my pillow a piece as large as a saucer, I realized my narrow escape. The window frame began to smoke, and we saw the house was on fire. He ran for a hatchet and I for water, and we put it out. Another [shell] came crashing near, and I snatched up my comb and brush and ran down here. It has taken all the afternoon to get the plaster out of my hair, for my hands were rather shaky."

Sergeant Tunnard could observe but "little apparent change in the situation," continuing:

198

☆ ☆ ☆ On the right hand bank, up the river, the enemy's trains were seen on a sandbar. At a distance they looked like a hive of busy bees, and were doubtless engaged in conveying stores to their troops.

The Parrott guns still annoyed the city and were heavily fired on by our batteries. The wreck of the *Cincinnati* was again shelled, the enemy being discovered at work on it, but were speedily driven away by our skillful gunners. Lieutenant Holt, of Company E, lying in a tent sick in the commissary camp, was shot in the leg, and badly wounded by a ball shot from a Belgian rifle, nearly a mile distant.

A courier arrived with dispatches and caps. He had floated down the Yazoo, through the fleet, on a plank, and was taken out of the water completely exhausted. His name, unfortunately unknown, assuredly deserves a place in the history of these daily events for his daring and determination in reaching the beleaguered city.

The day passed without any unusual occurrence. No light, as yet, glimmered through the dark cloud which hung like a funeral pall over the heroic defenders of the Hill City. ☆ ☆ ☆

To Winchester Hall, however, this was a sad Sunday since Major W. W. Martin, who had assumed some of the Colonel's duties following his wounding, fell in action. Hall wrote of the twenty-two-year-old Martin, second in command of the 26th Louisiana:

☆ ☆ ☆ Endowed with a fearless spirit, a cool head, judgment rare, no better soldier ever stood behind the battlements of Vicksburg. Had he fought under the eagles of Napoleon at an earlier day, the keen insight of that great captain would have marked him, and his transcendent worth would have made him, in time, a marshall of the empire.

As the enemy's work gradually approached our own, their picket line and ours was so near together, it was often understood, at various points there should be no picket firing. One night when our pickets were in charge of Lieutenant Sanders of Company B, he was making a tour about 2 A.M. when he heard a voice in ordinary tone near to him say "what o'clock is it, Reb?" It proved to be an officer in command of the enemy's picket!

Private Vileor Duhon of Company E, however, had a contrary experience, as mentioned to me by Lieutenant Gilbeau of the same company. Duhon being one of the outer line of pickets, on reaching his post behind a log, raised his head to look toward the front, when a shot from the enemy's picket made it prudent for him to protect himself behind the log. Not having been able to recognize the direction of the shot, he changed his position behind the log, and placing his hat at the end of a pole raised it at the point he had first occupied. As soon as the hat appeared a second shot was fired. Knowing now the position of his antagonist, he gave the latter time to reload, and then repeated the operation of raising the hat, having previously placed his gun in the direction of his opponent. The picket took another shot at the hat, and Duhon took a shot at the picket and threw himself behind the log where he began to reload. Before he had got through he heard a noise on the other side of the log and rising quickly was about to pierce his adversary with his bayonet, when he surrendered, saying that Duhon's first ball passed very near his head, and he was confident the next would kill him.

The days wore on wearily; with Colonel Crow in charge of the regiment, and Mrs. Hall in charge of my family camp—both approved soldiers—there was nothing more to be desired in their several lines of duty.

Mrs. Hall had driven into Vicksburg a cow Mrs. Downs had given to her. It was a treasure to us. She furnished milk for the children, and was a potent factor in our commissariat. As some soldiers were detected at one time driving her away, I had her guarded, and my eldest son performed some of his earliest military duty, at thirteen, in taking his tour of duty as sentry over her. But forage became very scarce, as my poor thin horses mutely attested, and I was compelled to have her killed. Indeed, as time passed by, food and forage were at a premium; the law of demand and supply was entirely ignored, and various expedients were resorted to.

The privates of the regiment successfully undertook a decrease in the rodent population. In my weakened condition, camp fare was repulsive. I sent out a man to shoot a rat for me, imagining I could eat it broiled with relish, but the hunt failed to secure the game, and the fancy passed. The men cut up the young growth of the wild cane, boiled it and made a delectable dish.

Peas were ground and mixed with cornmeal but proved unpalatable—the ever-faithful mule was looked upon with pitiless eye, and the scarcity of forage induced us to kill several and distribute the flesh among the officers' messes, by way of giving countenance to this novel addition to our menu, and preparing the men for it. ☆ ☆ ☆

Others were taking note of this so-called "squirrel stew," made of rats. "Our provisions," wrote Lucy McRae, "were becoming scarce, and the Louisiana soldiers were eating rats as a delicacy, while mules were occasionally being carved up to appease the appetite. Mother would not eat mule meat, but we children ate some, and it tasted right good, having been cooked nicely. Wheat bread was a rarity, and sweet potato coffee was relished by the adults."

The rugged Will Tunnard found no trouble in facing a plate of rodent meat. He recalled that he: ". . . made a hearty breakfast on fried rats, whose flesh [he] found very good, and fully equal to that of squirrels. The thought of such food may be actually nauseating to many, yet, let starvation with its skeleton form visit them, and all qualms would speedily vanish, and any food, to satisfy hunger, be voraciously devoured, and considered as sweet manna.

"It is a difficult matter for persons surrounded with abundance to realize the feeling produced by extreme hunger; no pen-picture, no grouping of words in all their forcibleness and power, can convey to those who have not experienced the sensation produced by this gaunt visitor. It must be felt to be realized; and if once felt, the idea of eating dogs, cats, rats, or even human flesh would contain nothing repulsive or repugnant to the feelings."

"Canards!" was, on the other hand, the incredulous reaction of young ladies such as Lida Lord, who went queasy at the thought of such rank fare involving "rats and mice and cats and puppies!"

At the same time, the young daughter of the Episcopal minister observed: "There was really no excuse for the city of Vicksburg being so poorly provisioned. The planters of Warren County offered General Pemberton the contents of their well-filled smokehouses and barns if he would furnish wagons and horses to bring them into town. His answer to the committee which waited on him was, according to common report:

" 'Gentlemen, when General Pemberton desires the advice or the assistance of the planters of Warren County *he will ask it!*' And so it was that the corn and sugar and bacon of rich plantations fed General Grant's army, while the defenders of Vicksburg starved."

Willie Lord, however, had heard talk of "feasting upon cats and dogs, and many seriously expressed their willingness to undergo the experiences of the defenders of Londonderry, where the besieged ate strips of rawhide and leather, rather than yield a city which was the key to the Mississippi Valley, and which would give the North the freedom of a great waterway penetrating the very heart and center of the Southwestern States. But alas for the realization of such extreme heroism!

"Whether General Pemberton was better advised than were the citizens and soldiers of Vicksburg regarding the impossibility of relief from the outside or whether, as was believed by many of his own men, he was too fastidious in the matter of his diet to relish the prospect of cat and dog ragouts or strips of leather made into soup. . .?"

Probably no woman in Vicksburg was making a meal on rats—as yet. But Mary Loughborough wrote of the emptiness inside being experienced by all the ladies, young and old:

☆ ☆ ☆ One day a friend brought us some fruit that had been presented to him. While we were conversing, my little hunger-besieged two-year-old daughter quietly secured it, and, sitting on the floor, ate with avidity. When she had finished nearly all of it, she turned around, with a bright and well-satisfied face, to me, saying, "Mamma, it's so good!"—the first intimation that I had that my portion had disappeared.

Dear child; I trembled for her in the greater trials I believed in store for us. Fruits and vegetables were not to be procured at any price. Everyone felt the foreboding of a more serious trouble, the great fear of starvation that stared all in the face, causing those who possessed any article in the shape of edibles to retain it for that period to which all looked forward with anxiety—when we would come to actual want.

The men in the rifle pits were on half rations—flour or meal enough to furnish bread equivalent in quantity to two biscuits in two days: many of them ate it all at once, and the next day fasted, preferring, as they said, to have one good meal.

So they sat cramped up all day in the pits—their rations cooked in the valley and brought to them—scarcely daring to change their positions and stand erect, for the Federal sharpshooters were watching for the heads; and to rise above the breastworks was almost certain death. Frequently, a Parrott shell would penetrate the entrenchments and, exploding, cause frightful wounds, and death most frequently. "Ah!" said M—— one day, "it is to the noble men in the rifle pits that Vicksburg will owe aught of honor she may gain in this siege. I revere them as I see them undergoing every privation with courage and patience, anxious only for the high reputation of the city."

They amused themselves, while lying in the pits, by cutting out little trinkets from the wood of the parapet and the minié balls that fell around them. Major Fry, from Texas, excelled in skill and ready invention, I think: he sent me one day an arm chair that he had cut from a minié ball—the most minute affair of the kind I ever saw, yet perfectly symmetrical. At another time, he sent me a diminutive plough made from the parapet wood, with traces of lead, and a lead point made from a minié ball.

I had often remarked how cheerfully the soldiers bore the hardships of the siege. I saw them often passing with their little sacks containing scanty rations, whistling and chatting pleasantly, as around them thickly flew the balls and shells.

Poor men, yet so badly used, and undergoing so many privations! ☆ ☆ ☆

The sight of half-famished soldiers prowling the city for sustenance particularly distressed Chaplain Foster:

☆ ☆ ☆ During this week our hungry men could be seen walking the streets in search of something to eat. Some would buy sugar at an enormous price and walk along eating it from their hands without any bread. Molasses was ten dollars a gallon—flour five dollars a pound— and meal $140 per bushel, and none to be had scarcely at that.

The poor soldier does not meet with the cakes and pies which once filled every corner of the streets. All the eating houses were closed. The poor in town are upon the verge of starvation. Lean and haggard famine stands at the door of the rich and knocks for admission.

All that our soldiers get for one day could be eaten at one meal and not be sufficient. Two common-sized biscuits, two rashers of bacon, a few peas and a spoonful of rice constitute one day's allowance.

Our eating at the hospital has been very scant. At first we had plenty of bread and beef. Now we are allowanced to a small piece of beef and pea bread. The pea bread is made of peas and corn ground up together and mixed in about equal proportions. It presented a black, dirty appearance and was most unwholesome—as heavy as lead and most indigestible. But we did not have enough of this.

We were thus kept half hungry all the time—consequently not in the best humor. But we fared better than our poor soldiers in the ditches. There were several orchards around and the apples were half grown. The trees were soon stripped of their premature fruit. Even soldiers in the line came out to share in the treat.

The doctors at the hospitals live like kings. There was no famine to them. Their tables groan with luxury and with every abundance. ☆ ☆ ☆

From across the lines a Union doctor, who would have been almost as surprised as his Southern counterparts to learn that he was subsisting in regal fashion, was writing his wife of his unflattering regard for Vicksburg's defending general.

"Pemberton is a fool!" snapped Dr. Tompkins, "or he would surrender. The rebs in Vicksburg must suffer terribly, nothing to eat and nothing for their sick and wounded. And what will they gain by holding out any longer? I do not believe they expect aid from Johnston any more. Goodnight, my darling wife. . . ."

Oldroyd drew a comparison in the provender for besieged and besieger:

☆ ☆ ☆ I was quite amused to see one of the prisoners brought in today, eating his supper. We gave him all he could eat, and that was no small amount. But he was certainly a very hungry man, and if he is a fair sample of those remaining in Vicksburg, Uncle Sam's commissary will have to endure quite a burden, for after the surrender, no doubt, Grant will have to feed them all.

We have eaten pretty well in camp today, and cooked everything we had on hand, since we may not get so good an opportunity again upon the march. When hardtack was first issued there was but one way to eat it, and that was dry, just as it reached us. Practice, however, taught us to prepare a variety of dishes from it. The most palatable way to dispose of hardtack, to my taste, is to pulverize, then soak overnight, and fry for breakfast as batter-cakes.

Another good way is to soak whole, and then fry; and still another is to soak a little, then lay it by the fire and let grease drop on it from toasted meat, held to the fire on a pointed stick. This latter is the most common way on a march. Sometimes the tack is very hard indeed by the time it reaches us, and it requires some knack to break it. I have frequently seen boys break it over their knees. Just raise your foot up so as to bring the bent knee handy, and then fetch your hardtack down on it with your right hand, with all the force you can spare, and, if not too tough, you may break it in two.

But one poor fellow I saw was completely exhausted trying to break a hardtack, and after resorting to all the devices he could think of, finally accomplished it by dropping on it a 12-pound shell. The objection to that plan was, however, that the fellow could hardly find his hardtack afterward.

There is a good deal of complaint, in our company at least, about the coffee. It seems not quite so good as that we have had, and I suspect it has been adulterated by somebody who is willing to get rich at the expense of the poor soldier, whose curses will be heaped strong and heavy on anybody who deteriorates any of his rations, and particularly his coffee. The only time a soldier cannot drink his coffee is when the use of that ration is suspended. In fact, there is nothing so refreshing as a cup of hot coffee, and no sooner has a marching column halted, than out from each haversack comes a little paper sack of ground coffee, and a tin cup or tin can, with a wire bale, to be filled from the canteen and set upon a fire to boil. The coffee should not be put in the water before it boils.

At first I was green enough to do so, but soon learned better, being compelled to march before the water boiled, and consequently lost my coffee. I lost both the water and the coffee. It takes but about five minutes to boil a cup of water, and then if you have to march you can put your coffee in and carry it till it is cool enough to sip as you go. Even if we halt a dozen times a day, that many times will a soldier make and drink his coffee, for when the commissary is full and plenty, we may drink coffee and nibble crackers from morning till night. The aroma of the first cup of coffee soon sets the whole army to boiling; and the best vessel in which to boil coffee for a soldier is a common cove oyster can, with a bit of wire for a bale, by which you can hold it on a stick over the fire, and thus avoid its tipping over by the burning away of its supports. ☆ ☆ ☆

"We had to buy water by the bucketfull and serve it out in rations," added Lida Lord, "so that we realized what thirst meant, and were often hungry, though when we knew our men were living on mule meat and bread made of ground beans we did not grumble at our scanty fare." Lida went on:

☆ ☆ ☆ In our cave we lived in constant danger from both rear and river. We were almost eaten up by mosquitos, and were in hourly dread of snakes. The vines and thickets were full of them, and a large rattlesnake was found one morning under a mattress on which some of us had slept all night. . . .

Our ears were always strained to catch the first sound of Johnston's guns; every extra-heavy cannonading was a message of hope, and every courier brought in, it was said, news of most encouraging victories. On Sunday, June 21, our friends, the young ordnance officers, were in jubilant spirits. They had seen an acquaintance, a St. Louis man, one Bob Lowder, who brought dispatches to Pemberton, and letters from home for them. They described him as a most daring man, but when cross-questioned admitted some doubts as to his being very reliable. He had passed the gunboats on the Yazoo, dressed as a fisherman, in a skiff full of lines and bait; but at the mouth of the river he saw so many men and boats that he had taken to the woods, and finally had floated down the Mississippi after dark on a plank canoe.

He stated that he had been sworn to secrecy, but when eagerly questioned he replied: "Now, boys, *don't*! I can only tell you that in three or four days you will hear the biggest kind of cannonading, and will see the Yanks skedaddling up the Yazoo."

He also said that Johnston's army consisted of the very flower of the South Carolina, Virginia, and Kentucky troops. This was corroborated by a courier, who came in the same day, and reported himself as only three days absent from Johnston's camps. Joseph E. Johnston was our angel of deliverance in those days of siege, but alas! we were never even to touch the hem of his robe. ☆ ☆ ☆

Postscripted her mother, Margaret Lord: "Tomorrow and the next we will listen so eagerly for the sound of the battle. May the Almighty who can save by many or by few fight for us and give us the victory."

JUNE 22

Thirty-sixth Day

> "President Davis expresses himself as thoroughly
> confident about the issue of the struggle in his
> own state. . . . It would appear that if Grant
> advances directly against the trench works at
> Vicksburg he is prepared to stake his all upon
> that cast of the die . . . the prospect does not
> seem very promising for the Federals."
> —LONDON *Times* CORRESPONDENT IN RICHMOND

"For the last two days," wrote Hugh Moss, "the mortars have left this place little peace. We hear that their silence is occasioned by General Grant sending Commodore Porter word that the people cared nothing for his shelling, and after extracting the powder, took shells for ornaments. The weather is quite cool and pleasant, at night so much so that we have to use a blanket."

The same days continued to pass "without any particular variation," it seemed to Chaplain Foster:

☆ ☆ ☆ At Hospital No. 1, my old home, the firing continues very dangerous. Well would it have been for some had they moved all the wounded to some more secure place when they were speaking of it. . . .

At this hospital there was a young man from some Louisiana Regiment dreadfully wounded upon his shoulder by a shell. Nearly all the flesh from one of his shoulders, down towards his back, was removed. By the closest attention his life may be saved.

The captain of the company to which this young man belonged happened to have his wife with him at the time and she was a particular friend to the wounded boy. She attended him to the hospital and for several days did not leave him, day or night. Then she made arrangements to stay in town at night and returned every morning.

No matter how severe the shelling was, she came as regular as the rising of the sun, always bringing some good nourishment for her friend. The wounded man improved under this kind treatment. Often I have noticed this brave woman make her visits at the peril of her life. She would go when the shells were falling all around, when the road to town was literally torn up by them, when even brave men would shrink from the danger. . . .

Now her cheek becomes pale from constant labor and her strength evidently begins to fail. About four weeks after the wound was inflicted, a young man of the same company attends upon his wounded friend at night. He remains in the ditches during the day and at night he watches at the bedside of his wounded friend. On a certain night the firing from the mortar shells was furious. One bursts overhead; a large fragment passes through the tent and takes off this young man's head, while he was sitting up with his wounded friend. . . .

This week the enemy began to plant guns on the other side of the river. At first they fire a small, movable cannon and change their position at every fire. Our old Columbiads thunder at the little impudent thing. Here comes another shot from this small cannon and strikes on the street before you hear the sound. Our guns fire at the smoke, but no doubt the active thing is far away from this for it seems to be drawn by horses.

After a while they plant a heavier gun on the opposite bank behind a mound. They open fire upon the town and make it dangerous to walk the streets. Our large guns open a furious fire upon this small gun. Old Whistling Dick tries his skill also, but in vain. They cannot dismount it.

Sometimes the shell would burst exactly over the spot and we would think that it was silenced, but after a while it would open again and send a defiant shot on Main Street again. Our guns, seeing that they could not dismount it, ceased firing, except occasionally, when the enemy would seem to be too saucy. The enemy, encouraged by their efforts, went to work and mounted other guns so that this part of town began to be quite dangerous. . . .

Thus passes the fifth week of the dreadful siege. No relief yet. Our men are discouraged, though some are yet hopeful. . . .

When will this long letter end? I must hurry to a conclusion.

The enemy occupied about this time a high hill in front of Hébert's Brigade and planted there a heavy battery within 50 yards of our works. . . . Now they begin to try the plan of undermining our works. Day and night they dig. Our men endeavor to countermine, and each party can hear the clinking of the tools of the other.

But our operations are not successful. The enemy push on the work with great energy. So close are the parties to each other that we throw hand grenades amongst them and sometimes they throw them back before they explode. Their ditches extend within 20 steps of our men.

General Hébert has a line constructed in the rear of our first works, and seeing that the enemy will shortly blow up the fort, hill and all, he orders them to abandon the threatened line. Everything is now ready. ☆ ☆ ☆

Meanwhile, Ida Barlow, from Winona, Mississippi, remained in the family's unhappy domicile position within the Union lines:

☆ ☆ ☆ A crowd of Yankees came into the room where my aunt was feigning sickness. One of her own house servants, a dining room boy, was leading the way, and called out, "Come this way, I'll show you where they keep the goodies," and led the way to the pantry. My aunt jumped from the bed and grabbed an old musket that my uncle always kept by the bedside and jerked out the bayonet that was the end of it and struck one of the Yankees in the breast. He was borne away to the surgeon, and the entire family thought our time had come and we would all be slain, but an officer was outside and he came in and had a private conversation with my grandfather and that was the end of it.

The two most horrible atrocities* that took place in our section were those of the Cook and Watson families. Mr. Cook was a planter who was said to be cruel to his slaves. It seems that his negroes had left their master and gone in a body to the Yankees as most all of them did over the whole country.

It is supposed they had reported their master's cruelty to them. A squad of soldiers went to the Cook home and overpowered the entire family except one little girl who hid under the house. The father was most horribly mutilated, both arms and legs were cut off. A candle was put into a gun and shot into the mother, a bayonet was thrust through one child, pinning her to the wall. After the soldiers left, the child under the house heard her father's groans and went to find him. Together they made their way to the nearest neighbors—the man just rolling along with both feet and hands gone and only lived a short time.

The Watsons were an old couple and he was a paralytic. They had several sons in the Confederate Army who were noted for their bravery.

*There is no way to prove or disprove Ida Barlow. Wanton killings, however, were associated with the infamous "bushwhackers," the ruffians following in the wake of armies. General Grant was known for the discipline he maintained and the swift punishment meted out to offenders.

The Yankees were supposed to have heard this and sought revenge on the parents. They rolled the old gentleman out on his gallery in his rolling chair. They then set fire to the house.

The mother they took in the yard, took her own feather bed and cut it open and while some were doing this others went into her own smokehouse and rolled a barrel of molasses into the yard, after removing all the woman's clothing, they put her in the feathers and emptied the molasses on her, leaving her thus to watch her husband burned to death sitting on his own gallery. We were told that General Grant was very indignant over this crime committed by his men and they in turn were severely punished.

One day my grandfather carried two bales of cotton into the quartermaster where he drew our rations and was given a good price for them. Not long after he reached home, several men who had seen him receive the money came, and placing a pistol to his temple, demanded the money. My grandmother went to the wardrobe and got several large rolls of Confederate money and gave that to them which they seemed to be satisfied with and left, not knowing it was not worth the paper it was printed on.

One night several Yankees brought in a Confederate spy whom they had captured and sat around our fire, saying that at 9 o'clock they would take him out and shoot him. My grandmother begged for his life but to no good, so the prisoner gave up his great Army coat and blanket and was led out behind the gin house. Out of the darkness came the report of pistol shots which sent him to his death.

Late one evening I was out in the yard with a cousin gathering bluebells which grew in our yard in abundance. We heard groans outside the fence, and saw a wounded man lying on the ground. We were so distressed that it turned us sick, and to this day the odor of the bluebell will cause me to feel as if I should faint. ☆ ☆ ☆

The same Monday, Charles Dana, "behind Vicksburg," was writing to Secretary Stanton about another and luckier spy, among other concerns of the moment:

☆ ☆ ☆ A spy of Admiral Porter, who got into Vicksburg some months ago and has served in an engineer company, came out to us last night. He reports that enemy have mines in front of Sherman, of Ransom and of Logan. He has worked on that before Sherman. It is made from the ditch of the principal fortifications, so that its explosion will leave the work unharmed, and extends toward the sap, which is now almost in contact with the ditch, there being but about 12 feet between them in front of Logan's position.

Of McPherson's lines he does not know the precise position of the mine, but as they talked of exploding it last night, he supposes it must be, like the others, outside of the work, which, as I have before reported, is on the most commanding height of this whole system of defense. On Ransom's front he is also ignorant of the exact position, and cannot say whether the mine covers the position gained by Ransom yesterday morning. Ord reports that at noon yesterday A. J. Smith had also gained the ditch and would mine.

The same spy tells us that the garrison, though weak from deficient food and excessive work, generally determined to hold out to the last. Their corn is nearly exhausted, and the ration includes a portion of wheaten flour. They say they can be starved out, but that the place can never be taken otherwise.

A private letter captured at Lake Providence contains the information, which the writer had from an agent of the Confederate Government, that Vicksburg has food enough to hold out to August 1. We have in position one and a half hundred and eighteen guns. There will be no attack unless a special opportunity should offer. From Joe Johnston we learn that the troops at Yazoo City and the other division this side of Big Black have been moved back across toward Clinton, leaving only detachments and a body of cavalry on this side. Joe Johnston has also notified C. C. Washburn, at Haynes' Bluff, who lately sent a flag of truce by steamboat up Yazoo River to Satartia, that no more flags will be received by the river, but that they must come by the front. General Grant is doubtful whether these movements of Joe Johnston indicate an attempt to avoid Haynes' Bluff by crossing Big Black near Bridgeport or elsewhere lower down. ☆ ☆ ☆

Thirty-seventh Day

"Yesterday morning a live Yankee was caught
on our streets and placed in jail. He is a
Dutchman affecting craziness and refuses to
give any account of himself. He cannot tell
the regiment he belongs to and says the
Yankees picked him up and forced him
into the army. We think such characters
ought to be hung as spies, as it is not likely
that the Federal government would enlist
idiots into its army."

—VICKSBURG *Citizen*

"On the night of the twenty-second of June," noted Will Tunnard,
"a couple of Georgia regiments charged a Federal breastwork, about
fifty yards in their front, which had been thrown up the night before,
and contained a regiment of the enemy. They succeeded in dislodging
this force at the point of the bayonet and captured a number of
prisoners with very slight loss. The work was filled up and the spades
and shovels of the enemy were taken and brought in.

"A little occurrence was spread through camp, afterwards, regarding
the lieutenant colonel of the Federal regiment. Seeing that he was
either to be captured or run the gauntlet in getting away, he laid
down among the dead in the ditch, expecting to remain 'perdue' until
our force retired, and then his escape would be secured.

"In this conclusion, however, he had not taken into account that
the ditch might be filled. A few spadesfull of earth had the salutary
effect of bringing him to, and the dead, to all appearance, rose up
and walked, declaring he was not ready to be buried alive. And the
strategic lieutenant colonel, notwithstanding his ingenious conceit,
became a prisoner."

This Tuesday Dr. Alison, who apparently had been too busy to notice previous storms and showers, observed in his diary:

☆ ☆ ☆ It is now raining for the first time since the siege commenced.
Today is the 37th since we have been surrounded, and no improvement in the situation, except that the mortars have ceased firing. I

think they must have worn out, as the last shots fired all fell short. The shelling from the lines continues. Twelve of our wounded were killed in Hospital No. 1, and some others have suffered equally.

Rations very short. We are all in good spirits and look for help *one of these days*. Our friends outside suffer more in mind, much more than we do. It would surprise anyone not accustomed to shelling to see how coolly we take it.

Incessant fire. Lieutenant Young was killed on the lines. He was as clever a gentleman as ever lived, and his loss will be long felt by all who knew him. He was the last of three brothers. All perished in this cruel war. The Vaiden Artillery has already lost four men, one more is dying from his wounds and another has had his arm taken off.

Rations very short. There is talk of our being compelled to eat mule beef if not relieved very soon.* There is a great deal of sickness in the army. Thirty-nine days in the trenches will kill up any set of men. ☆ ☆ ☆

Mary Loughborough, too, had noted the squall and the continuing discomfitures as chronicled by Dr. Alison:

☆ ☆ ☆ The clouds had been darkening around us all day, and at night we had the prospect of a storm. M—— sent George out with a spade to slope the earth about the roof of our home and widen the water ditch around it; yet, it was not until the next morning that the rain began falling. By daylight I heard M—— giving orders rapidly about packing the earth firmly, deepening the ditch and watching the rear of the cave.

I opened my eyes to see without the darkness and gloom of a rainy day—to feel the dampness of the mist upon my face, and to behold M—— standing at the entrance, with the movable articles near him piled out of reach of the driving rain, giving orders to George in regard to our doubly besieged fortress. I lay and listened to the dropping and splashing with a dreamy pleasure at first; but hearing M—— start out to see if all were right, I sprang up, thinking I might assist in keeping out the water. It was a very fortunate move; for I had scarcely begun dressing when the earth gave away at the head of my bed, and a perfect spout of muddy water burst through the embankment and fell in the center of the resting place I had so lately left.

To run and call M—— to stop the water in the back part of the

*Curiously, there were yet some units in Vicksburg who had not yet tasted mule.

cave, and, in the greatest haste, to assist Cinth in removing every article that was at all dry and let the water have free course through was the work of an instant; yet, in the short time that the water had flowed through the cave, we presented a miserably deluged appearance; trunks were piled on trunks—lines hanging from log to log in the roof, filled with the dripping carpet, blankets, sheets, and miscellaneous articles, dripping with a dreary patter on the floor—chairs turned up together, and packed out of the way—our homelike arrangements all in disorder.

And now that the water had been turned that flowed through the cave, I and the servant sat, disconsolately, with our skirts drawn around, and our feet on little blocks of wood to keep them out of the mud, with rueful faces, regarding the sweeping of the water and splashing of rain without.

The water, having overflowed the sides of the ditch, making a new channel and pouring down at the entrance, had completely washed away our little terrace, leaving a huge and yawning gulf immediately in front of us. I was thus contemplating, sorrowfully, the ruins of our little home when M—— came down, bringing cheer to us again in the expression of his bright, strong and calm face; the water was flowing in little streams from his hat down to his coat, flowing over his coat, making little pools on the floor as he stood. He declared that the storm was nearly over, and that we would have some breakfast in spite of it.

Taking his hat from his head and shaking the water from it and from his hair, he bade George take his spade and cut a fireplace near the entrance, bring up his camp kettles, which were full of water, kindle a large fire and have the breakfast on. He congratulated me upon the perfect safety of our residence, that the water was running around it in regular Venetian style, and that for the present we were perfectly waterproof.

Indeed, our home was in a precarious situation on a rainy day, for we were planted in the bed of the torrent of water that drained from the hill above; yet M—— assured me that now we had nothing to fear, for with George he had packed the earth perfectly firm and secure. He laughed heartily at my narrow escape; for I declared that I should never have felt in a pleasant humor again if that rush of muddy water had fallen on me.

Soon the fire blazed cheerfully up and George commenced the preparation of our simple breakfast, M—— going out to attend to some reports. I had always looked forward to the prospect of rain with pleasure, as procuring us some respite from the incessant noise of explosions, and from the whistling and falling of balls. The fury of the storm had scarcely abated when the tumult and din of the Federal batteries and musketry recommenced; and far from the rain extinguishing the fuse of the shell, there seemed to be an unusually large number falling this morning. I began to feel thoroughly thawed and revived when George set the breakfast on the table and M—— came in; so we sat down quite gaily in spite of the continued falling of the rain.

The pleasant fire was doing its work, and the earth was rapidly hardening around us.

M—— told me of a colonel of one of the regiments stationed at the foot of one of the fortified hills, who unfortunately slept too long, and the turbulent rush of the waters down the hill broke through all barriers, enveloping him completely in mud, water, sand and sediment. He sprang from the ground in a towering rage, and could scarcely be persuaded that he was not the victim of a practical joke. So soundly had he slept that he was entirely oblivious of the storm and could scarcely believe his rude awakening the work of the elements. M—— told me also, with a grave face, of the poor soldiers he had seen in the rifle pits that morning, standing in water—some with little pieces of carpet drawn around them; others with nothing but their thin clothes, which were saturated; and there they would lie through the day, with only the meal of yesterday to sustain them. ☆ ☆ ☆

As Willie Lord witnessed, mortar shells had the same effect as water freshets in undermining their imperfectly buttressed caves.

"One of these bombs," he wrote, "falling upon the summit of the hill containing our group of caves, detached a great mass of crumbling earth from one side of the roof of the main gallery at its central point. In its fall this mass crushed a young woman to the floor of the cave, and she would undoubtedly have been killed had it not been for the heroism of a visiting artilleryman."

Willie continued:

☆ ☆ ☆ This brave fellow broke the force of the falling earth by throwing himself forward and with his shoulder diverting it slightly in its course. So the girl's life was saved, at the expense to him of a badly bruised arm and shoulder, which he counted nothing.

Soon afterwards, the mouth of one of the entrance caves collapsed under similar circumstances and, as it happened, cut off from the rest of us my father and several others who were standing outside. My father's powerful voice, audible above the roaring avalanche of earth, as he shouted "All right! Nobody hurt!" quickly reassured us.

But after these narrow escapes there was no longer a feeling of security even in the more deeply excavated portions of the caves.

Another incident awakened all of my mother's fears for the safety of her little brood. During one of the intervals between bombardments, the mother of a charming boy about three years old sat watching him at play near the entrance to the caves, when suddenly and furiously the fleet again opened fire upon the city. Amid the booming of guns and the screaming of Parrott shells the startled mother ran from the shelter of the cave to bring into safety her baby boy. But the child, grown accustomed to the sound of the guns, knew no fear. Playing in the sunshine among the few straggling daisies along the roadside, he danced like a butterfly from point to point and laughed at his mother's vain attempts to catch and hold him, while in blissful ignorance he played tag with death.

With a sudden rush the frantic mother caught him with one hand, but, screaming with delight at his escape, he broke away and fell sprawling nearby upon the grass. In that very instant a shell exploded where he had stood a moment before, and it shattered his mother's outstretched arm and hand. This woman refused to call the loss of her hand and arm a misfortune because, as she explained, if she had retained her hold upon the child he surely would have been killed. . . .

The camp of the staff officers of a Missouri brigade was within sight of our new cave, and they proved to be, all of them, clever, merry gentlemen, who in defense of states' rights had come South as a matter of patriotic principle, and were proportionately devoted to "the Cause." They spent most of their leisure evenings in the cave, making its gloomy recesses echo with songs and laughter. By candlelight they carved silhouettes of our faces and their own in the soft clay walls, and made artistic niches and shrinelike shelves in which to place candles, books, or vases of flowers. They sang in gleeful parody of the old-time song, "Then Let the Old Folks Scold If They Will":

> *Then let the big guns boom if they will,*
> *We'll be gay and happy still,*
> *Gay and happy, gay and happy,*
> *We'll be gay and happy still.*

"Dixie," "The Bonnie Blue Flag," and "Maryland, My Maryland" were, of course, prime favorites, sung with patriotic zest by all except my father, who could not sing a note.

Our friends from Missouri had for their mess cook a Swede named Tallien, who was so arrant a coward that some desperate necessity must have driven him to enlist. This old man, in his shirtsleeves, as usual, was one day busily engaged among his pots and pans, when a shell burst near the cooking-tent and a small piece of it struck the thick curly hair of a handsome young officer who was standing nearby, seriously wounding him, but so numbing all sensation that he did not at the moment realize that he was hurt.

Another piece of the shell grazed the cook's back just below the shoulder blades, so neatly that it cut through his suspenders and shirt without drawing blood. Throwing himself upon the ground in abject terror and writhing in apparent agony, Tallien gave vent to such dismal howls that we all ran from the cave to his assistance, fearing that he was mortally injured.

The wounded officer also, dazed as he was, sought instinctively to help the unscathed cook, but in making the effort he fell unconscious and was hurried to the hospital, where, as the result of his wound, he lost his handsome curly hair and later his eyesight, but afterwards, as we were delighted to learn, strangely enough he recovered both.

Tallien, on the contrary, never recovered from the panic into which he was thrown by having his suspenders cut by a fragment of shell. He received no other apparent injury, but soon died. ☆ ☆ ☆

Willie's sister Lida also wrote of the same episodes:

☆ ☆ ☆ One memorable day two bombshells burst simultaneously in our small valley. This seems incredible, and still more incredible that none of us were killed. The ground was torn up, and the air was filled with flying splinters, clods, fragments of iron and branches of trees. The earth seemed fairly to belch out smoke and flame and sulphur, and the roar and shock were indescribable. The tents were in ruins. One of the officers was astride a table, without any idea of how he got there, and one was flat on the ground, with his scalp slightly grazed and bleeding. The mess-cook, a white man, was on his knees, with his hands clasped to his back, frantically clutching his suspenders and howling dismally. He was with much trouble convinced that he had escaped without a scratch.

That evening, in the reaction from our fright, we had quite a merry time. We made taffy, and the "boys" sang us many a rollicking song.

One young lieutenant had a beautiful voice, and gave us "Widow Malone" in fine style. Alas! he died of typhoid fever a few days after the siege ended. Another, his bosom friend, was an artist, and carved our profiles in basso-rilievo on the cave walls. A candle was held so as to throw a shadow, and with a penknife the work was very cleverly done. Even the baby in her nightgown was immortalized in clay. So we passed the time trying to be gay, though every face was pale from the recent shock and every heart heavy with grave anxieties. The entire force, except Cupid, the pony, slept in the cave that night, and before retiring we registered a vow to meet on every anniversary of the raising of the siege, and have a feast and frolic in our stout little underground home.

I mentioned Cupid, and he merits a chronicle of his own. His body was fat and his legs were lean and short, and he was much more like a pug-dog than a pony, but, representing in his own person all the livestock of the united party, he was the idol of every child in the camp. He belonged to the musical lieutenant and was named Cupid because *his* name was Archer, and Cupid was an archer! Everyday his master rode him off to water, and he was always followed down the road by an admiring bodyguard of youngsters and darkies. Cupid had something of the look and all of the peculiarities of a mule. He would buck and kick outrageously, and his capers provided fun for the whole camp. ☆ ☆ ☆

Osborn Oldroyd at this time was noting a less dramatic incident, one involving a Federal cook, "of the 96th Ohio [who] happened to be cooking beans when General A. J. Smith, commanding a division of the 13th Army Corps, came around on camp inspection. After being properly saluted by the cook, the general began a colloquy as follows:

"General Smith—'What are you cooking?'

"The Cook—'Beans, sir.'

"General Smith—'How long do you cook beans?'

"The Cook—'Four hours, sir.'

"General Smith (with a look of withering scorn)—'*Four hours! You cook 'em six hours!*'

"That cook's beans were tender enough that day."

Thirty-eighth Day

"From a private letter received here yesterday
we learn that General Grant was 'all right' and
had plenty of men. A large force of men were
on transports ready to be landed at any point
needed, and the army was in excellent spirits.
The letter states that Grant had commenced to
throw hot shot into the devoted city. The writer
speaks highly of the colored troops and says
the city must soon surrender or be destroyed."
—WASHINGTON *Evening Star*

The rain had started again in the night, according to Sergeant Tunnard, giving way to "a dark and lowering morning. About 12 P.M. at night a heavy skirmish commenced on the right. The mortars bellowed forth their hoarse thunder, and four rifled batteries kept up a continual fire on the city from the front. On the lower river batteries a heavy concentrated attack was made, resulting harmlessly. The enemy across the river were very busily engaged at their usual sport. The balls from their long-range rifles penetrated to Washington Street, killing one, and wounding two men.

"The evening was beautiful, and the moon shed its soft effulgence over the embattlements of the beleaguered city. The wearied mind of the soldier, with all the surroundings of grim-visaged war, could not but yield to the witching influence of the spell and dream of home and loved ones, and speculate on the probable destiny that awaited him. Of the inward soul-struggle of these heroic soldiers the world will never know. The hours of dark despair, succeeded by the presence of bright-winged hope, the treasured thoughts and pleasant dreams of the future, the bitter agony of perishing expectations, all the inward struggles of light and darkness are as a sealed book to the probing gaze of the world. But one mission was theirs; to defend to the last extremity the city wherein centered all their pride. Whether they did so, let History record and the world determine."

In his refugee's abode outside of Vicksburg, Max Kuner was finding less time for flights of prose than for the urgency of keeping himself fed. He wrote:

☆ ☆ ☆ For a time after moving into the plantation house I occupied my spare time at my trade of watchmaker. Some few watches came my way to be repaired. But very soon I found it to be more profitable to "hunt" provisions. With what money I had I rode about the country buying, when possible, ham and bacon and the like from neighbors. A neighbor and I killed a beef, and "jerked" the meat by drying it in the sun and smoke. It proved very acceptable.

However, in time my family was reduced to a main diet of eggs, milk, cottage cheese and corn bread. For a sack of coffee I paid $300; part of the coffee (a great luxury) I gave away to a neighbor—an act, the results of which were indeed far-reaching. Finally I was reduced to riding into the Federal camp and asking for supplies. "Hey! What you coming here for, Johnny Reb?" would tease the soldiers. "For something to eat," I would reply bravely; and it was the honest, even if humiliating, truth.

I have mentioned that the yard was overrun with blackberry bushes. In lack of anything better to do, my wife busied herself by picking some of the berries, and making blackberry cordial. A Federal soldier happening in upon us saw the cordial, and immediately besought that my wife put up some for the field hospital. He begged so hard, and said that he would furnish the liquor and the spices and sugar, that he won my wife over—particularly as it was for the hospital. The thought of the sick and wounded soldiers, whether wearing the gray or the blue, touched her heart.

In the burning, blistering Southern summer sun she labored, gathering berries and boiling them. The soldier took the cordial, and appeared very grateful. Then, my little girl being ill with a cold, it occurred to me that at the hospital I could buy some quinine for her. So thither I went. To the officer in charge I introduced myself as the man whose wife had been furnishing the blackberry cordial.

"The what!" he exclaimed, "Blackberry cordial? Why, I only wish that we had some."

I explained further. I told him about the soldier, and all.

"Thunderation!" he ejaculated. "That's why my patients have been getting drunk!" For the soldier had been the sutler, and not a drop of the cordial had reached the hospital save by an "interior" route! But I secured my quinine, and later the hospital *did* get some cordial. ☆ ☆ ☆

Sustenance, as Max Kuner had attested, or its lack, continued to be the *enfant terrible* of this ever-darkening, ever-forboding canvas that was the suffocation of Vicksburg.

"I am told by my friends," wrote Mary Loughborough, "that I am looking worn and pale. . . . I *am* tired and weary!"

She continued:

☆ ☆ ☆ I never was made to exist under ground; and when I am obliged to, what wonder that I vegetate, like other unfortunate plants—grow wan, spindling, and white! Yet, I must reason with myself: I had chosen this life of suffering with one I love; and what suffering, after all, have I experienced?—privations in the way of good and wholesome food, not half what the poor people around us are experiencing. . . .

The hill opposite our cave might be called "death's point" from the number of animals that had been killed in eating the grass on the sides and summit. In all directions I can see the turf turned up, from the shells that have gone ploughing into the earth. Horses or mules that are tempted to mount the hill by the promise of grass that grows profusely there invariably came limping down wounded, to die at the base, or are brought down dead from the summit.

A certain number of mules are killed each day by the commissaries and are issued to the men, all of whom prefer the fresh meat, though it be of mule, to the bacon and salt rations that they have eaten for so long a time without change. There have already been some cases of scurvy. The soldiers have a horror of the disease. Therefore, I suppose, the mule meat is all the more welcome. Indeed, I petitioned M—— to have some served on our table.

He said: "No; wait a little longer."

He did not like to see me eating mule until I was obliged to; that he trusted Providence would send us some change shortly.

That very afternoon I was looking out on the opposite hill, where the shells were falling frequently. I noticed a very large, fine cow slowly grazing on the side, and ascending higher and higher as she moved.

It was a matter of wonder with me where she came from, for beef cattle of all kinds had disappeared from Vicksburg. The cow was in fine condition; and I thought: Poor creature, you are not prudent in eating such dangerous grass. A short time before tea, M—— came up laughing, and said:

"Providence has indeed sent you fresh meat, so that you will not have to depend upon mule. A fine cow has been killed by a shell on the opposite hill. The General has taken the meat, and a large share has been sent to you."

I regretted the fate of the animal that I had so lately seen vigorous with life; yet now, "since fate was so unkind," I gladly received my portion, thinking of the old saw, "it's an ill wind," etc. George and some of the boys in the camp cut the meat in strips; and I was able to send some soup meat to the courier that rode continually among the shower of balls, and to a poor humped-back soldier, whose strength was giving way from the privation he had undergone. The remainder was rubbed with saltpeter, strung on canes laid across frames, with a slow fire underneath; and the heat of the sun and the fire combined jerked it nicely for future use.

I laughed heartily at the appearance of the cave a day or two after the process. The logs of the roof were hung with festoons of jerked meat that swung gracefully and constantly above us; and walking around under it, I felt, quite like an Indian, I suppose, after a successful chase, that starvation for a while was far in the background.

It was astonishing how the young officers kept up their spirits, frequently singing quarters and glees amid the pattering of minié balls; and I often heard gay peals of laughter from headquarters, as the officers that had spent the day, and perhaps the night, previous in the rifle pits, would collect to make out reports. This evening a gentleman visited us, and, among other songs, sang words to the air of the "Mocking Bird," which I will write:

> " *'Twas at the siege of Vicksburg,*
> *'Twas at the siege of Vicksburg,*
> *When the Parrott shells were whistling through the air.*
> *Listen to the Parrott shells—*
> *Listen to the Parrott shells . . .*

> " *'Oh! well will we remember—*
> *Tough mule meat, June sans November,*
> *And the minié balls that whistled through the air.*
> *Listen to the minié balls—"* ☆ ☆ ☆

Possibly it was the same cow that had provided dinner for Mary Loughborough alluded to by General Grant's son, Fred, in further reminiscences of the siege: "On one occasion while we were out on the line with General A. J. Smith, a flag of truce appeared, which General Smith advanced to receive, taking with him Colonel Lagow and myself. The Confederate General Bowen, Colonel Montgomery and another [came out to meet us]. Some of our guns, including those of the fleet, continuing to fire, our officers took steps to have them stopped, but Colonel Montgomery begged us that our fire did little or no harm.

"Asked if we had not inflicted great damage within the city, he acknowledged that during the previous week we had actually killed a cow! Later on, we suspected that Colonel Montgomery had been guilty of a little boasting."

The Federal soldiers, hardly in need of anything except a sight of home, nonetheless filled their waking moments and probably many of their dreams as well with visions of edibles.

"It is amazing," commented Oldroyd, "what progress soldiers make in foraging. They began committing such depredations as to cause an order on the subject to be issued, and on the eighth of May last the commanding General required a general order, prohibiting foraging, to be read throughout the army five times a day.

"Not long after that, two soldiers of the 13th Corps were arrested and brought before General A. J. Smith, at his headquarters in a fine grove of stately poplars, where the General was informed by the guard that the men had been caught in the act of stealing chickens. The gallant General appeared to be revolving the heinousness of the charge as he looked aloft among the poplars, and presently the guard inquired what should be done with the men, when the General, after another glance upward, turning to the guard, replied, 'Oh, damn 'em, let 'em go. There ain't any tree here high enough to hang 'em on.'"

Many in Vicksburg, too, probably should have been hung for stealing, by the estimate of Editor Swords of the *Citizen*:

☆ ☆ ☆ We have heretofore restrained from alluding to a matter which has been a source of extreme annoyance and loss to our citizens. We refer to the lax discipline of some of our company officers in allowing their men to prowl around, day and night, and purloin fruit, vegetables, chickens, etc. from our denizens and, in the majority of cases, from those whose chief subterfuge is derived therefrom. This charge is not confined solely to those at the works but equally if not mainly attributable to the wagoners and others in charge of animals.

Several cases have come to our knowledge wherein the offenders have, in open daylight, entered premises, seized cattle and other things, and defied the owners to their teeth. We are pained to learn that an esteemed citizen of Vicksburg, William Porterfield, was under the necessity in protecting his property to wound one or two soldiers and deprive another of his life. . . .

We make this public exposure, mortifying as it is to us, with the hope that a salutary improvement in matters will be made by our military authorities. ☆ ☆ ☆

Thirty-ninth Day

"The indications multiply that the rebel
army in Vicksburg must shortly surrender.
The fire upon the city is very heavy and
destructive."
—PHILADELPHIA *Bulletin*

Finally, the mine that the Federals had been boring in front of a troublesome fort on the north side of the Jackson Road was finished. As Chaplain Foster wrote, "The time comes to touch the fatal match. They intend making a charge at the time of the explosion. Their men are all drawn up in readiness."

"The enemy," observed another of the besieged, Alexander Abrams, "kept up a constant and concentrated fire on the works, and from the vigor with which he bombarded them, it became apparent that this position would be the principal point of attack. It was at first thought that the concentration of their fire on this particular point was an endeavor to destroy the works, but it was afterwards discovered as only intended to cover their mining operations, under the fort comprising a portion of our defenses on the left of the road, which from the advantages possessed by the enemy, progressed rapidly, and was soon in a state of completion." Abrams continued:

☆ ☆ ☆ As soon as this was discovered, General Hébert, who had shown considerable skill and valor during the siege, set to work and endeavored to foil them in their efforts. He first had a number of hand grenades manufactured, which he directed to be thrown at the enemy's working parties, and in a measure stopped the prosecution of their work for a time. But this even failed, as the enemy worked perseveringly in the night and succeeded in making an excavation under the fort of sufficient size to protect them from the hand grenades, while our men were unable to throw them in the hollow formed, in consequence of the slanting construction of the parapet.

Having failed in his endeavor to prevent the enemy from mining the fort, General Hébert immediately set to work and had a new line, of some length, built in the rear of the threatened point. The work

under his superintendence was pushed forward with as much alacrity
as the number of laborers he could command could push it forward.

The work having been at last completed by the twenty-fifth of June,
the majority of the Third Louisiana were removed from the mined
fort and positioned in the new line, which was very close to its rear.
Previous to this, the enemy must have completed their mine, and
made preparations to blow up the fort, for between four and five
o'clock on the evening of this same day, their train was fired. A terrific
explosion took place.

Huge masses of earth were thrown up in the air, and those who experienced it state that the ground was shook as if from an earthquake
or a volcanic eruption. As soon as the earth was rent, a bright glare
of fire issued from the burning powder, but quickly died away as
there was nothing of a combustible nature in the fort to ignite. In
consequence of the men having been previously removed from the work,
but few of them were injured, but all of them were considerably
jarred by the shock.

Perceiving the fort partially destroyed, a column of the enemy's
infantry, which had lain concealed in the hollow beneath the fort
all day, rushed forward with loud cheers for the purpose of gaining
possession of the ruins. They were gallantly met and a desperate struggle ensued. The Third Louisiana, which is without doubt one of the
best fighting regiments in the service, stood up manfully against overwhelming numbers, and despite every exertion on their part to storm
the line, held them in check until the Sixth Missouri, another gallant
regiment, under Colonel Eugene Erwin, had arrived and reinforced
them. As soon as they arrived, Colonel Erwin, who was ahead of his
men, immediately ascended the parapet of the ruined fort, when a
minié ball, from one of the sharpshooters, pierced his heart and he
fell dead. He was a grandson of Henry Clay, and from the commencement of the war an ardent supporter of the South.

The Missourians, enraged at the death of their Colonel, fought like
demons and, aided by the Third Louisiana, sprang into the ruined
fort. After a severe contest of two or three hours duration, they succeeded in repulsing the enemy with great slaughter.

From our men being very much exposed to the enemy in this engagement, our loss was not less than eighty-six in killed and wounded; a
very heavy list of casualties, for the small number of men engaged on
our side. So close were the enemy to our men during the fight that
they could have conversed in a low tone with one another. Brigadier

General Hébert, himself present during this engagement, acted with his usual coolness and intrepidity.

The loss of the enemy could not have been less than four hundred in killed and wounded as they lay in large numbers before our works after the fight, and a large number of wounded men were taken from the field as they fell. So severely punished were they in this attack that in the second attempt they made to blow up the remainder of this fort they did not try to storm the line.

While this struggle was going on, no demonstrations were made on any other portion of the line, beyond the accustomed amount of shelling and sharpshooting. Rumors of a speedy relief to the garrison were still spread among the troops, but from all the past reports proving false, the soldiers had begun to doubt everything they heard, leaving it for time to decide whether they should be believed or not. ☆ ☆ ☆

Tunnard, whose unit bore the brunt of the explosion, offered his own detailed account:

☆ ☆ ☆ Just after noon, the enemy sprung the mine beneath the Third Regiment, which they had been so long preparing. Six Mississippians, working in the countermine, were buried alive in the earth. This countermine counteracted the force of the explosion. The enemy immediately charged in heavy columns the gap made in the works, when a fierce hand-to-hand struggle ensued. The heroic and brave men of the regiment, sadly depleted in numbers as they were, undauntedly faced the foe, using their muskets and rifles with deadly effect upon the close columns of the Yankees.

While desperately fighting the fearful odds opposed to them, succor arrived. The Sixth Missouri Regiment, of Bowen's Brigade, led by Colonel Erwin, suddenly reinforced the regiment. Well the Louisianians knew their old comrades. Shoulder to shoulder had they stood together on many hard-fought fields, unmoved, unconquerable. They rushed into the desperate melee unfalteringly, and after a short struggle succeeded in repulsing the enemy with terrible loss. Colonel Erwin needlessly and rashly exposed himself by jumping on the top of the entrenchments and calling to his men, "Come on, my brave boys, don't let the Third Regiment get ahead of you!"

They were his last words, for he was killed almost instantly by the deadly aim of the enemy's sharpshooters. He was universally beloved, especially by the heroic troops whom he commanded, and his death was bitterly mourned.

[The *Citizen* printed by way of obituary that Erwin's "health had been delicate, and at times compelled his absence from the field. During the siege of this place he had more than once been driven to his bed, and on the day of his death he was out contrary to the advice and urgency of his friends, feeling as he said that it was his duty so long as he could stand, to stand at his post."]

Hand grenades were freely used in this fierce struggle. These missiles weigh about a pound, are an oval-shaped iron shell, a little larger than a hen egg and filled with powder. In one end is a small cylinder, at the bottom of which is a gun tube, on which is placed a common percussion cap. Into this cylinder is inserted a small rod, having a flat piece of circular iron on the end, about the size of a half dollar. This rod is drawn out to its full length and held in its place by a light spring pressing on it. The reverse end of the shell has a wooden rod inserted in it, about six inches long and feathered. This guides the shell. When thrown, the grenade usually falls on the bottom attached to the rod, which is forced on the cap, exploding the missile.

These shells were thrown in immense quantities, and with considerable effect. Many were caught or picked up when not exploding, and hurled back upon the foe.

This struggle was a severe test upon the courage of the Third Regiment, but they met the Federals with their usual determined valor, aided by the gallant Missourians, whom they loved and honored as fit compeers to stand by their side in the deadly breach.

A large number of the wounded were injured by the hand grenades. While this encounter was raging, the enemy's batteries in front and rear kept up a fierce cannonading. The day was very warm, and the sun sank below the horizon looking like a great ball of fire through the bluish haze—as if ashamed to shine bright and clear upon such a scene of butchery and bloodshed. ☆ ☆ ☆

As Dana reported to Washington, the grenades were not to be lightly passed off. "The wounds inflicted by those missiles are frightful," he wrote.

"The heat of the weather, the unexpected length of the siege, the absence of any thorough organization of the engineer department, and the general belief of our officers and men that the town must presently fall into our hands without any special effort or sacrifice, all conspire to produce comparative inactivity and inefficiency on our part."

Dora Miller thought it "a horrible day" for reasons other than the exploding of the mine or hand grenades:

☆ ☆ ☆ . . . the most horrible yet to me, because I've lost my nerve. We were all in the cellar when a shell came tearing through the roof, burst upstairs, and tore up that room, the pieces coming through both floors down into the cellar. One of them tore open the leg of H.'s pantaloons. This was tangible proof the cellar was no place of protection from them. On the heels of this came Mr. Jones to tell us that young Mrs. Porter had had her thighbone crushed. When Martha went for the milk she came back horror-stricken to tell us the black girl there had her arm taken off by a shell.

For the first time I quailed. I do not think people who are physically brave deserve much credit for it; it is a matter of nerves. In this way I am constitutionally brave, and seldom think of danger till it is over; and death has not the terrors for me it has for some others. Every night I had lain down expecting death, and every morning rose to the same prospect, without being unnerved. It was for H. I trembled.

But now I first seemed to realize that something worse than death might come; I might be crippled, and not killed. Life, without all one's powers and limbs, was a thought that broke down my courage. I said to H., "You must get me out of this horrible place; I cannot stay; I know I shall be crippled." Now the regret comes that I lost control, for H. is worried, and has lost his composure, because my coolness has broken down. ☆ ☆ ☆

The smoke had barely cleared by late afternoon and the disrupted earth settled, Chaplain Foster woefully observed, when "again they begin their mining operations, endeavoring to force our lines at this position. Like rats they work under the ground."

Fortieth Day

"A staff officer who left Vicksburg on Monday
reports the garrison as closely besieged. The
enemy kept up constant fire which was severer
than formerly, as they now have the range of the
town. An entire block of buildings on Washington
Street was destroyed by incendiaries.

"Every means was used to discover them but
without success. The sappers and miners on
both sides have hard work and are so close
together that they hear the sound of each
other's picks."

—JACKSON *Mississippian*

"The enemy has made but little progress in
destroying our works."

—PEMBERTON IN HIS DIARY

At eleven o'clock this Friday morning, "Ferd" Osman, the Maryland
Battery commander in Reynold's division, was "buried in a plain black
coffin, according to the forms of the Lutheran Church by Major Giesler
of the 59th Tennessee Rifles, a licensed minister."

The previous day, Ferd, who thought he glimpsed the foe approaching, borrowed a field telescope from his cousin, Claiborne, and hurried to a forward artillery position. He had barely given an order
to open fire when struck in the face by a shell fragment.

The word was quickly brought back to an incredulous William
Claiborne, who hurried to his cousin's side. Ferd Osman died a few
minutes later without regaining consciousness.

That night Captain Osman's body, in full uniform, lay in the commanding colonel's tent, attended by an honor guard, as mourning comrades filed past.

"I wished to have the service read by an Episcopal clergyman but
we failed to find one," noted Claiborne. "He was buried on a little
knoll about 100 yards north of Reynold's quarters. The place was
selected by Frank and Major Phifer. I was feeling too badly to go
out. I regret there are no trees near the spot to shelter it from the
sun and rains, but this was almost unavoidable. I will as soon as pos-

sible procure a stone with a suitable inscription to mark the spot. . . .

"His burial was attended by the colonel and staff, the members of his company and a large number of devoted friends. All were more affected than I remember to have seen on any former occasion. The general wept like a child. It was a strange sight—while shot and shell were falling thick and fast to see strong men used to war and blood and death all around them, bend the humble knee, forget their vengeful passions and by the grave of a soldier shed tears like a woman —but so is war.

"This is a terrible blow to me. I loved him more than language can express. . . ."

In his search for an Episcopalian minister, Captain Claiborne some-how had missed Dr. Lord, to whose presence and activity his wife and son bore testimony.

"Still in the caves," wrote Margaret Lord, "but with strong hope of being relieved in a few days. Last Sunday, I had readily become very desponding and weary living for weeks under guides and with children and servants becoming intolerable. In the morning I had service with Flora and the children, using the prayer for help and aid to our cause, and singing the hymns entitled 'Prayer and Hope' of the Almighty."

Walking around the entrenchments of Logan's division today was a man who "shouldn't be alive"—a slave from the Confederate side who had appeared the day before in Union lines after the smoke from the mine explosion had cleared. The apocryphal story that the frightened but unhurt Negro, named "Abe," had been blown high in the air was nonetheless attested to by General Grant. Possibly, doubting Thomases theorized, the fellow had merely wandered to freedom during the chaos, following the mighty blast.

For that matter Mary Loughborough marveled at her own continued existence. Her close daily brushes were constant. She wrote:

☆ ☆ ☆ I was sewing near one side of the cave, where the bank slopes and lights up the room like a window. Near this opening I was sitting, when I suddenly remembered some little article I wished in another part of the room. Crossing to procure it, I was returning, when a minié ball came whizzing through the opening, passed my chair, and fell beyond it. Had I been still sitting, I should have stopped it. Conceive how speedily I took the chair into another part of the room, and sat in it!

There is one missile, were I a soldier, that would totally put me to rout—and that is a shrapnel shell. Only those who have heard several coming at a time, exploding near and scattering hundreds of small balls around them, can tell how fearful the noise they make—a wild scream— a clattering and whizzing sound that never fails in striking terror to my heart! It seemed sometimes that as many as fifty balls fell immediately around our door. I could have sent out at any time, near the entrance of our cave, and had a bucketfull of balls from shrapnel and the minié rifle picked up in the shortest possible time.

One old, gray-headed, cheerful-hearted soldier, whom I had talked with often, was passing through the ravine for water, immediately opposite our cave. A minié ball struck him in the lower part of the leg; he coolly stooped down, tied his handkerchief around it, and passed on. So constantly fell projectiles of all descriptions that I became almost indifferent to them. Only the hideous noise of numerous shrapnel could startle me now. Generally at four o'clock in the morning the shrapnel were thrown more furiously than at any other time through the day. At about seven, the minié balls began falling, accompanied by Parrott, canister, solid shot and shrapnel shells; and through every minute in the day this constant play of artillery and musketry was kept up from the Federal lines. General Pemberton had ordered the Confederate batteries to remain silent, unless particular orders were given to fire, or an assault was made on the works.

One afternoon I remember so vividly! One of the surgeons of the staff was chatting with my husband when I heard a rushing and peculiar sound, as if someone were rapidly cutting through the air, near and around me, with a sword.

Both the doctor and M—— sprang to their feet, as the sound grew more confused, seeming as if the sudden rush of a volume of water was pouring down the hill. I saw M—— turn to the doctor and say: "They're coming!"

I dared not ask any questions; yet, I at first supposed the entrenchments were taken. M——, without a word, drew on another coat and threw the linen one he had worn to me, with a laugh. I suppose I must have looked rather wild; for I could not tell or imagine the meaning of the confusing and singular noise around us. Taking his sword, M—— started immediately. I feared every moment that he would fall, for the balls fell like hail. I turned to the doctor, questioning: "Are they coming over the hill?"

He laughed, and said:

"Oh! no; they are only making a charge on the entrenchments, and the rushing in the air you hear is the numerous small balls flying over us."

The strange, bewildering sound lasted for some time. The doctor soon took his leave, saying that the wounded would be brought in for him to attend. I sat for half an hour hearing the constant rushing and surging around me, and the quick dropping of balls; the ground trembled from the frequent discharge of the Confederate cannon.

What was likely to be the result, I could not tell; for the ravine below, lately so full of animation, seemed to be totally deserted, save now and then the rapid gallop of a courier through the shower of balls along the road. Soon there came a gradual cessation, quieting more and more down to the old interval of a minute between the discharges; soon M—— came home, reporting one or two wounded and one killed. It seems miraculous to me that, amid such a shower of balls, so few persons should be injured. ☆ ☆ ☆

Forty-first Day

"Indications multiply that the rebel army
must soon surrender. The fire on the city is
very heavy and is believed to be destructive.
The rebel reply is not heavy and is ineffectual.
News of its surrender may be expected at
any moment."
                            —*National Intelligencer*

"Vicksburg," wrote Dr. Tompkins, "has been a very nice city, one day, but the houses are either injured by our cannon or dilapidated and everything looks as if the city had been deserted years ago."

Sergeant Tunnard agreed:

☆ ☆ ☆ At this period, Vicksburg presented a fearful spectacle, having the appearance of being visited with a terrible scourge.

Signs wrenched from their fastenings; houses dilapidated and in ruins, rent and torn by shot and shell; the streets barricaded with earthworks, and defended by artillery, over which lonely sentinels kept guard. The avenues were almost deserted, save by hunger-pinched, starving and wounded soldiers, or guards lying on the banquettes, indifferent to the screaming and exploding shells. The stores, the few that were open, looked like the ghost of more prosperous times, with their empty shelves and scant stock of goods, held at ruinous prices.

"Ginger beer," "sweet cider," "beer for sale," glared out in huge letters upon placards or the ends of barrels, seeming the only relief to the general starvation. It would have puzzled a scientific druggist to have determined what were the ingredients of this decoction called "beer." Palatial residences were crumbling into ruins, the walks torn up by mortar shells, the flower beds, once blooming in all the regal beauty of spring loveliness, trodden down, the shrubbery neglected. No fair hands were there to trim their wanton growth; no light footsteps to wander amid nature's blooming exotics, or lovely forms seen leaning confidingly on some manly arm, while rosy lips breathed soft words of affection and trust.

Fences were torn down, and houses pulled to pieces for firewood. Even the enclosures around the remains of the revered dead were destroyed, while wagons were parked around the graveyard, horses tramping down the graves and men using the tombstones as convenient tables for their scanty meals, or a couch for an uncertain slumber. Dogs howled through the streets at night; cats screamed forth their hideous cries; an army of rats, seeking food, would scamper around your very feet, across the streets and over the pavements. Lice and filth covered the bodies of the soldiers. Delicate women and little children, with pale, careworn and hunger-pinched features, peered at the passerby with wistful eyes, from the caves in the hillsides.

Add to all these horrors, so faintly portrayed, the deep-toned thunder of mortars and heavy guns, the shrill whistle of rifleshot, or the duller sound of flying mortar shells; the crash of buildings torn into fragments; the fearful detonation of the explosions shaking heaven and earth; the hurtling masses of iron continually descending, and you may form some conception of the condition of the city.

Already, six weeks of unceasing battle had passed away—six weeks of such fighting as the world had seldom witnessed; yet the enemy, with all their material and appliances for conducting the siege to a speedy and successful termination, had most signally failed in every attempt. The Spartan band of Southern heroes held their position, utterly regardless of the furious storm of grape, canister, shell and shot poured upon them by the overwhelming forces of the Federals.

With the demon of famine gnawing at their heartstrings, they will daily shouted their defiance to the assailants, and their rifles were as actively handled, as skillfully aimed, as if nearly half their number were not disabled, and many sleeping peacefully beneath the green turf, above which rose the scream of shell, all the horrid din and saturnalia of the fierce conflict. ☆ ☆ ☆

A ranking officer to fall this day was Brig. Gen. Martin E. Green. The veteran commander of the 2d Missouri Brigade, with the angular face and long, gray beard, was familiar to all Confederates from the southwest.

Abrams wrote: "Two or three days after the destruction of our works by the explosion of the enemy's mine, an event of a most melancholy nature transpired. Brigadier General Green, commanding a brigade of Missourians and Arkansians, in Bowen's division, was shot in the neck by a minié ball, while in conversation with his staff. Although medical aid was promptly given to him, it was of no avail, his wound was mortal, and after lingering for about an hour he expired.

"Green was an aged man, esteemed by all who knew him for his unswerving devotion to the great cause for which he fell fighting, his intrepid valor, and his genial and amiable qualities. He was a quiet and unassuming man; all the unnecessary pomp and dignity of the high position he occupied were laid aside, and the meanest private in his command had free and uninterrupted access to his presence. So endeared was he to his men, that they looked upon him more in the light of a friend than that of a General.

"We were told that he wished, previous to his death, that he would not live to see the city surrendered."

Meanwhile, Captain Wise reached his destination bearing General Pemberton's instructions still more or less verbatim in his head. He had safely slipped through the Union lines, spending the night of the 22d in a house on Hall's Ferry Road and arriving in Jackson on the 24th.

Johnston, meeting the emissary this Saturday, a week after he had been ordered to start, asserted that he was "in no condition to move in Pemberton's favor." He emphasized his lack of soldiers, horses, artillery, or even supply trains.

The small, war-wearied General advised that he personally should not ask for surrender terms, "if it should become necessary," but Pemberton should do so.

Johnston then gave Wise a letter to General McPherson, for whom he apparently held great respect. In the event that Wise was captured, Johnston asked the Federal officer to "lessen the burden" of possible "imprisonment." The Confederate General's final words to the Captain were unequivocal: "Tell General Pemberton to consider himself authorized by me to surrender!"

At the same time, Johnston also started a dispatch to Pemberton: "The determined spirit you manifest . . . encourages me to hope something may yet be done to save Vicksburg, and to postpone both the modes suggested of merely extricating the garrison. Negotiations with Grant for the relief of the garrison, should they become necessary, must be made by you. It would be a confession of weakness on my part, which I ought not to make, to propose them. When it becomes necessary to make terms, they may be considered as made under my authority."

JUNE 28

Forty-second Day

"I am surprised that you have so small a
force, but as the enemy has separated his so
much and occupies so long a line, could not
a combined, vigorous effort even yet raise
the siege?"

—PEMBERTON TO JOHNSTON

Seth Wells, of the 17th Illinois, commenced this "hot, sultry," Sunday
with a familiar off-duty routine. He wandered down to a nearby
stream, "went after blackberries. Picked four quarts. Had a good wash
and returned to camp."

To Sergeant Tunnard:

☆ ☆ ☆ . . . the golden sunlight mellowed with its brilliant light the
hill-tops and the dark green foliage of the trees. Birds caroled their
matin songs, as if war was not holding its high carnival within and
around the besieged city. The mind would forget the unceasing din
of battle, and soar away into the realms of fancy. The hillsides have
a soft carpeting of emerald sward, upon which the soldier casts his
wearied body. He has forgotten his surroundings, is oblivious to the
screaming shells and singing bullets. A smile flits across his bronzed
features, as memory exhibits one of the beautiful pictures of the past.
The light of lustrous blue eyes is beaming upon him with a soft ten-
derness beyond portrayal. . . .

The Catholics of the city held services in their Cathedral, notwithstanding the danger of such a proceeding. As the congregation was
emerging from the building, the Argus-eyed enemy across the river
discovered the unusual number of people in the streets, and instantly opened on them with a Parrott gun. As the shells came screaming wickedly through the streets, exploding or entering the building,
men, women and children hastily sought shelter to escape the danger.

Several persons were struck by fragments of shells but, fortunately,
no one killed. Such an unheard-of, ruthless and barbarous method of
warfare as training a battery of rifled cannon upon an assembly of
unarmed men and worshiping women is unparalleled in the annals of
history.

237

["Mike Donovan," reported the *Citizen*, "an old and respected citizen of this place, had his arm frightfully lacerated by a shell which exploded in front of the Catholic Church while the early service of the day was progressing. A shell also entered and exploded in the sacred edifice but miraculously injured no one."]

Meat at this period became exhausted, and orders were issued to select the finest and fattest mules within the lines and slaughter them, for the purpose of issuing their flesh as food to the troops; a half pound per man was the ration. Several Spaniards belonging to the Texas regiments were also busily occupied in jerking this meat for future consumption. [The Third Louisiana apparently had not been served mule before.]

This meat was also supplied to the citizens from the market and sold for fifty cents a pound. We assume that the food was consumed with a keen relish worthy the appetite of a gourmand, or an epicure over the most dainty repast. Mule-flesh, if the animal is in good condition, is coarse-grained and darker than beef, but really delicious, sweet and juicy . . . besides this meat, traps were set for rats, which were consumed in such numbers that they actually became a scarcity.

Hunger will demoralize the most fastidious tastes, and quantity, not quality of food becomes the great desideratum. ☆ ☆ ☆

Writing home, Henry Ginder also found it to be "a very pleasant day, though rather warm, weather fine." He added:

☆ ☆ ☆ Notwithstanding the great amount of cannonading, there has been very little rain for the last six weeks. I am afraid to wish for that or anything else, for I don't know how it will affect our enemies. I am almost sorry to hear of Lee's progress northward, for it looks as if the importance of Vicksburg were not understood. Our existence almost as a nation depends on holding this place!

Why not then remain on the defensive and send troops hither, instead of employing them on useless expeditions, which are only raids on a grand scale, having no decisive results. Our rulers seem to have gone clean daft. Even if we are finally relieved, I shall not excuse them, for it is only owing to the total inefficiency of the enemy that we are not already captured, and no good general ever counts on such mistakes. I trust it is to the prayers of Christians we owe our continued safety, and that those prayers will continue to ascend till God sends us relief.

Our cook is improving; two kittens were killed by the same explosion, and our soup tureen and other dishes broken. This morning a man walking in town had his arm shot off. Major Reed's wife had her arm taken off by a piece of shell; and two ladies, day before yesterday, were struck by balls from a shrapnel shell and so severely wounded as not expected to live. The Yankees have placed sharpshooters on the opposite bank of the river to annoy our men as they go there to fill their casks with water.

Flour is selling at $600 a barrel, biscuits $8 dozen, pies $4 apiece. Our cornmeal has given out; the men now get 1/4 lb. bacon, 1/2 lb. flour or rice flour, sugar 1/8 lb., peas 1/12 qt., 1/50 gal. molasses. It said three couriers came in last night, but their news has not transpired. ☆ ☆ ☆

Margaret Lord was "still in this dreary cave. Who would have believed that we could have borne such a life for five weeks? The siege has lasted 42 days and yet no relief—every day this week we have waited for the sound of General Johnston's guns, but in vain.

"Provisions are getting scarce—but for the kindness of Lieutenant Donellan we should have been badly off—as it is I have paid $6 for a gallon of molasses and $3 for a miserable steak. The gentlemen here are still very kind. Captain Carlisle is a noble little gentleman and I only wish Willie may be such a man. Mr. Hutchinson, Hichcombe and Mr. Morrison are all very pleasant and kind. Dr. Cope, Major Williams and Mr. Mansfield have moved to town—where I hope to move next week if I can get a place to sleep in peace.

"This day a month ago was one of the most terrible of the bombardment—what if we should have some great change to record today?"

The minister's wife might have added that a pair of brogans were tagged at $100, if obtainable; a simple calico dress $40, and even sweet potato coffee had become a rarity. There were virtually no more sweet potatoes.

Three days after he had buried his cousin, Captain Claiborne wrote in doleful key: "Our horses are getting very lean. They have had no corn or forage since our return here on the 17th May, and live only on cane and the stunted grass herbage in the river bottom where they are driven every day to graze. What they get is barely sufficient to sustain life, and this even is rapidly being destroyed by the stock driven from the city.

"A few days after we came into this place most of the army mules were driven outside of our lines by order of General Stevenson. Though this was of course a heavy loss to the government, it was a wise measure because it saved our horses. The pastures here would not have sustained all the stock that came in with us."

Chaplain Foster, too, continued to mirror the increasing discouragement in Vicksburg: "The sixth week was now closed and nothing from Johnston. Our fate seems to stare us in the face. Still we hear rumors that he is coming with a mighty army. . . . Can't our government send us relief? Shall Vicksburg fall for want of energy on the part of our government? Will all the blood be spilled in vain? For the first time, dark doubts cross my mind. . . . Ever of a hopeful disposition, I would not listen to such fears, but would still believe that at the last hour the long expected help would come. Visiting the lines frequently, I discovered the men generally had almost given up hope of relief from without. They considered the place as lost, though they were willing to lie in the trenches another month if it would save the place."

Circulating through the forward lines this last Sunday in June was a curt, conceivably tempting propaganda leaflet. It was distributed perhaps by those Union pickets who dared show themselves:

TO OUR FRIENDS IN VICKSBURG

June 28th, 1863: Cave in boys and save your lives, which are considered of no value by your officers. There is no hope for relief for you. Sherman with 60,000 men is chasing Joe Johnston. Grant with 90,000 men, environs Vicksburg. *You can't escape in those boats,* that game is blocked on you. The 12,300 men under McCulloch,* on whom you depended to help you out, are retreating back to Harrisburg, well whipped, even Colonel H., who hopes to escape in his fast six (6)-oared whale boat, can't come in. Not one soldier of you will be heard of, as connected with the siege of Vicksburg, while your officers will all be spoken of as heroes. Your present form of Government crushes out the hopes of every poor man, distinction is kept for the aristocracy of the South. You have

*The allusion, erroneously enough, was to Brig. Gen. Henry E. McCulloch of the Texas Division, then near Monroe, Louisiana, west of Vicksburg.

better friends on this side than on that, the friends of
freedom.

LIBERTY

Conceivably more distracting, however, was an anonymous plea
slipped into Pemberton's headquarters at dusk. It read:

Sir: In accordance with my own feelings, and that of
my fellow-soldiers with whom I have conferred, I submit to your serious consideration the following note:

We as an army have as much confidence in you as
a commanding general as we perhaps ought to have.
We believe you have displayed as much generalship as
any other man could have done under similar circumstances. We give you great credit for the stern patriotism
you have evinced in the defense of Vicksburg during a
protracted and unparalleled siege.

I also feel proud of the gallant conduct of the soldiers
under your command in repulsing the enemy at every
assault, and bearing with patient endurance all the privations and hardships incident to a siege of forty-odd
days' duration.

Everybody admits that we have all covered ourselves
in glory, but alas! alas! general, a crisis has arrived
in the midst of our siege.

Our rations have been cut down to one biscuit and
a small bit of bacon per day, not enough scarcely to
keep soul and body together, much less to stand the
hardships we are called upon to stand.

We are actually on sufferance, and the consequence
is, as far as I can hear, there is complaining and general
dissatisfaction throughout our lines.

We are, and have been, kept close in the trenches
day and night, not allowed to forage any at all, and,
even if permitted, there is nothing to be had among the
citizens.

Men don't want to starve, and don't intend to, but
they call upon you for justice, if the commissary department can give it; if it can't, you must adopt some

means to relieve us very soon. The emergency of the case demands prompt and decided action on your part.

If you can't feed us, you had better surrender us, horrible as the idea is, than suffer this noble army to disgrace themselves by desertion. I tell you plainly, men are not going to lie here and perish, if they do love their country dearly. Self-preservation is the first law of nature, and hunger will compel a man to do almost anything.

You had better heed a warning voice, though it is the voice of a private soldier.

This army is now ripe for mutiny, unless it can be fed.

Just think of one small biscuit and one or two mouthfuls of bacon per day. General, please direct your inquiries in the proper channel, and see if I have not stated stubborn facts, which had better be heeded before we are disgraced.

From —

MANY SOLDIERS

Certain it was that the message reached General Pemberton. Less firmly established was the authorship. Some of the commanding officer's staff who read it would suggest it to be a clever bit of enemy propaganda. In fact, it was known that the canny Admiral Porter had floated small, hydrogen-filled balloons over the city, bearing similar leaflets, trying to break the will of the people to resist. Sharpshooters who drew a bead on these aerial messengers only served the Federals' purpose by helping to scatter the fluttery cargo.

"Many Soldiers"—but *whose* soldiers?

PART 3

LIKE
SO
MANY
HOGS
IN
A
PEN

JUNE 29

Forty-third Day

> "The Army is still advancing close to the
> works. General Sherman is so close that he
> cannot get nearer without going in. . . . Not
> a soul is to be seen moving in the city, the
> soldiers lying in their trenches or pits and
> the inhabitants being stowed in holes or
> caves dug in the pits."
> —*National Intelligencer*

"We were now nearing the end of our siege life," wrote Mary Lough-borough. The rations had nearly all been given out. For the last few days I had been sick; still I tried to overcome the languid feeling of utter prostration. My little one had swung in her hammock, reduced in strength, with a low fever flushing in her face. M—— was all anxiety, I could plainly see. A soldier brought up, one morning, a little jaybird as a plaything for the child. After playing with it for a short time, she turned wearily away.

" 'Miss Mary,' said the servant, 'she's hungry; let me make her some soup from the bird.'

"At first I refused; the poor little plaything should not die; then, as I thought of the child, I half consented. With the utmost haste, Cinth disappeared; and the next time she appeared, it was with a cup of soup and a little plate, on which lay the white meat of the poor little bird."

At least, as Sergeant Tunnard perceived:

☆ ☆ ☆ The firing on the lines was not so brisk as usual. The enemy were once more undermining the works held by the Third Louisiana Infantry, and the men went spiritedly to work digging a countermine. The laborers were so near each other that the strokes of the pickaxes could be distinctly heard, as well as the sound of the voices. Thus the deadly struggle went on.

A large number of skiffs were constructed and conveyed to the lower portion of the town. Speculation became rife as to the meaning of this new government. What could it possibly mean? The conviction seemed finally to settle on every mind that a desperate attempt would soon be made to cross the river with the army, and escape into the Trans-Mississippi Department. Whatever may have been the intention in building these boats, it was never divulged, and the accomplishment of such a design never carried into effect, or even attempted. It would have been an insane enterprise in the presence of the enemy's gunboats and troops.

The Federal sharpshooters very impudently wished to know how we like mule meat, proving conclusively that they were constantly informed of every event which occurred within the lines. Their question, however, was responded to in not very flattering or complimentary language. Thus affairs daily grew darker. . . . ☆ ☆ ☆

Captain Claiborne was aware of an unusual order issued this final Monday in June, "to arm teamsters and all other unarmed men connected with the several brigades, which smacks a little of an attempt to cut our way out."

He added: "Perhaps the lieutenant general has suddenly rallied from his lethargy and intends to do something. God grant it may be so, for dark shadows hang like a pall over this army, and unless some energy is shown and that quickly, I see no hope for us. . . ."

However, these Louisiana soldiers, and Tunnard, had not been eating mule. Claiborne continued, "Our rations are growing more scarce every day and we must eventually come to mule meat. We have a quantity of bacon yet on hand, but breadstuff is the great desideratum. The men receive only one-quarter rations of breadstuffs such as peas, rice, pea meal and rice flour—the corn has given out long since, rations of sugar, lard, molasses and tobacco are issued but this does not make amends for the want of bread, and the men are growing weaker every day."

Some of the neighboring Missourians were even treated to camel steaks after one of these Egyptian beasts of burden had been killed by a Federal sharpshooter. The animal was among the few remaining in the south and southwest from President Polk's experimental importation. The luckless camel, lamented Colonel Bevier, had been "a quiet, peaceable fellow, and a general favorite" with the 1st Missouri, which had adopted him.

Down on the river, aboard Admiral Porter's flagship *Black Hawk*, William A. Minard, a young naval officer, was in his cramped cabin writing a gossipy letter to "Friend Joe" in New York:

☆ ☆ ☆ . . . it isn't taken yet, I don't know when it will be either. . . . The damn Rebs are in it and may hold it for six weeks to come. It can't be taken by storm. The only way is to just set right down and starve them out. I saw in the papers that they get their supplies by means of an immense fleet of dugouts. Now that is all damn humbug! because I know better.

Vicksburg is played out. We are bound to have it. I heard that Banks had taken Port Hudson but don't know whether it is true. I am as busy as I can be keeping the mortar boats in repair.

I have been to work on a billiard table for the admiral, one that we got up to Haines Bluff. I suppose that after Vicksburg is ours General Grant and the Admiral will have a game of billiards on board the *Black Hawk.* ☆ ☆ ☆

Charles Dana, in more formal prose, also was advising that the city was "played out." He told Secretary Stanton:

☆ ☆ ☆ Two separate parties of deserters from Vicksburg agree in the statement that the provisions of the place are near the point of total exhaustion; that rations have now been reduced lower than ever; that extreme dissatisfaction exists among the garrison, and that it is agreed on all hands that the city will be surrendered on Saturday, July 4, if indeed it can hold on so long as that.

Colonel C. R. Woods, who holds our extreme right on the Mississippi, has got out five of the thirteen guns of the sunken gunboat *Cincinnati,* and this morning opens three of them from batteries on the bluff. The others, including those still in the vessel, he will place as rapidly as possible in a battery he has constructed on the river half a mile in the rear of his lines. Though this battery has no guns in it, yet the enemy has been firing its heaviest ordnance at it for several days past, and has done to the embrasures some little damage, easily repairable. It commands the whole face of the town. On McPherson's front a new mine is now nearly completed, and will at furthest be ready to spring at daylight tomorrow. It is intended to destroy internal rifle-pits with which the rebels still hold the fort whose bastion was overthrown by McPherson's former mine. If successful, it will give us complete possession of that fort, as the narrowness on the ridge on which it stands and the abruptness of the ravine behind it made it impossible that it should be defended by any third line in the rear of that now being undermined. The new line in Sherman's front will probably not be ready so soon, but the engineer's morning report has not been made. No news from Joe Johnston. . . .

General Grant this morning held a council of war with his army corps commanders to take their judgment on the question of trying another general assault, or leaving the result to the exhaustion of the garrison. The conclusion of the council was in favor of the latter policy, and as General Grant has himself previously strongly inclined to that course, it will no doubt be adhered to. ☆ ☆ ☆

And Alexander Abrams believed that:

☆ ☆ ☆ . . . no event of any importance transpired from this day [that of the mine explosion] to the twenty-ninth of June. The army and the citizens had almost despaired of ever seeing Johnston arrive. The couriers who ran the gauntlet through the enemy's lines, and arrived safely in Vicksburg, brought the most exaggerated reports possible of the strength and position of the army soon to march to our relief. They stated that General Johnston's force was not less than from fifty to sixty thousand strong, and were stretched from Jackson to Canton, Mississippi. With these reports, the people and garrison in general were surprised at his not making an advance on the enemy, as they felt certain that if his force was as strong as represented, there would be no difficulty in defeating any army the enemy could possibly send against him.

At this period, some unprincipled persons, actuated no doubt by animosity against General Johnston, spread a report in our lines that it was not his intention to relieve the garrison, as he had given Lieutenant General Pemberton orders to evacuate the city, which order not being obeyed, if he [Johnston] came to the relief of the beleaguered army and succeeded in raising the siege, it would compromise his reputation as a commander and an officer. Such being the case, the garrison would not be relieved, and Vicksburg would be left to her fate.

These reports, coming to the ears of the soldiers, caused some feeling of anger against General Johnston for a short time. All doubts of his desire or intention to aid them were soon laid aside, however, by the reports given to the men by the enemy's pickets. They determined to patiently await his arrival, being certain that as soon as he had organized a sufficiently large force, he would march to Vicksburg and raise the siege.

Among the many false reports brought into our line was one which stated that Major General Loring had crossed the Big Black at Hankinson's Ferry, and was advancing towards Vicksburg, when he was met by an overwhelming force of the enemy. A severe engagement was then said to have ensued, in which General Loring was repulsed and compelled to fall back. After retreating for some distance, he was reinforced by Major General Breckinridge's division and, making a stand the next day, fought a severe battle, routing the enemy, inflicting great slaughter on him and capturing six thousand prisoners.

We make mention of these reports to show the deceptions practiced on the men, although the statement narrated above was given by the enemy, so far as it relates to the repulse of Loring. They said nothing about the subsequent defeat of their army. As may be supposed, these reports, cheering the men as they did, when contradicted, did not tend to lighten the sufferings of the men, or relieve the anxiety which all felt for the advent of succor.

The brave men, nevertheless, still continued to bear up cheerfully against the hardships and sufferings they were then enduring, and there were but few who expressed any fear of our ability to hold the city, or who grew doubtful of final success.

After the explosion of their mine, on the 25th of June, and the partial destruction of the fort, the enemy set vigorously to work on a new mine for the purpose of completing its destruction. Having gotten everything in readiness, on the 29th of June, at about four o'clock in the afternoon, a second explosion took place, from which the enemy succeeded in destroying the remnant left standing. No effort was made to storm the works in the rear of the ruins, although several of our men were killed and wounded, either by the fragments of dirt or by the explosion.

The Third Louisiana regiment, which occupied this line throughout the siege, suffered more than any other body of men in the garrison. Several times their position was charged in the most desperate manner, and twice was it blown up by the enemy. The loss they sustained during the siege was not far from two hundred out of about four hundred and fifty contained in the regiment when the siege commenced. This was a fearful loss, when we consider it with that of the other commands.

In spite of the exposed position they occupied, these men, heroes of Belmont, Oak Hill, Elk Horn and Corinth, stood up manfully to their posts and held their position against every effort of the enemy to force their line. We make particular mention of this regiment without disparagement to any other of the commands, as all fought with a valor unsurpassed in the annals of war, but merely as an act of justice to a gallant body of men, the survivors of what was once a regiment nearly twelve hundred strong. In giving them this praise, we but echo the opinion of every soldier in the Confederate army who has seen them in battle.

The firing from the peninsula, with mortars and siege guns on Vicksburg, had meanwhile continued with violence. Additional guns were brought to bear upon the devoted city, making it almost untenable. Starvation, in its worst forms, now confronted the unfortunate inhabitants. All the beef in the city was exhausted by this time, mules were soon brought in requisition, and their meat sold readily at one dollar per pound, the citizens being as anxious as they were before the investment to purchase the delicacies of the season. It was also distributed among the soldiers to those who desired it, although it was not given out under the name of rations. A great many of them, however, accepted it in preference to doing without any meat. The flesh of the mules was found equal to the best venison. The author of this work partook of mule meat for three or four days, and found the flesh tender and nutritious and, under the *peculiar circumstances*, a most desirable description of food.

The enemy, forgetful of or disregarding all rules of civilized warfare, exhibited a refinement of cruelty in firing at our hospitals. There were between four and five thousand sick and wounded soldiers in the different hospitals in Vicksburg, over each of which the usual yellow flag floated to designate that they were hospitals. Without appearing to care whether they were or not, the enemy deliberately fired into them, killing and wounding several of the unfortunate beings, whose ill-luck it was to be quartered there for medical treatment. That this barbarous act was committed intendedly was apparent when the Washington Hotel, which had been converted into one of the hospitals, in full view of the enemy, on the banks of the river, was struck by a twelve-inch mortar.

We have not been able to learn whether Lieutenant General Pemberton ever protested against the shelling of our hospitals, or remonstrated with General Grant at permitting it; if he did, no regard was paid to his complaint, as they continued their barbarity. The Federal officers, in explanation, stated that the guns on the peninsula were manned by raw troops, and served the double purpose of annoying the city and practising the men, but that General Grant never countenanced or gave his consent to the hospitals being shelled. ☆ ☆ ☆

Also remarking on the second mine, Chaplain Foster wrote:

☆ ☆ ☆ They are checked by our countermining operations at times; still, they progress. On the 29th, another mighty explosion takes place. At this time several of the brave 3rd Louisiana were killed and wounded. A mighty chasm is made in our lines and the enemy occupies the position which was once our lines, but they dare not show their heads above the embankments.

The firing from the other side of the embankments was now becoming furious. The sharpshooters across the river keep up a fire at the teamsters that go to the river to water their stock and at those who come after barrels of water for our soldiers, for they hauled water to our lines.

At twilight they would converse with our men across the river. "How far is Johnston in the rear? We are coming over to see you on the Fourth of July for dinner." Some fellow replies: "You had better come pretty early in the morning for we will eat it all up pretty soon."

They would talk and joke every evening. ☆ ☆ ☆

To which Abrams added his own "overheard": "The enemy's pickets told our men that preparations were being made to storm our works on the fourth of July, as Grant had determined to sup in Vicksburg on that night, or sup in h——l to which remark one of our pickets replied that as there was no chance of Grant's supping in Vicksburg on the fourth of July, it was very likely he would sup in the latter place. Not a man had the least idea that the city would be yielded up to the enemy on that day, all of them thinking that when the worse came we would cut our way out of the city.

"Our men were so weak and exhausted from the want of a sufficiency of food, that such an attempt would have resulted in the annihilation of the entire army, as we do not believe that out of the eighteen thousand men reported for duty, three thousand could have succeeded in reaching Big Black safely."

JUNE 30

Forty-fourth Day

"Grant's forces on Saturday made a considerable
fuss, and for some time the opinion was
entertained that a serious demonstration would
be made on our lines: but the little good
judgment they possess prevailed, and further
than wasting considerable ammunition nothing
was done. Sunday was a day of rest with them
and was quieter than any Sabbath since our city
has been invested by the enemy. Yesterday was
also extremely quiet and we are led to the
belief they are sick of their undertaking."
—VICKSBURG *Citizen*

In the same wallpaper issue, Swords's newspaper announced that "last week the following ladies of our city were wounded: Mrs. Major T. E. Reed, Mrs. C. W. Peters, Mrs. W. S. Hazzard, Mrs. W. H. Clements, Miss Lucy Rawlings and Miss Eileen Canovan. Most of the ladies were severely though not dangerously injured and it affords us pleasure to state that they are doing well. The wounds were all from fragments of shell and splinters, with the exception of Miss Rawlings who was struck with a minié ball."

And in another column:

"General Pemberton, in an address said to have been made to the soldiers within our lines, is reported to have stated that he would not surrender our city so long as there was a mule or dog left whereon the men could subsist. The possibility being that such animals will ultimately be brought into requisition as food induced some of our officers the other day to try mule meat, and accordingly a couple of these animals were slaughtered, dressed and properly cooked, whereof a large company bountifully partook.

"We learn the flesh is not only very palatable, but decidedly preferable to the poor beef which has been dealt out to the soldiers for months past, and that a willingness was expressed among those who tried the meat to receive it as regular rations. We have not as yet learned of any one experimenting with the flesh of the canine species. The proprietor of the *Citizen* insinuates that the above officers omitted to extend the customary courtesy to the press and broadly assert that mule meat would not 'go bad.' "

"The last day of June," wrote Sergeant Tunnard. "The sun shone brightly, while groups of summer clouds floated gently across the heavens. The sharp-shooting was slow but constant—unceasing all day. The gunboats approached the terminus of the lines below, and poured a concentrated fire of shells into the entrenchments, doing little damage or injury. Across the river, the peninsula looked lonely and deserted. The general apathy in fighting appeared ominous, and a dull, leaden weight unaccountably oppressed the mind, giving a gloomy hue to every object."

All in all, Vicksburg was far from a desirable dwelling place. Those who had not previously attempted to leave tried now. Among them was Dora Miller.

☆ ☆ ☆ Some months ago, thinking it might be useful, I obtained from the consul of my birthplace, by sending to another town, a passport for foreign parts. H. said if we went out to the lines we might be permitted to get through on that. So we packed the trunk, got a carriage and drove out there. General V. offered us seats in his tent. The rifle bullets were whizzing so *zip, zip* from the sharp-shooters on the Federal lines that involuntarily I moved on my chair.

He said, "Don't be alarmed; you are out of range. They are firing at our mules yonder." His horse, tied by the tent door, was quivering all over, the most intense exhibition of fear I'd ever seen in an animal. General V. sent out a flag of truce to the Federal headquarters, and while we waited wrote on a piece of silk paper a few words.

Then he said, "My wife is in Tennessee. If you get through the lines, give her this. They will search you, so I will put it in this toothpick." He crammed the silk paper into a quill toothpick, and handed it to H. It was completely concealed. The flag-of-truce officer came back flushed and angry. "General Grant says that no human being shall pass out of Vicksburg; but the lady may feel sure danger will soon be over. Vicksburg will surrender on the 4th."

"Is that so, general?" inquired H. "Are arrangements for surrender made?"

"We know nothing of the kind. Vicksburg will not surrender."

"Those were General Grant's exact words, sir," said the flag-officer. "Of course it is nothing but their brag."

We went back sadly enough, but today H. says he will cross the river to General Porter's lines and try there; I shall not be disappointed. ☆ ☆ ☆

And, on other concerns, Pvt. Hosea Rood of the 12th Wisconsin recalled:

☆ ☆ ☆ One night, I think it was the 30th of June, Lieutenant Cobden Linnell had charge of our part of the picket line, and he thought it practicable and wise to move our outposts across the deep ravine in our front and establish them on top of the opposite bank, and at least halfway up to the Rebel lines. It was a bold plan, but the lieutenant was willing to undertake its execution. The night was dark, a circumstance greatly in our favor. About nine or ten o'clock we took several spades and some rails on our shoulders, and started out.

We filed down into the ravine and up on the other side. Lieutenant Linnell posted some sentinels well up toward the Rebel lines to keep watch while the rest of us did the digging. We were very still, scarcely speaking even in a whisper, and handling our spades rather gingerly for fear of making racket enough to be heard by the sentinels of the enemy. But, for all this, we made pretty good progress. The ravine had a trend from near the Rebel line at our right towards our picket posts and then at our left it curved slightly back toward the Rebel lines again.

We knew that if the enemy understood our position it would be very easy to send a hundred men down the ravine until they should get between us and our lines, when they could climb the hill to where we were at work and invite us to go up with them inside their lines and partake of their mule-meat with them, which we preferred not to do.

While we were digging away . . . we heard a rushing noise in the bushes, on the bank below us. We instinctively dropped our spades and grabbed our muskets, sure that the rebs were surrounding and cutting us off from our lines. The noise in the bushes came louder and louder, but as we listened with bated breath it seemed to be made by only one person. . . .

And indeed it was—Lieutenant Linnell posted there just to watch out for the "rebs." ☆ ☆ ☆

JULY 1

Forty-fifth Day

"The indications are that the great struggle
   is at hand."
                                    —CHICAGO *Tribune*

General Sherman at this time had established himself at the plantation "of one Trible," northeast of the city, from which he "frequently
reconnoitered the whole line and could see the enemy engaged in like
manner on the east side of the Big Black."

He continued:

☆ ☆ ☆ . . . but he [the enemy] never attempted actually to cross over,
except with some cavalry, just above Bear Creek, which was easily
driven back. In a small log-house near Markham's was the family of
Mr. Klein, whose wife was the daughter of Mrs. Day, of New Orleans,
who in turn was the sister of Judge T. W. Bartley, my brother-in-law.
I used frequently to drop in and take a meal with them, and Mrs.
Klein was generally known as the general's cousin, which doubtless saved her and her family from molestation, too common on the
part of our men.

One day, as I was riding the line near a farm known as Parson
Fox's, I heard that the family of a Mr. Wilkinson, of New Orleans,
was "refugeeing" at a house nearby. I rode up, inquired, and found
two young girls of that name, who said they were the children of
General Wilkinson, of Louisiana, and that their brother had been at
the Military School at Alexandria. Inquiring for their mother, I was
told she was spending the day at Parson Fox's. As this house was on
my route, I rode there, went through a large gate into the yard,
followed by my staff and escort, and found quite a number of ladies
sitting on the porch.

I rode up and inquired if that were Parson Fox's. The parson, a
fine-looking, venerable old man, rose, and said that he was Parson Fox.
I then inquired for Mrs. Wilkinson, when an elderly lady answered
that she was the person. I asked her if she were from Plaquemine
Parish, Louisiana, and she said she was. I then inqured if she had a
son who had been a cadet at Alexandria when General Sherman was
superintendent, and she answered yes.

I then announced myself, inquired after the boy, and she said he was inside of Vicksburg, an artillery lieutenant. I then asked about her husband, whom I had known, when she burst into tears, and cried out in agony,

"You killed him at Bull Run, where he was fighting for his country!"

I disclaimed killing anybody at Bull Run; but all the women present (nearly a dozen) burst into loud lamentations, which made it most uncomfortable for me, and I rode away. ☆ ☆ ☆

"The hour had come," wrote Sergeant Tunnard wearily, "that tried the souls of men. The dark cloud of disaster hovered over the devoted garrison. . . . Our batteries were very quiet. . . . The hospitals were sad scenes of agony, suffering and death, with their numerous occupants."

To Dora Miller, Vicksburg was "now like one vast hospital!" And General Lee, the friend of Emma Balfour, wrote his own affirmation: " . . . near 6,000 men were in the hospitals and not one-half of the men actually in the trenches were fit for duty.

"The hospitals were full and the men actually in the trenches sick, with friends, afraid of erysipelas [fever and inflammation of the skin] prevalent in hospitals.

"I do not believe one-half of the men in the trenches could have stood up and fought had they been attacked by the enemy a few feet off and undermining the principal forts."

Thus, it did not come entirely as a surprise this hot Wednesday when Maj. Gen. John H. Forney, one of the defending division commanders, received a "confidential note" from Pemberton: ". . . informing me that unless the siege of Vicksburg was raised or supplies thrown in, it would be neccessary very shortly to evacuate the place; that he saw no prospect of the former, and that very great if not insuperable obstacles were in the way of the latter, and calling for a report as to the condition of my troops, and their ability to make the marches and undergo the fatigues necessary to accomplish a successful evacuation. I laid the matter clearly before my brigade commanders, and they in turn before their regimental and battalion commanders.

"It was their unanimous opinion, in which I concurred, that although the spirit of the men was good, their physical condition and health was so much impaired by their long confinement in narrow trenches, without exercise and without relief, being constantly under fire and necessarily on the alert, and living upon greatly reduced rations, that they could not make the marches they would have to make and fight the battles they would have to fight against the greatly superior numbers that would be brought against them in making the attempt to break through the enemy's lines. I therefore favored a capitulation rather than make this attempt, attended, as I thought, with such little hope of success."

JULY 2

Forty-sixth Day

"A severe battle was fought yesterday about
a mile and a half north of Gettysburg, Pa.
... General Meade is at the front today
superintending operations."
—PHILADELPHIA *Inquirer*

The Union troops continued to feel the effects of the siege.

"On the morning of the 2nd of July," wrote Pvt. George Crook of
the 21st Iowa, "[Brig. Gen. Michael K.] Lawler's brigade was ordered
out to meet and repulse a reported movement of Johnston across the
Big Black, for the relief of Vicksburg. The march was a forced one,
the day was hot and sultry, the roads dusty, water scarce, the men
unused to marching for nearly two months. A General on horseback,
who had never marched a mile in his life on foot." Private Crook
continued:

☆ ☆ ☆ The suffering of the troops was intense. The men were
marched all day with great rapidity, and all afternoon were falling,
fainting by the roadside, with blistered feet, parched throats, swollen
veins and blood-shot eyes. When halted for the night, late in the afternoon, the regiment could not muster a hundred men. A relief corps
was sent back to gather up the fallen and exhausted and bring them in.
Others had to go on picket immediately. The boys came in by twos
and threes all evening, and it was midnight before all were accounted
for. It was the most distressing march yet made. There was no enemy,
or sign of one, and so, after a night of disturbed sleep, the men got
up stiff and sore in every joint and muscle, to be marched back again
over the same road. . . .

The suffering from fatigue and sleeplessness was very great.

As every elevation and open space was completely covered by the
enemy's sharpshooters and swept by his artillery, the men were necessarily confined in close quarters, and this, with its attendant absence
of sanitary provisions, together with the meagerness of the diet, the
constant excitement, the intense heat and unwholesomeness of a Mississippi June, so undergone, told with sad and terrible effect upon
the health of the troops.

The hospitals were crowded with the victims of disease, and every day the burial parties performed their sad duties at the graves of newly departed comrades. ☆ ☆ ☆

These were, indeed, dark apprehensive days, for everyone.

"A sad accident," noted Mary Loughborough, "cast a gloom over all the little community encamped in the ravine—officers, soldiers and servants." She went on:

☆ ☆ ☆ A soldier, named Henry, had noticed my little girl often, bringing her flowers at one time, an apple at another, and again a young mocking bird, and had attached her to him much by these little kindnesses. Frequently, on seeing him pass, she would call his name, and clap her hands gleefully, as he rode the general's handsome horse for water, causing him to prance past the cave for her amusement. She called my attention to him one morning, saying:

"O mamma, look at Henny's horse how he plays!" He was riding a small black horse that was exceedingly wild, and striving to accustom it to the rapid evolutions of the Texas troops, turning in his saddle to grasp something from the ground, as he moved speedily on. Soon after, he rode the horse for water; and I saw him return and fasten it to a tree.

Afterward I saw him come down the hill opposite, with an unexploded shrapnel shell in his hand. In a few moments I heard a quick explosion in the ravine, followed by a cry—a sudden, agonized cry. I ran to the entrance, and saw a courier, whom I had noticed frequently passing by, roll slowly over into the rivulet of the ravine and lie motionless, at a little distance: Henry—oh, poor Henry!—holding out his mangled arms—the hands torn and hanging from the bleeding, ghastly wrists—a fearful wound in his head—the blood pouring from his wounds.

Shot, gasping, wild, he staggered around, crying piteously, "Where are you, boys? Oh boys, where are you? Oh, I am hurt! I am hurt! Boys, come to me!—come to me! God have mercy! Almighty God, have mercy!"

My little girl clung to my dress, saying, "Oh mamma, poor Henny's killed! Now he'll die, mamma. Oh, poor Henny!" I carried her away from the painful sight.

My first impulse was to run down to them with the few remedies I possessed. Then I thought of the crowd of soldiers around the men;

and if M—— should come and see me there—the only lady—he might think I did wrong; so I sent my servant, with camphor and other slight remedies I possessed, and turned into my cave with a sickened heart.

In a few moments, the litters passed by, going toward the hospital, the blood streaming from that of Henry, who still moaned and cried "for the boys to come to him," and "for God to pity him."

But the other bore the still, motionless body of the young courier, who, in the strength of his life, had been so suddenly stricken. It seems that the two men had been trying to take out the screw from an unexploded shell for the purpose of securing the powder; in turning it, the fuse had become ignited, communicating the fire to the powder, and the fatal explosion ensued.

Henry had been struck in the head by a fragment—his hands torn from his arms; one or two fragments had also lodged in his body. The courier had been struck in two places in his head, and a number of balls had entered his body. Poor soldier! his mother lived in Yazoo City; and he was her only son. So near was she, yet unable to hold his head and set the seal of her love on his lips ere the breath fled from them forever! He lived until the sun went down, speaking no word—making no moan; only the quickly drawn breath told that life still flickered in the mangled body. Henry died, also, that night, still unconscious of the sorrowful comrades around his bed—still calling on God to pity him.

After the bodies of the wounded men had been carried away, we heard loud wailings and cries in the direction of the city. I was told a negro woman, in walking through the yard, had been struck by a fragment of shell, and instantly killed. The screams of the women of Vicksburg were the saddest I have ever heard. The wailings over the dead seemed full of a heart-sick agony. I cannot attempt to describe the thrill of pity, mingled with fear, that pierced my soul, as suddenly vibrating through the air would come these sorrowful shrieks!—these pitiful moans!—sometimes almost simultaneously with the explosion of a shell. This anguish over the dead and wounded was particularly low and mournful, perhaps from the depression. Many women were utterly sick through constant fear and apprehension. It is strange that the ladies were almost constantly in caves. Yet, did one go out for a short time, she was almost certain to be wounded, while the officers and soldiers rode and walked about, with very little destruction of life ensuing.

An officer was telling me of two soldiers near his camp who had been severely wounded by minié balls—one shot through the hand and lung, the other through the side.

A new cause for apprehension came to me about this time: the mortar boats were endeavoring to throw their bombs as far as the entrenchments, and almost succeeded. I could see them at night falling near the opposite hill; and I was in a constant state of trepidation lest they should be cast still nearer us. After witnessing the brilliant streams of light that they created in the heavens, one night, and feeling repeatedly thankful that they always fell short of the hill we inhabited, I gradually grew sleepy in utter loneliness, for M—— seldom finished receiving reports until eleven. I wearily turned to the little mattress on the floor, said my prayers, and retired. I had been sleeping some time, for the moon was shining brightly, when I was awakened by loud cries and screams: "Where shall we go? Oh! where shall we go?" My immediate conclusion was that some woman had been killed or wounded, as every now and then I could see the mortar shells dropping on the hill opposite. I therefore thought that I had been spared in Vicksburg, as long as I reasonably could hope, from the variety of changes through which I had passed; and immediately I was seized with a severe panic. If shells had not been falling from the battlefield also, I fear I should have started in that direction—so great was my dread of the mortars!—and run, I cared not where, out of their range.

But the counter awe of Parrott shells kept me where I was. I sat up in bed in a fearful state of excitement; called M—— again and again, without the slightest response; at last, a sleepily uttered "What is the matter?" gave me an opportunity of informing him that we would all be killed, and telling him, while the cold moisture of fear broke out over my forehead, that the mortar shells were nearer than ever, and that the next one would probably fall upon our cave.

Awakening at last to my distressed state of mind, and hearing me say that I knew some woman had been killed, he got up, dressed, took up his cap, and went out to see what had happened, telling me he would return shortly—looking back, laughing as he went, and saying to me that I was fearfully demoralized for so good a soldier. He soon returned, telling me that a negro man had been killed at the entrance of a cave a little beyond us, toward the city; that his mistress, wife, and the young ladies of the family were very badly frightened, having taken refuge in the adjutant's office. ☆ ☆ ☆

Others also died or were injured in the city, according to the *Citizen*:

"Mrs. Cisco was instantly killed on Sunday, on Jackson Road. Mrs. Cisco's husband is now in Virginia, a member of Moody's artillery, and the death of such a loving, affectionate and dutiful wife will be a loss to him irreparable.

". . . Jerre Askew, one of our most esteemed merchant-citizens, was wounded at the works in the rear of our city a few days since, and breathed his last on Monday. Mr. Askew was a young man of quiet integrity, great industry and an honor to his family and friends. He was a member of Cowan's artillery, and by the strict discharge of his duties and his obliging disposition, won the confidence and esteem of his entire command."

James Bradley, a Confederate dispatch rider who carried the mails, happened to be in Vicksburg this afternoon during an especially heavy cannonading by the defenders. It was as if the gunners felt that this might be their last chance for a substantial barrage.

"The battery commander," wrote Bradley, "would show his 'friends' across the river how dexterously he could handle his guns. Turning them directly upon the enemy's batteries, he poured such a storm of shell and shot plunging down into their midst where they had but little protection; as soon dismantled most of their guns and swept the whole bottom beyond of a single foe.

"In the language of Captain Lowry, of the Third Regiment, Missouri troops, who was watching the battle, 'You could see brass flying in the air for half an hour after the firing was over.' "

Late that evening, Pemberton at a council of war informed his generals, "I am a northern man. I know my people. I know we can get better terms from them on the 4th of July than any other day of the year."

As Abrams would report the meeting: ". . . we understand that Major General M. L. Smith was the only one who absolutely opposed surrendering on any condition, preferring to remain behind the breastworks and starve rather than give up the city. A majority of the council, being of a contrary opinion to him, however, he was, of course, necessitated to abide by their decisions."

At 3 A.M. Friday, a messenger was sent into the Federal lines bearing this proposal from Pemberton to Grant:

> General: I have the honor to present to you an armistice for——hours, with the view to arranging terms for the capitulation of Vicksburg. To this end, if agreeable

to you, I will appoint three commissioners, to meet a like number to be named by yourself, at such place and hour to-day as you may find convenient. I make this proposition to save the further effusion of blood, which must otherwise be shed to a frightful extent, feeling myself fully able to maintain my position for a yet indefinite period.

This communication will be handed you under a flag of truce, by Major General James Bowen.

Very respectfully, your obedient servant. . . .

Forty-seventh Day

"Last evening at sunset the cannonading at
Vicksburg was heard distinctly in Jackson. The
Ordnance was evidently of a heavy caliber and
it is probable that the enemy has renewed the
siege in the rear of the city. It may be that the
enemy is making his last desperate and prolonged
effort to capture our garrison. The firing
continued with unabated fury until a late hour
of the night."

—JACKSON *Mississippian*

"I hope to attack the enemy in your front the
7th, and your cooperation will be necessary
. . . our firing will show you where we are
engaged. If Vicksburg cannot be saved, the
garrison must."

—JOHNSTON TO PEMBERTON
(DISPATCHED THE 3D,
RECEIVED THE 10TH)

Before dawn, Grant's reply was moving toward the Confederate lines
under the customary white flag of truce. It read:

General: Your note of this date, just received, pro-
poses an armistice of several hours, for the purpose of
arranging terms of capitulation, through commissioners
to be appointed, etc. The effusion of blood you propose
stopping by this source can be ended at any time you
may choose, by an unconditional surrender of the garrison. Men who have shown so much endurance and courage as those now in Vicksburg will always challenge the
respect of an adversary, and I can assure you will be
treated with all the respect due them as prisoners of war.
I do not favor the proposition of appointing commis-

sioners to arrange terms of capitulation, because I have no other terms than those indicated above.

I am, General, very respectfully, your obedient servant,

This Friday, in spite of "the confusion prevailing" in Vicksburg and the fact that suddenly—and, to some, mysteriously—business was "entirely suspended," Claiborne received the "slab I have had prepared for Ferd's grave and placed it in position. It is a plain slab of white marble, neatly carved with a simple inscription and a piece of artillery above."

Then, his regiment "received orders . . . to cease firing as a flag of truce had been sent out. A thousand conjectures and rumors afloat as to the meaning of the flag. Some say it is to send out some prisoners captured a day or two since; others, to point out the locality of our hospitals so they will not be fired on; while they again say it is to ask permission to remove the women and children to a place of safety.

"*I* know what it means, tho' we have as yet no official information on the subject and the army will know very shortly."

Next, he mused, in smaller penmanship, as if in private, "Is Pemberton a traitor? Has he sold us?"

The word spread through Vicksburg.

"Early in the morning," wrote Margaret Lord, "came the startling news that Generals Pemberton and Bowen with other officers were to have an interview with General Grant. We were all hopeful, sanguine and becoming accustomed to our place and scant fare. The soldiers and we saw almost hundreds every day altho pale and wasted, as enthusiastic and determined as ever.

"What could it mean? A sickening dread and anxiety filled our hearts. Mr. Lord's face was so anxious and apprehensive. Charlie Hitchcock's bright eye was clouded, but still he would not even whisper that it could mean surrender."

Chaplain Howard, of the 124th Illinois, noticed "at 8 o'clock in the morning a white flag away to our left on the rebel works."

☆ ☆ ☆ Soon another appeared, and another and, directly, one in front of us. The firing ceased, and all was still, the first time since May 25th, thirty-nine days. Soon greybacks began to show themselves all along the lines. Heads first, cautiously, then bodies, and we straightened up too, in many places only a few yards from them. The works were mounted and we looked each other in the face, the line of motley and the line of blue.

How eager we all were to see, and what did it all mean? Was it to bury the dead again—their dead—or the prelude to a surrender? And so the forenoon wore away. About half-past one a scare occurred. We all dropped, and a few shots were fired, but "cease firing" rang out everywhere, and no one was especially anxious to disobey; we had all had about enough of that.

A few minutes later, and a stir near the white house on our left indicated something unusual, and all eyes were turned in that direction. Soon our quiet Captain, the determined, self-possessed, heroic Grant, came riding down our covered way, with McPherson, Logan, Ord,* A. J. Smith and other officers, and half a score of orderlies, and passed on toward the rebel works. As they left the trench and emerged into open view, three horsemen, followed by orderlies, came out from the rebel lines and advanced to meet them. These were Pemberton, Bowen and Col. Montgomery, Pemberton's chief-of-staff.

All dismounted as they met, a general hand-shaking followed, and then Grant, McPherson and A. J. Smith were seated with the rebel three, under a large, narrow-leaved oak, in peaceful conference. This augured favorably, but still the mortar fleet kept thundering away. At four o'clock the conference had ended, and our men were all ordered down. The rebels, too, had disappeared, but there was no firing. ☆ ☆ ☆

As Fred Grant reported the confrontation between his father and Pemberton:

"General Grant betrayed no excitement. But in the afternoon he rode out with his staff to a point opposite Fort Hill, I accompanying them. Here our group was joined by Generals McPherson, Logan, A. J. Smith and others.

"Soon a white flag appeared over the enemy's works, and a party of Confederates were seen approaching. Firing ceased; and General Grant met his opponent. The other officers separated into groups and conversed, while the works on both sides were lined with soldiers."

And General Grant himself wrote: "Our place of meeting was on a

*Maj. Gen. Edward O. C. Ord, who succeeded late in June to the command of the 13th Corps, relieving General McClernand. The latter's dismissal came as the culmination of long-standing differences, if not rivalry, between him and Grant.

hillside, within a few hundred feet of the rebel lines. Nearby stood a stunted oak tree.

"General Bowen, I saw, was very anxious to see that the surrender should be consummated. . . . After awhile, Bowen suggested that the Confederate army should be allowed to march out, with the honors of war, carrying their small arms and field artillery. This was promptly and unceremoniously rejected. The interview here ended."

The only strain during the conference, Dana observed, was occasioned by Pemberton, who appeared "much excited, and was impatient in his answers to Grant."

The latter's small son continued: "The consultation of the commanding generals lasted a short while, and presently both parties retired to their own quarters. Father was immediately joined by the largest assemblage of general officers which I had ever seen—the heroes of the most brilliant campaign and siege recorded in the history of the world: deciding upon the settling of the fate of their foes. They had conquered and taken into their power the largest number of men, the greatest number of war materials and spoils ever surrendered in battle. . . .

"After conversation, General Grant dispatched a note to the defender of Vicksburg, and the group of officers dispersed."

Dora Miller and her husband, Anderson, had the misfortune to have picked this day—of all times—to attempt to leave the city on their pass:

☆ ☆ ☆ H. was going to headquarters for the requisite pass, and he saw General Pemberton crawling out of a cave, for the shelling has been as hot as ever. He got the pass, but did not act with his usual caution, for the boat he secured was a miserable, leaky one—a mere trough.

Leaving Martha in charge, we went to the river, had our trunks put in the boat, and embarked; but the boat became utterly unmanageable, and began to fill with water rapidly. H. saw that we could not cross it and turned to come back; yet in spite of that the pickets at the battery fired on us.

H. raised the white flag he had, yet they fired again, and I gave a cry of horror that none of these dreadful things had wrung from me. I thought H. was struck. When we landed H. showed the pass, and said that the officer had told him the battery would be notified we were to cross. The officer apologized and said they were not notified.

He furnished a cart to get us home, and to-day we are down in the cellar again, shells flying as thick as ever.

Provisions are so nearly gone, except the hogshead of sugar, that a few more days will bring us to starvation indeed. Martha says rats are hanging dressed in the market for sale with mule meat—there is nothing else.

The officer at the battery told me he had eaten one yesterday. We have tried to leave this Tophet and failed, and if the siege continues I must summon that higher kind of courage—moral bravery—to subdue my fears of possible mutilation. ☆ ☆ ☆

Sherman, who was not with the surrender party, once more met his friend, Mrs. Wilkinson. He wrote: "On the 3d of July, as I sat at my bivouac by the roadside near Trible's, I saw a poor, miserable horse, carrying a lady, and led by a little negro boy, coming across a cotton-field toward me. As they approached I recognized poor Mrs. Wilkinson, and helped her to dismount. I inquired what had brought her to me in that style, and she answered that she *knew* Vicksburg was going to surrender, and she wanted to go right away to see her boy. I had a telegraph-wire to General Grant's headquarters, and had heard that there were symptoms of surrender, but as yet nothing definite.

"I tried to console and dissuade her, but she was resolved, and I could not help giving her a letter to General Grant, explaining to him who she was, and asking him to give her the earliest opportunity to see her son. The distance was fully twenty miles, but off she started, and I afterward learned that my letter had enabled her to see her son, who had escaped unharmed. Later in the day I got by telegraph General Grant's notice of the negotiations for surrender; and, by his directions, gave general orders to my troops to be ready at a moment's notice to cross the Big Black, and go for Joe Johnston."

Officers such as Colonel Bevier—the Russellville, Kentucky, attorney —found the day one of mingled beauty and astonishment when, at long last, they were permitted to see their enemy's works:

☆ ☆ ☆ Beautiful masses of clouds flecked the azure sky, through which the sun was sending down the fervid heat of a Southern July. The unceasing roar of the bombardment had almost become music to us and lulled us in our very slumbers, so that when on the third a slight hush occurred, my attention was at once attracted.

To the right of me, a white handkerchief, attached to a ramrod, was fluttering in the breeze, and behind, grimly awaiting the result, stood Pemberton and his staff.

Soon silence settled on the scene; the "confusion worse confounded" that had prevailed all around the circle from the crescent to the river, gave place to a sweet, serene, quiet summer day—lovely with the slight haze of white smoke drifting slowly away. The blue tint of distant hills and the far-off Louisiana woods made all nature look pure and innocent; a picture of calm and holy repose, in which "man alone was vile"; the "sunny sky of vine-clad Italia," with the gloomy recesses of Borgia's damp dungeons and noisome cells underneath.

What a time it was for instilling the precepts of "Divine philosophy"; how the inquiring intellect could seek for similes and the treasures of ancient lore, and in his dreams of nymph or naiad, still prosecute his researches into the unexhausted wells of the Stagyrite or the golden fountains of Plato, forgetting the misfortunes of his lot, and extinguishing the hoarded enthusiasm of his soul for the lost opportunities of the sinking but yet buoyant and hopeful cause.

For forty-eight days we had been fighting, and hardly caught a glimpse of each other, save hurriedly and beneath the black smoke of a charge or the rush of a retreat.

Now the two armies stood up and gazed at each other with wondering eyes.

Winding around the crests of hills—in ditches and trenches hitherto undreamed of by us—one long line after another started into view, looking like huge blue snakes coiling around the ill-fated city.

They were amazed at the paucity of our numbers; we were astonished at the vastness of theirs.

We recognized acquaintances and fellow-countrymen in the opposing host; and as I recalled the friendships of olden days, I remembered that sentence in the aerial invocation of Volney's Genius of the Ruins: "What accents of madness strike my ear? What blind and perverse delirium disorders the spirits of the nation?"*

Their parallels, in many places, had been pushed to within twenty feet of us. Conversation was easy, and while the leaders were in consultation, the men engaged in the truly national occupation of "swapping" whatever our poor boys could muster to "dicker" for coffee, sugar and whiskey. ☆ ☆ ☆

*Comte Constantin François de Volney, a late eighteenth- and early nineteenth-century French philosopher, wrote of the crumbling of empires in "The Ruins" and the need for equality of mankind. For all his espousal of brotherhood and freedom, he was arrested and nearly guillotined in the French Revolution.

And on the opposite side, Hosea Rood of the 12th Wisconsin was recording similar emotions and reactions:

☆ ☆ ☆ It was hot and sultry as most of our days there were. We boys in the pits were employed in various ways. Where I was on duty three or four were blazing away at the rebel works; about as many were using the bottom of the rifle-pit for a card-table; two or three were going into the depths of their haversacks after bits of hard-tack with which to stay their stomachs till time to go to camp; one or two tired fellows had dropped to sleep and were, perhaps, dreaming of mother, Mary or Alice; just at one end of the pit one of the boys was lying on his back and reading the home newspaper his father had sent him; and another had his portfolio spread out on his knees and was writing to his mother all about the siege, his health, giving his opinion about how much longer the war would last, and telling how much he wanted to see his little brothers and sisters again.

Suddenly Henry Marston cried out, "Joe, come here with your gun, *quick*—mine isn't loaded! Look at that Johnny right on top of the works! What does he mean by getting up there in that way! There's another, and *another!* Why, the whole Rebel army is coming up! What in the name of General Grant is going to happen now!"

Hank's animated remarks brought every man to his feet, and, sure enough, the whole Rebel line was swarming with men in gray who seemed to have nothing to do but gaze towards us. . . .

Presently, a fellow belonging to the 11th Wisconsin, and who was visiting us that day, said, "I'm going down into the ravine and shake hands with them Rebs!"

To the suggestion that they might take him he replied, "Who's afraid of that! I ain't!" and then he started on a run down the hill.

When he got across the creek below, a Johnny saw him and came to meet him. Both armies watched the performance with much interest. Soon they approached each other with outstretched hands which they clasped in a hearty *shake*. This was a signal for hundreds of men from both sides to rush down, and then the handshaking became general. Men who but ten minutes before were firing bullets at one another's heads, and taking the best possible aim, were shaking hands as cordially as if they were brethren.

While giving the best of attention to the berries around them, they entered into lively conversation. They asked us how we liked the southern climate, and our boys assured them that we were all delighted with it. They wanted to know whether our men kept their health in such hot weather, to which question we replied that we never felt so well before in all our lives. We also spoke of the probable outcome of the siege; they did not seem hopeful. They told us they had breakfasted on mule meat. But for all that, some of them said they were glad that Pemberton intended to hold out just as long as possible; others cursed him for it. The war was discussed in general. We even touched upon state sovereignty and the tariff.

One poor fellow sitting upon a log and listening to the talk drawled out in a doleful sort of way, *"I want to see my ma!"* The men of one side told those on the other when particularly good shots had been made, and with what results.

No one seemed to know just what was the cause of this strange freak of ours.

While thus enjoying our visit, a colonel came down from the Vicksburg side and in no very mild terms ordered his men to go back to their works. They reluctantly obeyed, and we, not caring to be there after our newly made acquaintances should get back to their guns, made good time in the direction of our pits. A few of our boys lingered behind for just a few more of the berries, but when someone shouted to them that hostilities would, no doubt, be resumed the minute the Rebels got back, they fairly scrambled up the hill and tumbled over into the pits.

The last man was no sooner out of sight than firing was resumed, and everything went on pretty much as before. ☆ ☆ ☆

With dusk, Chaplain Howard continued:

☆ ☆ ☆ As night drew on, the silence began to be fearfully oppressive. For so many long days and nights it had been a continuous battle. Not a minute but the crack of the rifle or the boom of the cannon had been in our ears. And much of the time it had been deafening. Now it was still, absolutely still. The tremendous tension was over.

We had not felt it so overwhelmingly earlier in the day when we could look and see, but now it began to pain us.

It was leaden.

We could not bear it; it settled down so close; it hugged us with its hollow, unseen arms till we could scarcely breathe. Only those whose experience has been similar can imagine the weight we carried through that otherwise happy night.

Few of us slept much, and none well. ☆ ☆ ☆

The children—Lucy McRae, for one—were especially sensitive to

Vicksburg's sudden, unfamiliar atmosphere of silence and foreboding. She found that: "All was quiet; people could be seen walking around, concluding that the silence meant dreadful things on the morrow. We were all sitting outside the cave, twilight approaching, when father came in sight.

"Mother thought father had decided to die with his family the next day, for everybody thought that General Grant would make the effort of his life to take the city on the 4th. Father came to mother, looking sad, with tears in his eyes, and said, 'You can all come home for a night's rest. General Pemberton has surrendered, and General Grant will enter the city in the morning.' "

The correspondence between the commanding generals that had been initiated earlier in the day continued into the night. Grant, who had served in the same division with Pemberton in the Mexican War, remained firm on his original demand for "unconditional surrender."

Finally, Pemberton, who had, it seemed to Grant, acted "rather snappishly" at the meeting, hastened across the lines a final offer. Midnight had almost struck:

"At 10 o'clock AM tomorrow I propose to evacuate the works . . . and to surrender the city and garrison under my command, by marching out with my colors and arms, stacking them in front of my present lines, after which you will take possession. Officers to retain their side arms and personal property, and the rights and property of citizens to be respected."

Fred Grant was still at his father's side. He wrote: "I remained in the tent, sitting on my little cot, and feeling restless, but scarcely knowing why. Father sat at his writing table.

"Presently a messenger handed father a note. He opened it, gave a sigh of relief, and said calmly, 'Vicksburg has surrendered.'

"I was thus the first to hear the news officially, announcing the fall of the Gilbraltar of America, and, filled with enthusiasm, I ran out to spread the glad tidings. Officers rapidly assembled and there was a general rejoicing."

Margaret Lord, meanwhile, observed that "Mr. Hutchinson was still sick, scarcely able to move. We missed him very much from our little circle. Just before dark Major Hauer came over to see us. Of course we were all eager to know what he thought as he belonged to General Bowen's staff." She went on:

☆ ☆ ☆ He said he did not know what to think, that General Bowen had returned and seemed as chipper as usual, but he greatly feared the meeting was to arrange terms for surrender, at all events there was to be no firing that night and in the morning we would know it was all right if they resumed firing. Major Hauer said he had been requested by General Bowen to express his thanks to me for embroidering the wreath round the stars on his collar.

I told the Major to say to General Bowen, I had felt it an honor to be employed in such a manner for so brave a man, but if he had worn it in an interview with General Grant for the surrender of Vicksburg I could only wish that I could take out every stitch I had put in.

A few moments after I had retired to my hard bed in the cave, Charlie Hitchcock came to the door to say he had just learned the cause of the interview to be our General wishing to protest against the constant firing on the hospital, by which so many men had been injured and killed. Knowing there was a necessity for such a protest and scarcely thinking General Bowen would accompany General Pemberton on a mission for surrender, to sleep with relieved heart, and in the early morning of the 4th I heard a slow firing in the distance which reassured me. ☆ ☆ ☆

JULY 4

Headquarters Department of Tennessee,
Before Vicksburg, July 4, 1863.

Lieutenant General Pemberton, commanding forces in Vicksburg:

General: I have the honor to acknowledge your communication of the 3d of July. The amendments proposed by you cannot be acceded to in full. It will be necessary to furnish every officer and man with a parole signed by myself, which, with the completion of the rolls of prisoners, will necessarily take some time. Again: I can make no stipualtion with regard to the treatment of citizens and their private property. While I do not propose to cause any of them any undue annoyance or loss, I cannot consent to leave myself under restraint by stipulations. The property which officers can be allowed to take with them will be as stated in the proposition of last evening—that is, that officers will be allowed their private baggage and side arms, and mounted officers one horse each. If you mean by your propositions for each brigade to march to the front of the lines now occupied by it, and stack their arms at ten o'clock, A.M., and then return to the inside and remain as prisoners until properly paroled, I will make no objections to it. Should no modification be made of your acceptance of my terms by nine o'clock, A.M., I shall regard them as having been rejected, and act accordingly. Should these terms be accepted, white flags will be displayed along your lines to prevent such of my troops as may not have been notified from firing on your men.

I am, General, very respectfully, your obedient servant,

U.S. GRANT,
MAJOR GENERAL UNITED STATES ARMY.

"Two days bring about great changes. The banner of the Union floats over Vicksburg. General Grant has 'caught the rabbit.' He has dined in Vicksburg and he did bring his dinner with him. The *Citizen* lives to see

it. For the last time it appears on wallpaper. No more
will it eulogize the luxury of mule meat and fricasseed
kitten—urge Southern warriors to such diet never more."

—VICKSBURG *Citizen* [a box in the lower right-hand
corner of an edition set in type earlier contained
the comment, "Ulysses must get into the city before he dines in it. The way to cook a rabbit is 'first
to catch the rabbit, etc.' "]

In the wan, predawn light, Dr. Alison was scribbling a final diary
entry. Too busy in the wards to be aware of what had transpired,
or in likelihood to care, he was wholly perplexed as to the sudden stillness:

☆ ☆ ☆ Strange to say all is quiet this morning, but how long it will
last no one knows. Yesterday the shelling was terrible. My end of the
town was too hot to stay in, however it quieted down about dusk. All
the men I have seen today are very much depressed, and look for a
surrender soon. I am still hopeful and try to keep their spirits up.
Our troops have laid in the trenches for forty-seven days. We have been
eating mule "beef" for nearly one week, but it has not been issued to
the whole army as rations yet, but I presume will be tomorrow. I have
not tasted it yet but hear it is very good.

I still look for relief, but fear Johnston will put it off until the last
moment. The men in the trenches are suffering very much from short
rations and the distress of the wounded is horrible to think of. Many
of them die for the want of proper food to support their strength.
Erysipelas is prevailing, and where that will end, none can say. So
far, my health is better than I could have expected under the circumstances. Although far from well, I have always been able to attend to my duties. This morning is the only quiet we have had in
47 days. ☆ ☆ ☆

"About half past 8 o'clock," continued Mrs. Lord, "before I was
dressed, Mr. Lord came into the cave, pale as death and with such
a look of agony on his face as I would wish never to see again, said,
'Maggie take the children home directly, the town is surrendered, and
the Yankee army will enter at 10 o'clock.'

"Judge my feelings, I was speechless with grief, no one spoke, even

275

the poor children were silent. As I left the cave *forever*—with dear little Loulie by the hand, Charles Hitchcock made a step towards [me] with such a look of shame on his usually bright and happy face, but I waved him back. I could not, I could not have spoken.

"As I started up the hill with Flora, the children, the tears began to flow and all the weary way home I wept incessantly, meeting first one group of soldiers and then another, many of them with tears streaming down their faces."

At the Jackson Road, Lida Lord recalled, "we met group after group of soldiers and stopped to shake hands with all of them. We were crying like babies, while tears rolled down their dusty cheeks, and eyes that had fearlessly looked into the cannon's mouth fell before our heartbroken glances.

" 'Ladies, we would have fought for you forever. Nothing but starvation whipped us,' muttered the poor fellows, and one man told us that he had wrapped his torn battle-flag around his body under his clothes."

All in all, as Colonel Bevier sorrowed, they might have been members of "the funeral cortege of some chieftain."

"How sad," added Lucy McRae, "was the spectacle that met our gaze: arms stacked in the center of the streets, men with tearful eyes and downcast faces walking here and there; men sitting in groups feeling that they would gladly have given their life-blood on the battle-field rather than hand over the guns and sabers so dear to them! The drummer-boy of a Tennessee regiment, rather than give up his drum, gave it to my brother, but it was very soon taken away from him. One poor fellow gave me his horse, which was branded with the letters *C. S.*, and my two brothers hid him in the yard; but it was only a little while before a Federal soldier came in and took him. The instruments of the band of the Tennessee regiment were stacked on the corner in front of our house, while the guns were stacked in the middle of the street. Men looked so forlorn, some without shoes, some with tattered garments, yet they would have fought on.

"While this gloom hung over the Confederate forces a glance over the hills to the north and east of the city brought into view the bright-shining bayonets and sabers of a mighty host approaching the city by way of Glass Bayou bridge and Jackson Road. General Grant led that part of the army that came by way of Jackson Road. An old negro, it was said, greeted him with these words, 'De long-looked-fer done come at lass'—for the negroes thought they would be given liberty to plunder and do as they pleased. While the army was entering the city from the rear, the river-front presented a scene of unsurpassed grandeur. To say that the scene looking from the upper porch of our residence, where we commanded a fine view, was superb in its magnificence is to say little. The inspiring grandeur of gunboat after gunboat, transport after transport, with flags flying to the breeze, broadside after broadside belching forth in honor of a victory dearly won, bands playing, made a picture that can never fade from memory."

At ten o'clock, Mary Loughborough "put on my bonnet" and "sallied forth beyond the terrace for the first time since I entered."

☆ ☆ ☆ On the hill above us, the earth was literally covered with fragments of shell—Parrott, shrapnel, canister, besides lead in all shapes and forms, and a long kind of solid shot, shaped like a small Parrott shell. Minié balls lay in every direction, flattened, dented, and bent from the contact with trees and pieces of wood in their flight. The grass seemed deadened—the ground ploughed into furrows in many places; while scattered over all, like giants' pepper, in numberless quantity, were the shrapnel balls.

I could now see how very near to the rifle pits my cave lay: only a small ravine between the two hills separated us.

M—— came up, with a pale face, saying: "It's all over! The white flag floats from our forts! Vicksburg has surrendered!"

He put on his uniform coat, silently buckled on his sword, and prepared to take out the men, to deliver up their arms in front of the fortification.

I felt a strange unrest, the quiet of the day was so unnatural. I walked up and down the cave until M—— returned. The day was extremely warm; and he came with a violent headache. He told me that the Federal troops had acted splendidly; they were stationed opposite the place where the Confederate troops marched up and stacked their arms, and they seemed to feel sorry for the poor fellows who had defended the place for so long a time. Far different from what he had expected, not a jeer or taunt came from any one of the Federal soldiers. Occasionally, a cheer would be heard, but the majority seemed to regard the poor unsuccessful soldiers with a generous sympathy. ☆ ☆ ☆

From other perspectives, the canvas was a somewhat brighter one. Wrote Chaplain Howard:

☆ ☆ ☆ The morning of Saturday, the 4th of July, dawned gloriously.

It was our nation's birthday, and we felt it. We sympathized with it as never before. The oppression of the day and night had given place to light feeling. We seemed to tread on air. We put our feet down in a sort of uncertain way, and it was so strange to stand up straight whenever we chose. But as yet we had no news. No orders.

A little later a report said the city was to be surrendered at ten o'clock. Then rumor said Grant's stern terms had been rejected. Soon we were ordered to black our boots, which was done with a will. All the finery we had, whether paper collars or white gloves, was in speedy requisition. And, thanks to our efficient Quartermaster, despite the rigors of the siege, we were far from being a shabby lot. What the battle and sickness had left of us looked well.

Just before 10 o'clock, "Fall in!" was the word, and in a moment we were in our places, shoulder to shoulder, as we had often been, but never with such a feeling, never so proud of each other before.

A moment later our brigade band, one of the best in the service, startled the leaden air and us together, by bursting out with "Hail Columbia," hidden from us in the white house on our left. We had not thought of music; it had been so long since we had heard any, that its place had dropped out, or been filled with shot and shell. Since Utica Cross Roads [17 miles southwest of Raymond], May 10th, but few of us had heard a note, save a bugle call one evening in the direction of Pleasant Dale, some miles away. And now as these strains welled out so exultingly, and the chords of our hearts were swept, we went down before them, and strong men wept like babes. This was followed by "The Star-Spangled Banner," during the playing of which we received a mail. While the Johnnies marched out in front of us, and at many other places along the line, stacked arms, and marched back again. "See the rebs," we cried, under our breath, lest we should lose a note of the music, then "Forward, march!" rang out, and the gallant 1st brigade, General M. D. Leggett commanding, of Logan's fighting 3d Division, took up its line of march into Vicksburg.

Past the rebel gun stacks, over the works, with our field bands playing, through the gazing Johnnies, right down the Jackson Road we went, the 45th leading. Not a dog barked at us, not a cat shied round a corner. Poor things, they had all been eaten in the straitness of the siege.

The roads were dusty and the day was hot, but this was our celebration, and our steps did not falter. On we went through the scorching road cuts, sweltering. It was farther than we thought. When should we reach the retreating city? But at last the houses grew thicker, the hospital was passed, and cheer upon cheer was heard. "Ah! that is the courthouse, and, see? the Stars and Stripes are floating from the cupola where the 45th have placed them. Now boys, hip, hip, hurrah." And we shouted lustily. Our wild huzzas rent the air. We shall never, we can never shout so again. The long beleaguered, stoutly defended, and sadly punished city was ours at last, and it has ever since seemed to us, who shared in the glories of that day, that we had two Fourths to celebrate. One for our national birth, and one for Vicksburg. ☆ ☆ ☆

Dr. Tompkins entered along with "bands playing and colors flying":

☆ ☆ ☆ I straggled from the regiment soon after we got into the city. It has been a very nice place once here. Nearly every house has a hospital. The Rebs, although protected by their works, have suffered far more than we have. Nearly half the force in Vicksburg were sick or wounded. It was afternoon before we entered the works and I did not have time to visit any of the hospitals. . . .

The natural fortifications of Vicksburg are superb, and the Rebs have exercised great skill in fortifying, but their works were not better than ours outside of theirs. They had abundance of ammunition on hand but were eating mule meat for two days before they surrendered and the hospitals have been using mule beef for several weeks. . . .

The mosquitoes have been very bad for several days, but I have a net and they do not bother me much after I go to bed. They are singing around my ears now, thick enough. I dreamed last night that I was home. . . .

[At home, however, all was not entirely as it might be. Mollie was even then penning, "I have not been very well for the last two weeks, but am better today . . . I have had a pain under my left shoulder."] ☆ ☆ ☆

There was a certain amount of bitterness, and even anger in the fallen city.

"We were there just 48 days and nights, penned up like so many hogs in a pen," asserted Corporal Abner J. Wilkes of the 46th Regiment, Mississippi Infantry. "We never could have been wiped out there but General Pemberton sold us to the Yankees at some price. But I can say we gave them Hail Columbia for 48 days and nights!"

The tough, spirited Louisianans, who had sustained the worst the Federals could throw at them, including the mine, were perhaps the only defenders demonstrably outraged at the surrender. Their behavior proved a marked contrast to that of their comrades.

The order to his division from General Forney became "the signal for a fearful outburst of anger and indignation seldom witnessed," asserted Will Tunnard. "The members of the Third Louisiana Infantry expressed their feelings in curses loud and deep. Many broke their trusty rifles against the trees, scattered the ammunition over the ground—in many instances the battle-worn flags were torn into shreds."

As General Shoup himself put it, "the men were full of indignation." But he hastened to add, "Though they have had very scant fare and had been exposed to a merciless and almost continuous fire, remaining at their post in the trenches without relief, I have rarely heard a murmur or complaint. The tone has always been, 'This is pretty hard, but we can stand it.' "

Alexander Abrams thought that the "indignation" of at least some troops "knew no bounds." He observed: "Having been among the troops, we can truthfully speak what we heard and saw of the expressions of sentiment on their part relative to the surrender. With almost an unanimous voice the soldiers declared that General Pemberton had yielded the city without their will, and against any desire on their part. All expressed a determination never to serve under him again, many stating that rather than be under the command of such a man, they would desert from the army, if they were afterwards shot for it. It is not to be denied that the feeling among the men amounted almost to a mutinous one—to such a degree, indeed, was it, that many threats were made, which only the argument and supplication of the officers prevented the men from putting into execution."

Colonel Bevier added: "Dismissing the regiment, I rode into the city to see the vast Federal fleet come down to the landing, with pinions and streamers fluttering, and blaring music and blowing whistles, evidently in gayer spirits than we were.

"When returning to camp I was politely accosted by an officer in blue, who overtook me. We had some conversation, chiefly complimentary, on his part, to the stubborn bravery of our troops, when, noticing that a large staff followed him, which I had not observed before, as the road was crowded with equestrians, I looked at him closely and found it was General Grant himself, the accidental hero of the hour."

"Up in the city," wrote Ida Barlow, "the scene would not be described by mortal tongue. Starving men, women and children with rags hanging to them stalked the streets in utter despair. They had given all for their country, and had naught left but a feeble claim on life, and this they were ready to give also but our great General Pemberton said 'No, we must give up,' and on July 4th, 1863, Vicksburg was given over into the hands of the enemy, and a death blow fell upon the Confederacy, for from that day those in authority knew that hope was vain and the cause for which so many brave men had given up their lives was lost, that the death knell of the beloved Confederacy was sounded.

"For days and weeks we had to endure the pitiable sight of our own men straggling homeward, there were no trail roads in running order and with bare feet, gaunt, and partly naked on they came in a steady stream. But the poor starved creatures were still afraid and would only stop for a drink until out of the Yankee lines, and many was the poor fellow who fell by the wayside.

"One by one our own dear ones returned to us, one with an arm gone, another with a leg gone."

Max Kuner "rode in beside, it happened, General Herron of Iowa. Poor old Vicksburg! The bombardment had done its work. I saw my own store a mere heap of ruins, but strange to say, this affected me not at all; everything was the same. I rode on to the family home. The house had a great hole in the side, where a shell had penetrated. This shell burst in the basement, which had been our dining room, and had splintered the table there so that the remains were about the size of matches." He continued:

☆ ☆ ☆ Before the house I dismounted, and was about to enter, when I encountered a negro whom I had left in charge as caretaker.

"I'se mighty glad to see you again, Massa X," said old Joe. "But you better not go in theah. They's Yanks in theah."

I pushed past him and entered. In the hall, upon the sofa, there was sitting a man well sprawled out in white trousers and his shirt, and without insignia. He was speaking with another man in uniform, a colonel. The colonel told him that the house was ready, and then passed me and went out. As the man on the sofa appeared to be staying indefinitely, I asked: "By what authority, sir, do you take possession of another man's house?"

"That's none of your damned business," he answered, never moving. "Who are you?"

"I'm the owner of this house," I said.

"Are you a loyal citizen?" he demanded.

"That," I replied, for I was furious, "is none of *your* damned business."

At this he began to swear violently, and started to rise, lifting his foot as if, actually, he was about to kick me out of my own house! I did not wait to be kicked. Instead, I ran down the steps and overtook the colonel. I inquired where I could find General Grant, for I was bound to go to the head of the army.

The colonel asked me if I knew to whom I was talking in the hall.

I answered: "No, except that I knew it was not a gentleman." The colonel informed me that it was General Mills,* Grant's medical adviser, and second only to him in rank, being head of the medical division of the army. But I did not care. I had been treated rudely in my own house, so to General Grant I went. Grant's headquarters were then upon the steamer *Grosbeck*; immediately after the surrender a great flock of Federal steamers had descended from just above the city.

General Grant gave me an order, directing that my house be vacated to me, and upon the back he noted that I would find General Mills another house just as good. ☆ ☆ ☆

By late afternoon Chaplain Foster observed the Federal soldiers moving freely about the streets and within the stores:

☆ ☆ ☆ Sugar, whiskey, fresh fruit and air-tight cans are enjoyed in great abundance. They invite our men to share in the abundance and they feel no reluctance in participating. Now the steamers come pouring down the river as if by magic. Ten or 12 can be seen landing at the same time. In a short time these line the levee up and down the river for nearly a mile in distance. They are loaded down with provisions of every kind.

At the close of day I visit once more the "Sky Parlor." How changed the scene. Spread out before me are the splendid steamers of the enemy, exhibiting the riches and power of our strong and wealthy foe. As I looked upon the scene and reflected upon the mighty blow we had just received—upon a long and protracted war that now awaited us—upon the streams of blood yet to be shed—upon the future strength

---

*Max Kuner obviously was alluding to Dr. Madison Mills, a New Yorker and veteran of the Mexican War. Formerly Medical Director of the Department of the Missouri, the surgeon was thought of so highly for his Vicksburg service that he was brevetted brigadier general.

of our young men and the carnage and desolation and destruction which should sweep over our beloved South—as I thought upon these things, tears of bitter anguish fell from my eyes and a cloud of darkness and gloom settled upon my mind.

Farewell ye mighty hills, upon whose rugged peaks I have stood and with solemn awe admired and adored the power of the Almighty, to whom belongs the strength of the hills. No more shall I roam over those lovely hills and deep valleys, for they are now in the possession of a hateful foe, desecrated by the vile footsteps of a heartless, cruel and unprincipled enemy who came with the felonious purpose of desolating our homes, of spreading the shadow of death over our firesides and of enslaving a free and noble people.

And thou great Father of Waters upon whose lovely banks I have stood as sentinel in the lonely watches of the night, looking with covert eyes across the dim and dark waters for the approach of the enemy's boats, no more shall I guard thy rolling waves nor walk up and down thy friendly banks. Thy proud waves, unguarded by Southerners, shall now roll on to the mighty ocean upon no friendly errand but for us beating upon thy placid bosom the power and wrath of our deadly foes.... ☆ ☆ ☆

It was a strange, melancholy and consummately quiet dusk that settled over Vicksburg, affecting not alone Foster, but all in a fallen city.

"All is still," observed Mary Loughborough. "Silence and night are once more united. I can sit at the table in the parlor and write. Two candles are lighted. I would like a dozen. We have had wheat supper and wheat bread once more. H. is leaning back in the rocking chair. He says: 'G., it seems to me I can hear the silence, and feel it too. It wraps me like a soft garment; how else can I express this peace?'"

"Just before dusk," wrote Mrs. Lord, "someone belonging to the Yankee army—I have forgotten his name—but a kind, gentlemanly man having something to do with the St. Louis papers, a member of the church, called to see Dr. Lord and stayed a long time, asking questions and expressing sympathy which, though kind in intentions, was hard to bear.

"It grew darker and we had not a candle. Gas, of course, there was none. I had scarcely spoken a word but then in the suppressed, coldest manner I said,

" 'It is hardly necessary for me to apologize for a want of light. We have none.'

"He answered with a good deal of feeling, 'Mrs. Lord, I am very sorry. I have influence in the army and will be very glad to send you what you need.'

"I felt the proud blood rush to my face and tingle in my veins as I said, 'Sir, we stand in need of everything, but you must excuse me, I can receive nothing from you.' "

Will Claiborne then penned his own short amen: "The deed is done—after so long and gallant a defense Vicksburg is at the mercy of her foes."

And so while the saddest day in Vicksburg's history came to a close, the victor would have to admit that as a prophet he had missed his mark—maximum though it was—by exactly 29 years and 318 days. His son Fred could not resist reminding General Grant that, just after the Battle of the Big Black, he had asserted to a woman at whose house he had stopped for water that he "would capture Vicksburg if it took thirty years to do so!"

Certainly, as the Confederate Brig. Gen. John B. Gordon, who fought at Gettysburg, observed, "The shock of Vicksburg's fall was felt from one end of the Confederacy to the other."

"Gen. Meade Surrendered! Forty thousand prisoners
taken. Yankee accounts confess the capture of
our troops of Gen. Meade's army. This number
comprises his whole army excepting perhaps
remnants of stragglers here and there.
Washington City, Baltimore, Harrisburg and
Philadelphia at the mercy of our army. . . .
"Many of our people are not willing to believe
that Vicksburg has capitulated."
                              —JACKSON *Mississippian* (July 7)

"Great and Glorious News—The Union arms
victorious in the greatest battle of the century.
. . . The enemy withdrew his force from the
city of Gettysburg yesterday."
                              —WASHINGTON *Evening Star*

The interesting report in the Jackson *Mississippian* had already filtered
through the south. Chaplain Foster himself wrote from Vicksburg, in
one of his final letters to his wife: "We also heard that General Lee
had again defeated Meade and had demolished his entire army, and
that he held Arlington Heights and was shelling the City of Washington,
after having demanded a surrender. This intelligence was said to have
been received from a Northern paper. This, however, was not generally
credited, though all believed that Meade's army had met with a great
defeat.

"These rumors for a while cheered the heart. We felt more confident of success. Besides, couriers would come in stating that Johnston
had an army of 90,000 men; that they had organized and were coming
to our relief, that he would attack the rear of the enemy in 10 days
at most. . . ."

Indeed, the leaders of the Confederacy were just as ignorant in
Richmond as to the progress of the war in the west. On July 8, Jefferson Davis telegraphed Governor J. J. Pettus at Jackson: "What is the
state of affairs at Vicksburg? The old key is used. Answer by telegraph."

As a matter of fact, Jackson was already under attack by General
Sherman's troops, and would fall on the 17th.

In Vicksburg there remained differing opinions on almost all matters: How the occupation was administered, the manner in which the

soldiers in blue conducted themselves, even the extent of ruin visited upon the city by the long enemy bombardment.

Franc Wilkie, the correspondent for the Dubuque *Herald* and *New York Times*, found, somewhat to his surprise, that an: ". . . . innumerable number of buildings had been hit by shells, but no considerable damage had followed. The shells from the mortars had dug their way into the earth where, as a rule, they exploded, if at all, without damage. . . ."

Wilkie located rooms "for a few days with a lady who had remained in her house during the entire siege. It had been struck several times by the mortar-shells and they had dropped all about in the yard and street, but despite this she refused to leave for a safer locality.

"One shell had exploded in the wall and thrown the entire side of the dining room into the street. Another had alighted in the kitchen, and had blown everything into flinders, 'leaving,' as the hostess informed me, 'scarcely anything recognizable save some bricks and a couple of stove-legs.' "

Abrams found no basis of agreement with Wilkie, as he wrote angrily of:

☆ ☆ ☆ . . . a scene of pillage and destruction which beggars all description. Houses and stores were broken open, and their contents appropriated by the plunderers. The amount of money and property stolen in this way was enormous, and the Yankee soldiers appeared to glory in their vandalism. One merchant, by the name of G. C. Kress,* had his safe broken open, and twenty thousand dollars in money, with a large supply of clothing, taken away. Another merchant and well-known citizen of Mississippi, by the name of W. H. Stephens, had his store broken open and nearly all the contents taken away. In fact, every place that they could possibly enter without fear of resistance, was broken open and robbed of what was contained in them. The enemy appeared to glory in their course, and on one occasion, in reply to a remonstrance on the part of a gentleman whose residence they had broken open, they said, "We have fought hard enough to capture Vicksburg, and now we have got it, we intend to plunder every house in the d——d rebel city."

*This Kress may have been an uncle or other relative of the brothers who founded the S. H. Kress chain in Memphis in 1896. Executives of the variety stores, now aggregating more than three hundred, were unable to establish a definite family connection.

As soon as General Grant heard of the wholesale pillage of the city that his followers had commenced, he ordered guards to be stationed over the town, and issued an order prohibiting any of his men from entering any other residence than that in which they were quartered, and threatening to punish any soldier who might be caught in the act of robbing citizens; at the same time he gave no satisfaction whatever to those parties who had already suffered at the hands of his army. Several applications were made to him for redress, but he told the applicants he was unable to assist them, or give any permission to have the camps of the men searched; although, if any of his soldiers were discovered with stolen property in their possession, he would have it returned to their owners, on their proving it belonged to them. This was, of course, but poor consolation to the losers, who were necessitated to be satisfied with this answer, and submit to their loss.

With that enterprise and greed for gain which characterizes the universal Yankee nation, on the same day that the Federal army entered Vicksburg, several places of business were opened, and signs informing the public that metallic coffins were on hand to remove the dead bodies of friends, and that express offices, book and fruit stores were "within," were to be seen upon several establishments on Washington street. ☆ ☆ ☆

But Willie Lord was not so displeased, unrelievedly, as Abrams. He alluded to "the very favorable terms of capitulation" given by Grant. He continued:

☆ ☆ ☆ In their knapsacks the men of the rank and file, now waifs of war, carried for the first time in many months ample rations, pressed upon them by a hospitable and admiring foe. Men who, to tantalize the starving Confederate soldiers, had shaken well-filled coffee-pots and inviting morsels of good in grim derision, and in the face of death, across the embattled trenches, now vied with each other in seeing that their former enemy was laden with such good food and luxuries as had not been enjoyed since the capture of the well-provisioned Union camps and wagon trains at Shiloh.

This spirit of brotherly appreciation for a brave though fallen foe was reflected in the men from the qualities of their heroic leader, General Grant, who, paradoxical as it may seem, was even then a popular conquering general. He suppressed with an iron hand looting, violence and vandalism. He collected and listed all stolen goods which could be found among his men, and placarded the city and surrounding country with a proclamation calling upon all citizens who had been despoiled to call at headquarters and identify and reclaim their property. We learned this, however, too late to save our own effects. If they had been stored in the cellars of the church they would have remained intact.

A group of camp-followers invaded the Flowers plantation; and though they left the homestead standing, they destroyed all within it which they could not take away.

The story of the destruction of our household goods and of my mother's wardrobe, as told by one of the Flowers' family servants, is worth relating as an illustration of the barbarous methods resorted to by these unofficered and lawless men.

Our trunks were broken open. Then arraying themselves in my mother's dainty gowns and wraps, the men indulged in a devil's dance around a tree upon the lawn, tearing the garments from each other, one by one, amid ribald shouts and songs. With the butt ends of muskets, pictures, mirrors and bric-à-brac were shattered, while curtains, rugs, and carpets were slashed and torn into shreds by sabres and bayonets.

A huge plantation wagon was loaded with my father's invaluable library, and with less respect for literature than was shown by the Turks at the taking of Constantinople, the contents were scattered broadcast upon the muddy road between Flowers's plantation and the Big Black River, so that for a mile and a half, as we were told, one might have walked on books. Some of the less-damaged books were afterwards gathered from the roadside, and with the mud stains still upon them they are preserved today.

All of this, I believe, might have been prevented if our former host had remained at home upon his plantation instead of taking to the woods, which he did upon the first news of the fall of Vicksburg. Men who wantonly destroy are presumably cowards, and if Mr. Flowers had been at hand to confront the marauders, the dread of his identifying them before their silent and iron-willed commander, General Grant, as violators of an imperative order against looting and wanton destruction, would probably have saved both his property and our own.

We found the rectory in deplorable condition. A bombshell had exploded in the center of the dining room, completely demolishing the table spread for our guests of the officers' mess; and tearing away the roof of the apartment, it had made a hole in the floor six feet deep and 12 feet in circumference. Not a vestige of the table or its contents was ever found, except two or three solid glass saltcellars, such as were used in those days. It seemed as though the table and all else that was on it had been blown into dust and atoms and dissipated by the winds. In the library a solid shot had torn its way through the side-wall directly above a settee. As it happened, my father, with two of his friends among the officers, was seated upon this settee, discussing the folly of dodging while under fire, when this particular cannonball crashed through the wall just above their heads and caused them all to dodge, and one of the officers to fall upon his hands and knees. None was hurt, though all were powdered with splintered wood and crumbled plaster. ☆ ☆ ☆

His mother confirmed the "deplorable" spectacle:

☆ ☆ ☆ Such a scene of desolation you can hardly imagine. The dressing room was in ruins, the end where the fireplace had been was blown entirely out. The nursery was uninhabitable, a hole deep almost as a cistern in the middle of the floor, every room in the house injured and scarcely a window left whole, but this is a small matter. Our poor soldiers soon came in a continuous stream past the house so pale, so emaciated and so grief-stricken, panting with the heat and Oh! saddest of all without their colors and arms.

Some of them had determined not to give up their battle flags which had been carried victorious in so many hard won battles, so bound them round their bodies under their clothes. We all congregated on the piazzas with buckets of water to quench their thirst and [hear] their "God bless you, ladies."

Nothing but starvation whipped us, could be heard on all hands. ☆ ☆ ☆

Soon, however, the Lords were receiving rations from the occupation forces.

"I told General Grant I had no objection to that," Margaret continued, still aggrieved and full of spite toward the Northerners, "as the U.S. Army had robbed me of far more than their rations could ever repay.

"At night our house being in such ruins, we had to lock Flora Tulley, Lida, Sallie and Marianie in the pen. Afterwards things were more orderly as my family got a protection paper from the Provost Marshal. But how sad those two weeks were to see our brave soldiers without arms, paroled and passing sadly out of the place they had so long and so bravely defended. To feel for ourselves that the time had come when honor and duty required that we should leave the happy home and kind friends of twelve years and go out poor, saddened and homeless with our five children.

"Every day families were moving away in wagons, carts, any conveyance that could be obtained, in the hot July sun but we felt that it would be impossible for us to expose our children in that way and hope they would live after their confinement in the cave and its poor scant fare."

And soon the Lords were joining the exodus from Vicksburg, themselves destined for Mobile by way of New Orleans aboard a steamer overflowing with sick and wounded Confederates. Many who had survived battle would nonetheless not be among this conceivably fortunate number. Some, such as Charlie Hitchcock, who had shared the Lords' cave, would die in a few days of wounds. Others, including General Bowen, would succumb to malaria, yellow fever, or the varied diseases that scavenged in the wake of nineteenth-century battle.

The cost to the Union forces for Vicksburg, commencing May 18, was incredibly low: 766 killed, 4,063 wounded and missing. The Confederates in the same period lost 875 killed, 2,327 wounded and missing.

These statistics, laboriously compiled in 1905 by the Vicksburg National Military Park Commission, were less than Grant himself had estimated for his troops, and about one-third the losses some Confederates had believed their enemies had sustained.

Civilian or soldier, the refugeeing multitude presented a pitiable sight. The soldiers, carrying with them little but their clothing, limped off to their homes in Mississippi, Louisiana, and other portions of the south and southwest. A few would have the heart and the strength to rearm and fight again.

Noncombatants, almost all of whom left by riverboat, took not a great deal more with them than the troops—whether headed north, after swearing the oath of allegiance to Old Glory, or south to continue like so many embittered Chauvinists their espousal of an already lost cause.

The scene of departure described by Willie Lord was repeated over and over those waning weeks of Vicksburg's tragic summer:

☆ ☆ ☆ As we stepped aboard the boat which was to bear us on toward the unknown experiences that awaited us during the death struggles of the Confederacy, a group of our loving friends and my father's devoted parishioners waved us a sad farewell from the wharf-boat; and as we swung from the shore amid the songs of negro "roustabouts," now no longer slaves, we became, without realizing all the hardships and bitterness the word implied, refugees adrift upon the hopeless current of a losing Cause. ☆ ☆ ☆

Surely, as Lincoln himself remarked, "the Father of Waters again goes unvexed to the sea."

This dramatic change in the status of a vital national artery of commerce, combined with the smashing of Lee's forces at Gettysburg, left no doubt in the Great Emancipator's mind that victory was coming. There remained but one question—when?

EPILOGUE

What happened to the defenders of Vicksburg?

Among those paroled was forty-year-old Lt. Col. Sid Champion of the 28th Regiment, Mississippi Cavalry, on whose farm had been fought the decisive battle of Grant's advance upon Vicksburg. He elected to rearm himself following this gloomy word from Matilda, on July 10, who had been a refugee at "Brae Mer," Rankin County, east of Jackson:

☆ ☆ ☆ . . . well, our beloved Vicksburg has fallen, the city of a southern heart's pride. Our own Mississippi is now invaded and what is to become of us? We must suffer as others have done long since, our property destroyed and negroes taken away, etc. I am willing to work, but oh God, when will this war end and let several families be reunited?

Our home is destroyed, torn to pieces and perhaps burned by this time. I was there on the 2d and 3rd of this month to get away all we had left there; much is destroyed, but we have enough yet if we could only be permitted to enjoy it once more.

Our little ones are all well except little Liddy. He has been cutting four jaw teeth and has been quite unwell for a month . . . is some better now. ☆ ☆ ☆

Sid returned after Appomattox to the heartbreaking job of rebuilding. But he never recovered from wounds received at the Battle of Franklin (Tennessee.) He died not quite three years later, leaving four children and Matilda, who again could wonder, "What is to become of us?"

Matilda, however, was molded of strong and resilient fibers. She raised her children and—more or less—reestablished the farm on Champion Hill. A shrunken, white-haired lady, wearing a country bonnet, Matilda Champion was photographed in 1906 at the dedication of the Illinois Memorial, a handsome marble-domed structure on the Vicksburg Battlefield Park.

The name "Champion" persists with familiarity to residents of Hinds and adjacent Warren counties (the latter being the location of Vicksburg). A Champion still resides on what is left of Champion Hill.

Dora Miller, like so many others in Vicksburg during the siege, sought only to "go home." She finally was successful in moving through the

Federal lines—south to New Orleans, where she was widowed just two years afterward.

Dora taught school for the remainder of the century, sometimes seeking counterpoint to classroom tedium through newspaper and magazine writing. George Washington Cable, the prolific author and editor, persuaded her to refurbish her already diaried experiences in Vicksburg, which she obligingly did. For a time she wrote the woman's page for the New Orleans *Times-Democrat*.

World War I was entering its fourth month when Dora, just turned seventy-nine, was found dead one morning by a servant in her Arabella Street home in New Orleans. She had outlived both of her sons, although they had attained adulthood. No longer would the lawyer's widow have to worry that she had "lost my nerve" because of the cruelty of mortal man.

Early widowed, too, was Mary Loughborough, who had set up housekeeping in Little Rock, Arkansas. In 1884 she founded one of the country's pioneering women's magazines, the "Arkansas Ladies Journal," later named the "Southern Ladies Journal." The increasingly frail little author of "My Cave Life in Vicksburg" never fully recovered, however, from that summer's tension and privation. She died in August, 1887, two days before her fifty-first birthday.

The handsome, airy old mansion on East Eighth Street, in which she had reared four children, would itself survive for another eighty years to become a scene and symbol of protest and picketing. Conceivably pragmatic Little Rock businessmen had decreed its extinction in favor of something no more esthetic or nostalgic than a gasoline station.

Of all those men and women who had resolved—at first cannon blast—to share their experiences with posterity, only Emma Balfour remained in Vicksburg. There she died and was buried, also in 1887, just a decade after her doctor-husband had passed on. The man who, she thought, considered her "a great favorite" had predeceased her by six years.

A semitragic figure, General Pemberton breathed his last in Allentown, Pennsylvania, discredited if not despised by what once was known as the Confederacy. His final years in his native state had proven, as Grant had at least hinted, that the defender of Vicksburg could still count his best friends in the north.

Lucy McRae was no little surprised, after Appomattox, to greet a brother, Allen, dusty, thin, exhausted, having ridden on horseback the

1,000-some miles from Richmond. Her other older brother had been among the defenders of Vicksburg.

"Allen McRae," she wrote, "was the last man who stood guard at President Davis' tent and, when discharged by him, was given a letter, a horse and a $20 gold piece. My brother rode from Virginia to Vicksburg on that horse, carrying the gold piece in the bottom of his boot."

Lucy soon moved north, as the bride of John Walton of Lewisburg, West Virginia. Upon his death she married Henry T. Bell of the same city. Lucy died in 1930, outliving her only child—a daughter, also named Lucy—by nineteen years. The Lucy who survived the siege of Vicksburg is buried in the Old Stone Presbyterian Church cemetery in Lewisburg.

Lucy McRae Bell's Vicksburg home, a museum, "Planters Hall," evokes curious images of a long-distant yesterday. For some visitors, however, it might not be easy to reconcile the presence of Lucy's mother "on the upper porch of our house to see the gunboat" with the extrusion of a TV antenna from much the same spot.

Mollie Tompkins, to whom her husband, Charles, had scribbled so many letters from his surgical tent, was immensely saddened a few days after the surrender of Vicksburg to learn that her favorite brother, Michael "Mike" Gapen, had been killed in the final hours of struggle. Dr. Tompkins apparently had not paid sufficient heed to the complaint Mollie voiced in at least one letter concerning the "pain under my left shoulder." She died of a heart attack in 1873 leaving four children.

Dr. Tompkins, however, married four more times, to become the father of a total of seven children, two of whom followed the MD's profession. He became a well-known druggist and businessman in Fulton County, Illinois, being active in the campaign for a narrow-gauge railroad to that region.

Upon retirement, Dr. Tompkins moved to Florida. He died in 1913 at the home of a son, Dr. Raymond Dean Tompkins. Another son, Claude, the offspring of Dr. Tompkins' fourth marriage, still resides in Florida, in his ninety-first year.

Another medical man, Dr. Richard Hall, as some had wondered after reading his letter in the *Citizen*, did indeed survive the sinking of the *Cincinnati*. In fact, the gunboat herself was raised, and it finished out the war under the Union flag.

The navy surgeon who had come from Fairfield, Jefferson County, Indiana, went on to private practice in Wichita, Kansas. There he achieved a blend of civic leadership and medical specialization in "female diseases"—the predecessor of today's gynecologist—which he proclaimed in large type on his own letterhead, complete with self-portrait. Personal tragedy struck when his son was slain by marauders.

Hall, who had remained immune to Confederate cannon and a sunken warship, died of old-age complications in 1896.

From Mobile, Dr. Lord took his family first to Charleston, South Carolina, where he continued his ministry until General Sherman captured that city in February, 1865. Driven inland to Winnsboro, South Carolina, the much-refugeeing Episcopalian remained there until invited to become first pastor of the freshly constructed Holy Trinity Church in Vicksburg.

Before he left his adopted land, Dr. Lord helped found the University of the South at Sewanee, Tennessee. In his later years the poet-preacher returned belatedly to the north as pastor of Christ Church, Cooperstown, New York, not far from his birthplace. He retired only when he was almost too feeble to walk, or talk. Outliving many members of his family, he died in a New York City sanitarium on April 22, 1907, a white-bearded patriarch of eighty-eight.

Another chaplain of Vicksburg, William Lovelace Foster, joined the faculty of what is now Baylor University, in Texas, as professor of mathematics and astronomy. He was also the Baptist minister of a church in Ladonia, Texas. But time was short. The Reverend Foster crammed a great deal of teaching and thinking into a few years. He died, suddenly, in 1869 of what was apparently a ruptured appendix. He was but thirty-nine years old. Buried beside him is his "Dearest Mildred."

Will Tunnard, the faithful if outspoken chronicler of the siege, went on to fame and modest fortune—a mere sergeant in the trenchworks who rose to "General" in the General Leroy Stafford Camp, United Confederate Veterans, Shreveport, Louisiana, which he had served in many posts. He never stopped writing, being the editor at different times of the Shreveport *Times* and Shreveport *Journal*.

Almost as spry as when he watched for Yankee minié balls, Tunnard showed his age only in the increasing whiteness of his beard and thick shock of hair. He did not know sickness. One hot, breathless Sunday at the end of July, 1916, "General" Tunnard bade a customary goodnight to a granddaughter, Mrs. H. T. Gladney, with whom he was living in Shreveport, turned out the lights and went to bed. It was midnight.

Will Tunnard never awoke.

Another Louisianan, Winchester Hall, after serving in the Louisiana legislature and as a judge, migrated northward to New York City. There he engaged in law practice until his retirement at seventy-five, when he moved to Pocomoke City, on Maryland's eastern shore.

Colonel Hall in 1905 wrote a small book, "Self-Development," which was, as the subtitle noted, "addressed to youth on the threshold of a career." None could dispute his assertion: "Over fourscore years have I walked the earth, and the scars of battle are mute reminders of a record." The old soldier died four years later. He is buried at St. Mary the Virgin Episcopal Cemetery, Pocomoke.

The resting place of James M. Swords, on the other hand, is obscure. The publisher of the Vicksburg *Citizen*, in spite of all his barbs at the Federals, nonetheless proved adaptable. Under the occupation forces, he edited the new *Weekly Herald*, and without ever a harsh word for the Yankees.

Swords left the paper in 1871, and other than a flowery obituary clipping from an unknown newspaper and unknown date, on file at the Old Court House Museum, Vicksburg, nothing is readily known of the editor's subsequent career.

Almost two decades after the siege had ended, Max Kuner was eating dinner in a Cincinnati restaurant, one which surely offered better fare than mule steaks or pea bread. He was recounting to a dining companion how he had fled his horse cart, after a mortar shell had landed close behind him with a *whirr-r-r-r!*, sending shrapnel through the vehicle and through an oil painting he was moving. When, however, Max found "the old horse jogging on behind me with ears not even pricked," he decided to be "as unconcerned as the horse," and the pair proceeded on their way together.

He had barely finished telling this favorite anecdote when a man at the next table "jumped to his feet," shouting, "I fired that shot, I fired that shot!" He introduced himself as a Captain Hoffman, who said he had been in command of that particular mortar boat close inshore, and had indeed watched the whole episode, bemused, through a telescope.

After that the trail and life story of Max Kuner fades into oblivion.

Annie Wittenmyer and Mrs. A. H. (Jane Currie) Hoge, who had accompanied Grant's army, continued in their same fields of welfare. The widow Wittenmyer, from Keokuk, Iowa, helped the 52d Congress pass a law pensioning army nurses, and also founded a soldiers' home in

Kentucky. From 1874 until 1879 she was national president of the Women's Christian Temperance Union.

The heavyset, outspoken Mrs. Hoge, who became president of the Women's Board of Foreign Missions, died in Chicago in 1890. Mrs. Wittenmyer outlived her by exactly a decade.

But four of those who chronicled the struggle for Vicksburg lived, so far as is known, measurably past World War I. They were Hosea Rood, Osborn Oldroyd, and Alexander S. Abrams, in addition to Lucy McRae Bell.

Rood, of the 12th Wisconsin, distinguished himself in veterans' affairs, being instrumental in the establishment of a rest-and-retirement home in Waupaca, in east central Wisconsin, in 1888. His last reporting on affairs pertaining to the rapidly thinning ranks of Blue was in 1926. Sadly enough, the Roods who live in Wisconsin today do not seem to remember Hosea at all.

Oldroyd, of the 20th Ohio, operated a book store in Springfield, Illinois, after the war. Then he moved to Washington, where he was custodian of the house opposite Ford's Theater in which Lincoln died. He had accumulated a large collection of Lincoln relics during his lifetime, never losing his nostalgia for "Old Abe," whom he had met during the Lincoln-Douglas debates.

Oldroyd died in Washington in October, 1930. He was eighty-eight.

Alexander S. Abrams, paroled, went on to Atlanta where he reported for the *Intelligencer* before once again shouldering a musket to face Sherman in the summer of 1864. Wounded at the battle of Jonesboro, the climactic assault before the fall of the Georgia "arsenal" city of the Confederacy, Abrams was no longer fit to bear arms.

The youthful Louisianan, taking the loyalty oath, moved to New York City where he joined the staff of the *Herald*. As foreign editor, he handled the dispatches from the Franco-Prussian War.

Later he moved to Orlando and Jacksonville, becoming one of Florida's most prominent lawyers. He represented the Seaboard Air Line Railroad and other corporations. Somewhere along the way he acquired the rank "Major."

A political figure in the state who once contemplated running for Congress, "Major" Abrams now was spelling out his middle initial, which was "St. Clair." Somehow he managed the time in a busy life to found the town of Tavares, twenty-four miles northwest of Orlando. It remains an important citrus-packing center.

When Alexander St. Clair Abrams slept away, in Jacksonville in 1931 at the age of eighty-six, leaving a daughter and three grandsons, he was quite likely the last of the gallant little band who survived the heaviest General Grant could bestow upon Vicksburg.

. . . they are all gone now, the people of Vicksburg, Confederates and Federals, the citizens and the soldiers, the old and "the little ones" who "without a word would slip on their shoes and run like rabbits"— Lida and Little Loulie, Ida, Mary Ann, the slave girl, Willie and Fred —all of them who perhaps grew up to become mothers and fathers themselves, as well as grandparents.

. . . they are all gone now, and have become names on mostly forgotten tombstones, statistics in moldering, brittle files in one hundred country courthouses.

. . . they are all gone now, and only the cold regimental markers in the battlefield park hint at where a Ferd Osman fell, a Union soldier lamented that he was "tired, tired, tired . . ." or yet another sang "Widow Malone."

The wind whistles through the gullied hillsides and the slanting shadows of dusk imbue with curious aura the inscription:

. . . here brothers fought for their principles, here heroes died for the country and a united people will forever cherish the precious legacy of their noble manhood.

It says that on a plaque before the Pennsylvania memorial. The names are there, too, the forgotten names.

. . . they are all gone now. It is all over and one might ask: What was it all about? And what would it mean in the unfathomable enigma of tomorrow, or the day after tomorrow?

Vicksburg would have no heart to celebrate the Fourth of July for eighty-two years. Then, in 1945, two months after V-E Day, it did so. General Eisenhower himself was there for the 1947 celebration. Now the memories of that Fourth in 1863 have lost some of their bitterness.

ACKNOWLEDGMENTS

The author and editors acknowledge the kind assistance of the following persons, libraries, historical societies, colleges, universities, and other institutions, without whose help this documentary history could never have been realized. In fairness, their names must be presented an on alphabetical basis:

ALLEN T. AKIN, Vicksburg attorney. His wife was a great-granddaughter of Emma Balfour. The original of her diary, with some pages long since torn out, and an oil portrait are in Mr. Akin's possession.

WILLIAM K. ALDERFER, State Historian, Illinois State Historical Library, Springfield: Osborn Oldroyd data.

MISS JOYCE AMEDEE, Secretary, Department of the Archives, Baton Rouge, Louisiana: Tunnard manuscripts.

DR. PAUL BALLARD of Vicksburg, who owns the last remaining siege cave.

EDWIN BEARSS, Historian, Office of Archaeology and Historic Preservation, National Park Service, United States Department of the Interior, a sometime resident of Vicksburg, author and leading authority upon that phase and locale of the Civil War. Great appreciation is due him for his painstaking proofreading of this manuscript, his corrections and suggestions.

V. L. BEDSOLE, Head, Department of Archives and Manuscripts, Louisiana State University, Baton Rouge: general information.

EDMUND BERKELEY, JR., Assistant Curator of Manuscripts, University of Virginia Library: general background.

EDWIN FOSTER BLAIR of New York, who made available the letters of Chaplain Foster, his grandfather. They appeared in the Mississippi State *Times*, Jackson, in 1960.

MRS. MARGARET BURKHEAD, Director, Little Rock (Arkansas) Public Library: Mary Loughborough information.

ALFRED E. CAIN, Senior Editor, Trade Book Division, Prentice-Hall, who, if not quite parent to this book, was untiring midwife in its delivery. He largely inspired the scope and magnitude of the present treatment of the siege.

MAJ. CALVIN COLLIER of Little Rock, authority on this area in the Confederacy.

DR. J. ISSAC COPELAND, Director, Southern Historical Collection, University of North Carolina Library, Chapel Hill: the W. H. Claiborne diary, the Pemberton files (which include the Captain George Wise account and letter from General Lee), Dr. Joseph Dill Alison papers, and the William A. Minard (officer on the *Black Hawk*) letter.

MRS. MARIANNE D'ARTOIS of Mobile, Alabama, who made available photographs and biographical information pertaining to her great-grandfather, William Tunnard.

MRS. EVA W. DAVIS, founder and long-time director of the Old Court House Museum, Vicksburg, recently retired, who tapped her vast memory for facts about the siege. Buried in the Davis' back yard, according to rumor, is one "McGill," among the first civilians to lose his life in the siege. Neither Mr. or Mrs. Davis has yet gotten to digging to prove or disprove this legend.

REAR ADMIRAL E. M. ELLER, USN (ret.), Director of Naval History, Department of the Navy, who assisted in matters pertaining to Admiral Porter's fleet. Thanks go, as well, to all of his staff, including those of the Navy Library.

SISTER EMMANUEL, St. Francis Xavier School, Vicksburg.

WILLIAM EDWARD FINANE, Director, Old Court House Museum, Vicksburg, and his staff, who helpfully searched files for text and photographs and arranged interviews. The J. Mack Moore print collection, representing the life work of a late Vicksburg photographer, is one of the best local picture-histories available in the South. Among manuscript material consulted at the Old Court House Museum were the Dr. Joseph Dill Alison letters (copies), Mrs. Richard Groome diary, and the Corporal Abner Wilkes diary.

MRS. KATHRYN M. FINNEY, Public Relations Assistant, Association of American Railroads, Washington: information on old Mississippi timetables and fares.

THE REVEREND GEORGE F. FRENCH, Rector, Christ Church, Cooperstown, New York: Doctor Lord.

J. CARRINGTON GRAMLING, JR., of Miami, great-grandson of Alexander St. Clair Abrams.

MRS. VIRGINIA R. GRAY, Assistant Curator, Manuscript Department, William R. Perkins Library, Duke University, Durham, North Carolina: the extensive Dr. Charles Brown Tompkins correspondence, Matilda Champion letter, and the "Hotel de Vicksburg" menu.

THOMAS B. GREENSLADE, College Archivist, Chalmers Memorial Library, Kenyon College, Gambier, Ohio: Tunnard data.

MRS. CONNIE G. GRIFFITH, Director, Special Collections Division, Howard-Tilton Memorial Library, Tulane University, New Orleans: the Dora Miller diary, sometimes listed as "War Diary of a Union Woman in the South," the Henry Ginder letters, also the "To Our Friends in Vicksburg" surrender plea. George Washington Cable published and edited a version of the Miller diary in 1889, in a volume entitled *Strange True Stories of Louisiana*, under Scribner's imprint.

MRS. JOSEPHINE L. HARPER, Manuscript Curator, The State Historical Society of Wisconsin, Madison. Also Miss Judith Topaz, for general information as well as specific on "Old Abe," mascot for the 8th Wisconsin Volunteers.

MARY HOEHLING, also an author, who did some of the original research when this book was but a glimmer, nearly ten years ago.

THE REVEREND WILLIAM T. HOLT, Minister of Christ Episcopal Church, Vicksburg, who supplied much information about and a portrait of his long-ago predecessor, Dr. Lord.

MILO B. HOWARD, JR., Director, Department of Archives and History, State of Alabama, Birmingham: general research.

MRS. ANNABELLE JAMISON of Vicksburg, the present occupant of "the Mundy house" on Mundy Street, in front of which Mrs. Gamble was killed.

COLONEL ALLEN P. JULIAN of Atlanta, eminent Civil War historian, who was of great help in "leads" toward the researching of this book.

MRS. DELLA BEL KRAUSE of Lake Charles, Louisiana, keeper of the diary of A. Hugh Moss, an ancestor.

MRS. HENRY L. McKNIGHT of Vicksburg, an author, editor, and untiring helpmate in the preparation of this book. Virginia McKnight is the widow of a Mississippi State Representative, who died in 1969.

MRS. LIMERICK McRAE of Vicksburg, whose late husband was a descendant of Lucy McRae.

MISSISSIPPI STATE ARCHIVES, Jackson: Emma Balfour diary copy, Ida Barlow Trotter account, the "Yankees are come, vile thieves. . . . !" verse, another copy of the "Hotel de Vicksburg" menu, and the "Many Soldiers" plea to General Pemberton, which is also in the *Official Records, War of The Rebellion* and in the Pemberton papers, Southern Historical Collection.

JOHN E. MOREHISER, JR., of the New Orleans Public Schools, who aided in the quest for additional biographical information on Dora Miller.

MRS. AMY S. OLLENDIKE of the Worcester County Library, Snow Hill, Maryland, for information on Winchester Hall.

JOHN C. PEMBERTON of New York, grandson of General Pemberton.

MRS. VIRGINIA S. POWELL, librarian, Shreveport (Louisiana) *Times*: Tunnard research.

MRS. ANNIE LEE SANDERS of the Vicksburg *Evening Post*. This newspaper published an exceptionally complete centennial edition on July 1, 1963. It contains, among other accounts, the Fred Grant reminiscences based on a subsequent visit to the city.

MISS MARY E. SCHERMANN, parish secretary, Trinity Episcopal Church, New Orleans: Dora Miller research.

The late GILBERT TWISS, cable desk, Chicago *Tribune*, and Civil War Round Table member, who was most generous in supplying names of those acquainted with the history of Vicksburg.

DR. PETER WALKER, Professor of History at the University of North Carolina, author of *Vicksburg, A People at War*, who kindly gave of his time to make suggestions for further research.

THE REVEREND E. STEWART WOOD, recent Minister of Holy Trinity Church, Vicksburg, who volunteered information on Dr. Lord. He uses as a paperweight an unexploded two-pound shell.

MISS MARION WORLEY of Jasper, Florida, granddaughter of Dr. Tompkins: biographical material and a portrait.

The typists of the manuscript: MRS. RUTH CHENAULT, who also performed a measure of the research and editing, MRS. MARY HUIE, MRS. JO HUMPHREY, and MRS. IRIS MEADOR.

No acknowledgments of a Civil War study would be complete without a tip of the historian's hat to those laboring ancestors who assembled the 128 volumes of *The War of the Rebellion, A Compilation of the Official Records of the Union and Confederate Armies*. The War Department portion was published between 1880 and 1901. The guiding hand of this undertaking was Lt. Col. Robert N. Scott, an aide-de-camp to Grant before Richmond, who supervised the first twenty-six books from 1877 until his death in 1887.

This monumental effort was not only a kind of prophetic WPA writers' project but also a best-seller from the start, some of the volumes running to printings of 10,000 weighty copies. Inspired by the success of the battlefield series, Congress authorized the Navy Department to prepare and the Government Printing Office to produce the naval equivalent. This continued to thirty volumes, between 1894 and 1922. The interruption was occasioned by World War I.

And last, but hopefully not least, the grandfather of the author-editor of this book, ADOLPH A. HOEHLING, one of 118 assistant surgeons then in the United States Navy. Dr. Hoehling served on Porter's mortar boats during the siege, and was narrowly missed by shore fire at least once. He also left a treasure of letters to his mother, which somehow, most unfortunately, have vanished into the limbo of misplaced antiquity.

BIBLIOGRAPHY

Abrams, A. S., *A Full and Detailed History of the Siege of Vicksburg*, Intelligencer Steam Press, Atlanta, Georgia, 1863.

Anderson, Ephraim McDowell, *Memoirs, Historical and Personal, First Missouri Confederate Brigade*, Times Printing Company, St. Louis, 1868.

Andrews, Edmund, *Record of Surgery and Battles Near Vicksburg*, Chicago, 1863.

Bearss, Edward, *The Rebel Victory at Vicksburg*, Vicksburg Centennial Commission, 1963.

Beck, Stephen C., *A True Sketch of Army Life*, privately printed, Nebraska, 1914.

Bel, Mrs. Ernest (Floy), *A. Hugh Moss Diary*, Scribner's, New York, 1948.

Bettersworth, John K. (ed.), *Mississippi in the Confederacy*, for the Mississippi Department of Archives and History, Jackson, Mississippi, 1961.

Bevier, R. S. *History of the First and Second Missouri Brigades, 1861-1865*, Bryan, Brand and Company, St. Louis, 1879.

Bradley, James, *The Confederate Mail Carrier*, privately printed, Mexico, Missouri, 1894.

Brown, Alonzo, *History of the Fourth Regiment, Minnesota Infantry Volunteers*, Pioneer Press, St. Paul, Minnesota, 1892.

Brown, Willard J., *The Signal Corps USA in The War of The Rebellion*, U.S. Veterans Signal Corps Association, 1896.

Bruce, Robert V., *Lincoln and the Tools of War*, Bobbs-Merrill Company, New York, 1956.

Catton, Bruce, *Mr. Lincoln's Army*, Doubleday, Garden City, New York, 1951.

——, *Grant Moves South*, Little Brown and Company, Boston, 1960.

Crater, Lewis, *History of the 50th Regular Pen Regiment, Pennsylvania*

Volunteers, Coleman Printing House, Reading, Pennsylvania, 1884.

Crooke, George, *The 21st Regiment of Iowa*, privately printed, Milwaukee, Wisconsin, 1891.

Dana, Charles A., *Recollections of the Civil War*, D. Appleton and Company, New York, 1902.

Flower, Frank A., *Old Abe and the 8th Wisconsin*, Curran and Bowen, Madison, Wisconsin, 1885.

Foote, Shelby, *The Civil War—A Narrative*, Vol. 2, Random House, New York, 1963.

Gordon, General John B., *Reminiscences of the Civil War*, Scribner's, New York, 1905.

Grant, Ulysses S., *Personal Memoirs*, C. L. Webster and Company, New York, 1894.

Greene, F. V., *The Mississippi*, Scribner's, New York, 1882.

———, *Battles and Leaders of the Civil War*, Century, New York. 1887–88.

Hall, Winchester, *History of the 26th Louisiana Infantry Regiment*, privately printed, 1890.

———, *Self-Development*, Broadway Publishing Company, New York, 1905.

Hoge, Mrs. A. H., *The Boys in Blue*, E. B. Trent and Company, New York, 1867.

Horn, Stanley F., *The Army of Tennessee*, Bobbs-Merrill, New York, 1941.

Howard, Chaplain R. L., *History of the 124th Regiment, Illinois Infantry Volunteers*, H. W. Rokker Company, Springfield, Illinois, 1880.

Jackman, Captain Lyman, *History of the Sixth New Hampshire Regiment*, Republican Press, Concord, New Hampshire, 1891.

Johnson, Robert U., and Buel, Clarence C. (eds.) *Battles and Leaders of the Civil War*, The Century Company, New York, 1884–88 (4 Vols.).

Johnston, Joseph E., *Narrative of Military Operations*, D. Appleton and Company, New York, 1874.

Johnston, Mrs. Maria I., *The Siege of Vicksburg* (novel), Pratt Brothers, Boston, 1869.

Kellogg, Captain J. J., *War Experiences*, privately printed, 1913.

Lane, David, *A Soldier's Diary*, privately printed, 1905.

Livermore, Mary, *My Story of the War*, A. D. Worthington and Company, Hartford, Connecticut, 1888.

Loughborough, Mary Ann, *My Cave Life in Vicksburg*, D. Appleton and Company, New York, 1864.

Mabbott, Thomas O. (ed.,) *Complete Poetical Works of W. W. Lord*, Random House, New York, 1938.

Miers, Earl Schenck, *The Web of Victory*, Alfred A. Knopf, New York, 1955.

Miller, Francis Trevelyan (ed.), *The Photographic History of the Civil War*, The Review of Reviews Company, New York, 1911.

Morison, Samuel Eliot, *The Oxford History of the American People*, Oxford University Press, New York, 1965.

Oldroyd, Osborn Hamline, *A Soldier's Story of the Siege of Vicksburg*, privately printed, Springfield, Illinois, 1885.

Parker, Thomas H., *History of the 51st Regiment of Pennsylvania Volunteers*, King and Baird, Philadelphia, 1869.

Pemberton, John C., *Pemberton, Defender of Vicksburg*, University of North Carolina Press, Chapel Hill, 1942.

Plum, William R., *The Military Telegraph During the Civil War in the United States*, Jansen, McClurg Publishers, Chicago, 1882.

Pratt, Fletcher, *Battles That Changed History*, Hanover House, Garden City, New York, 1956.

Rood, Private Hosea W., *Story of the Service of Company E, 12th Wisconsin Regiment*, Swain and Tate, Milwaukee, 1893.

Russell, William Howard, *My Diary, North and South*, Bradley and Evans, London, 1863.

Sandburg, Carl, *Abraham Lincoln, The War Years*, Harcourt, Brace and World, New York, 1939.

Scott, Colonel H. L., Inspector-General, U.S.A., *Military Dictionary Comprising Technical Definitions and Information of Troops, Actual Service, Materiel and Administration*, D. Van Nostrand, New York, 1861.

Sherman, William Tecumseh, *Memoirs*, Fourth Edition, C. L. Webster, New York, 1891.

——, *The Memoirs of William Tecumseh Sherman*, Vol. 1, D. Appleton and Company, New York, 1913.

Sketches of War History, papers read before the Ohio Commandery, Military Order of the Loyal Legion of the United States, Robert Clarke Company, Cincinnati, Ohio, 1881.

Tunnard, William H., *The History of the Third Regiment, Louisiana Infantry*, privately printed, Baton Rouge, 1866.

Walker, Peter F., *Vicksburg, A People At War, 1860–65*, University of North Carolina Press, Chapel Hill, 1960.

Wells, Seth (Diary of), *The Siege of Vicksburg*, W. H. Rowe, Detroit, 1915.

Wilkie, Franc Bangs, *Pen and Powder*, Ticknor and Company, Boston, 1888.

Wittenmyer, Annie, *Under the Guns*, E. B. Stillings and Company, Boston, 1895.

Young, Agatha, *The Women and The Crisis*, McDowell, Obolensky, New York, 1959.

Periodicals

Harper's, December, 1908, W. W. Lord, Jr., "A Child at the Siege of Vicksburg."

Harper's Weekly, June, 1912, reminiscences of Lucy McRae Bell.

Century, April, 1901, Lida Lord, "A Woman's Experiences."

Frank Leslie's Illustrated Newspaper, general artists' work.

Sewanee Review, October, 1907, Max Kuner, "Vicksburg and After."

These newspapers not already mentioned in the text or acknowledgments were also of great help: The Arkansas *Gazette*, Baltimore *Sun*, *The Democrat* (Lewistown, Illinois), *Illinois State Journal* (Springfield), London *Times*, and the New Orleans *Times-Picayune*.

Libraries, Historical Societies, Archivists

Army Library; Atlanta Historical Society; Department of Archives, Diocese of Baton Rouge; District of Columbia Public Library; Duke University Library; Illinois State Historical Library; Library of Congress; Little Rock Public Library; Louisiana State University, Archives; National Archives; New York Public Library; Supervisor of Research, New Orleans Public Schools; Department of Archives and History, State of Alabama; State Historical Society of Wisconsin; Tulane University Library; University of Virginia Library; Worcester County (Maryland) Library.

GLOSSARY

ADJUTANT—an officer responsible for communicating orders from the commander of a corps, division, brigade, or regiment to the next smaller unit.

ADJUTANT-GENERAL—the principal channel of a commander of the army for publishing orders.

ADVANCED LUNETTES—works resembling bastions or ravelins, having faces and flanks (see drawing of bastion) and formed up and beyond the *glacis*.

AIDES-DE-CAMP—confidential officers selected by the general officers to assist them in their military duties.

ARTILLERY—weapons for discharging missiles. In the United States military, an arm of the service designed to use mountain, field, and heavy ordnance and with the knowledge for such use.

ASYLUM (military)—the Soldiers' Home in Washington, D. C., serving as a retreat for honorably discharged soldiers, disabled veterans, or soldiers who have contributed to the upkeep of the asylum. In nonmilitary terminology, protection from arrest and extradition, given especially to political refugees of a nation or by an embassy or other agency enjoying diplomatic immunity.

BARBETTE—guns are in barbette when, elevated by raising earth behind a parapet, or by placement on a high carriage, they fire over a parapet instead of through an embrasure.

BASTION—a work of two faces and two flanks, all of the angles being salient.

BATTALION—an aggregate military force of from two to six companies.

BREACH—a rupture or gap in a fortification wall made by battering or cutting to facilitate the assault.

BREASTWORK—a hastily arranged parapet not high enough to require a banquette.

BREVET—commission in the army at large. The 61st Article of War provides that within a regiment or corps officers shall take rank and do duty according to the commissions by which they were mustered into their corps or regiment, but brevets or former commissions may take effect in detachments and courts-martial composed of different regiments or corps.

CAISSON—a two-wheeled carrier of artillery ammunition attachable to a two-wheeled horse-drawn gun or vehicle, called a limber.

CAPS—paper or metal containers holding an explosive charge.

CARBINE—a cavalry weapon intermediate in weight and length between a rifle and a pistol, frequently breech-loading.

CASEMATE—see *Fortification*.

CHEVAUX-DE-FRISE—a defense consisting of lumber or an iron barrel covered with projecting spikes and often strung on barbed wire. Used to obstruct a passage or breach or against cavalry.

COLUMBIAD—an American cannon of very large caliber, invented by Colonel Bomford, used for throwing solid shot or shell. When mounted in barbette with a center pintle, it has a vertical field of fire from 5 degrees depression to 39 degrees elevation, and a horizontal field of 360 degrees.

COMMISSARY—one who provides subsistence stores for the army either by contract or direct purchase. Also used to denote a store for equipment and provisions.

CORPORAL—grade between private and sergeant.

COUNTERMINES—galleries dug by fortress defenses to intercept mines or destroy works of besiegers.

COUNTERSCARP—see *Fortification*.

DEFILADE—to raise parapets of fortress or fieldwork or to lower the level space between parapets where guns are mounted to hide the interior of a work from the view of the enemy on an elevated position.

DEFILE—any narrow passage, such as a ford, a bridge, a road running through a village, a mountain pass.

DEPLOYMENT—tactical maneuvers widening a column to the order of battle. In a general sense, the placement of troops in battle formation or appropriate position.

EMBRASURE—an opening, with sides flaring outward, cut through a wall or parapet of a fortification, usually to allow a greater extent of firing for artillery.

ENFILADE—to sweep with gunfire the whole length of the face of any work or line of troops, usually by a battery on the prolongation of a face or line.

ESCALADE—a surprise attack on, or the capture of, a fortified place.

ESCARP—the inner side of a ditch below the parapet of a fortification.

FORTIFICATION (from old military dictionary) —a fortification in its most simple form consists of a mound of earth, termed the *rampart*, which encloses the space to be fortified.

The *parapet* surmounts the rampart and covers the men and guns from the enemy's projectiles.

The *scarp wall* sustains the pressure of the earth on the rampart and the parapet, and presents an obstacle to an assault by storm.

A wide and deep *ditch* is another obstacle that prevents the enemy from approaching near the body of the work.

A *counterscarp wall* sustains the earth on the exterior of the ditch.

A *covered way* occupies the space between the counterscarp and a mound of earth, called a *glacis*, which is thrown up a few yards in front of the ditch to cover the scarp of the main work.

All works immediately enveloping the fortified space is called the *enciente* or *body of the place*. Other works added to the enciente to strengthen fortification weak points or to slow a breach by the enemy are the *outworks*, when enveloped by the covered way. *Advanced works* have some connection with the main work but are outside the covered way, while *detached works* are entirely beyond the glacis.

In a *bastioned front* the principal outwork is the *demi-lune*, in front of the curtain, which covers the main entrance.

The *tenaille*, a small low work in the ditch, covers the scarp wall of the curtain and flanks from nearby besieging fire.

The *place of arms*, outside a work, is an assembly point for troops acting against that work. The *reentering places of arms* are small redans at juncture points of bastion and demi-lune covered ways. *Salient places of arms* are covered-way parts in front of bastion and demi-lune salients.

Redoubts, small permanent works, are put inside demi-lunes and reentering places of arms to strengthen them. These *interior retrenchments*, when high enough to command the exterior ground, are called *cavaliers*.

Caponniers cover the passage of the ditch from the tenaille to the gorge of the demi-lune, then to the covered way, to maintain communications between the enciente and outworks.

Posterns and *sortie passages*, also covered, preserve communication from the body of the place to some outwork or through the glacis.

Traverses are small works on the covered way to intercept enemy fire.

Scarp and *counterscarp* galleries in the ditch have loopholes through which the garrison troops fire on the besiegers without exposure to enemy batteries.

In seacoast defenses, and sometimes in the land front of the ditch, embrasures are made in the scarp wall for firing artillery; the whole being protected from shell by a bomb-proof covering overhead; this arrangement is termed a *casemate*. Sometimes double ramparts and parapets are formed, so that from the interior one can fire over the more advanced, the latter in this case being called a *fausse braie*. When the inner work is separated from the outer (*a retrenchment*) and has a commanding fire, it is a *cavalier*.

All works included between the capitals of two adjacent bastions are called a *front*.

FORTIFICATION (natural)—naturally formed objects that are capable of impeding the enemy, and a station is said to be naturally fortified when it is on top of a steep hill, or surrounded by impassable marshes, rivers, etc.

FORTIFICATION (regular)—one in which the works are built in a regular polygon, with corresponding parts equal to each other.

GALLERY—in permanent fortifications, a passage to that part of a mine where the powder is lodged. The principal gallery, from which the others originate, is built under the banquette of the covered way and follows that part throughout the entire works.

INVEST—to take initiatory measures in besieging a town to secure every road and avenue leading to the town, thus preventing ingress and egress.

LOGISTICS—the procurement, maintenance, and transportation of military materiel, facilities, and personnel.

LUNETTES—redans having flanks parallel to their capitals.

MINIE BALL—a rifle bullet having a cylindrical body, conical head, and hollow base. In 1851, experiments established the peculiar advantages of a method devised by French army officer and inventor Charles Étienne Minié for quick loading and forcing shot into the rifled state. Although not in French service, a large supply of what has been called the regulation minié musket was ordered for the United States army. The term *minié ball* was generally but improperly applied to all elongated shot for musketry despite differences, one from another, in form and weight.

MORTAR—a muzzle-loading cannon having a tube short in relation to its caliber, that is used to throw projectiles with low muzzle velocity at high angles.

ORDNANCE—military supplies including weapons, ammunition, combat vehicles, and the necessary maintenance tools and equipment. Also the service arm responsible for procuring, distributing, and safekeeping of ordnance.

PARROTT GUN—a 10-, 20-, 30-, 100-, 200-, and 300-pounder rifled bore cannon with reinforced breech, named for its inventor, Robert Parrott, whose arsenal was at Cold Spring, New York. Used continuously during the siege of Vicksburg, this gun possessed accuracy, although its destructive power was limited by the poor quality of the shell's explosives of the day.

PONTOON BRIDGE—a floating bridge.

PROJECTILE—a missile for a firearm, cannon, or other weapon. The projectiles for unrifled ordnance are solid shot, shells, canister, and grape.

PROVOST MARSHAL—an officer appointed in every army in the field to secure prisoners confined on charges of a general nature.

QUARTERMASTER—an army officer who provides clothing and subsistence for a body of troops.

RAMPART—see *Fortification*.

RAVELIN—work beyond the main ditch, opposite the curtain, composed of two faces, forming a salient angle and two demi-gorges, formed by the counterscarp; separated from the covered way by a ditch that runs into the main ditch.

REDAN—small work with two faces ending in a salient angle, used to cover a camp, the front of a battlefield, advance posts, avenues of a village, bridges, etc.

REVETMENTS—facings that enable the inner slopes of the parapet of permanent and field works to endure the action of the weather. They are made of close, regular bunches of green brushwood, sod, timber, sandbags, etc.

REDOUBT—see *Fortification*.

SALIENT ANGLE—an angle of a fortification projecting outward toward the country.

SAP—an apparently slow method of constructing trenches within themselves that was continued ceaselessly to form an extension, sometimes to a point beneath an enemy's fortification.

SHARP's—a breech-loading rifle.

SHELL—a hollow projectile for cannon containing an explosive charge. Also, a metal or paper case that holds the charge of powder and shot or bullet used with breech-loading small arms.

SIEGE—a military blockade of a city or fortified place to compel it to surrender. This explanation comes from an old military dictionary:

An army, to undertake the siege of a fortress, must have superiority in the field, so that while some of the corps are occupied in besieging the place, others are employed in covering this operation, or in repulsing the enemy whenever he endeavors to succor the place. The army covering the siege is called the Army of Observation, and that which endeavors to give aid to the place is called the Succoring Army. The Besieging Army is that which, protected by the army of observation, throws up all the works necessary to take the place, such as trenches, batteries, etc. It begins its operations by investing the fortress; that is, it will advance with the greatest secrecy and rapidity, and occupy positions on every side, to cut off all communication with adjacent country, and confine the garrison entirely to its own resources. The positions thus occupied are strengthened by field works, and a sure communication is kept between them.

It is absolutely necessary to invest the fortress attacked, so as to prevent the garrison holding any intercourse with the neighboring country; for if this precaution be not taken, the defenders will be able to draw fresh supplies of men, provisions, and ammunition from the country, increasing greatly the duration of the siege, and reducing chances of ultimate success.

SKIRMISH—a loose, desultory engagement usually made by light infantry troops.

SPENCER—a repeating rifle, the most remarkable of the war, invented by Christopher Spencer of Hartford, a former employee of Colt's Firearms. The cartridges, themselves among the most advanced of the day, were loaded through the stock directly into the breech. Some Federal commanders professed that this rifle, along with its companion carbine (formerly for cavalry use) were major factors in winning the war. In quantity production by the time of the Atlanta campaign in the summer of 1864, "the Spencer" exacted shocking toll of the enemy. At one time the spectacle of a squad of "Billy Yanks" fording a stream, ducking under while reloading the revolutionary weapon, caused a platoon of Confederates to surrender. They were incredulous at a gun that could be loaded and, seemingly, fired under water.

SUTLERS—provisioners to an army post, often established in a shop on the post.

TIN-CLADS—these light draft river craft (drawing as little as two feet of water) figured prominently in Mississippi actions as well as in the Yazoo and other tributaries. With armor plating less than one-inch thick, they were said to be able to "go anywhere where the ground was a little damp." The true *ironclads*, with upwards of one hundred tons of iron plating bolted onto wooden hulls, boasted armor three inches or more thick in places, on top of fifteen inches of oak. The *monitors*, dubbed "iron coffins" by their crews, were wholly different, being constructed of metal and using wooden beam armor for what little freeboard was presented. They did not figure at Vicksburg.

VEDETTES—sentries upon outposts, so placed that they can best observe the movements of an enemy and communicate by signal to their respective posts and with each other.

WOODRUFF—a $2\frac{1}{8}$-inch smooth-bore cannon.

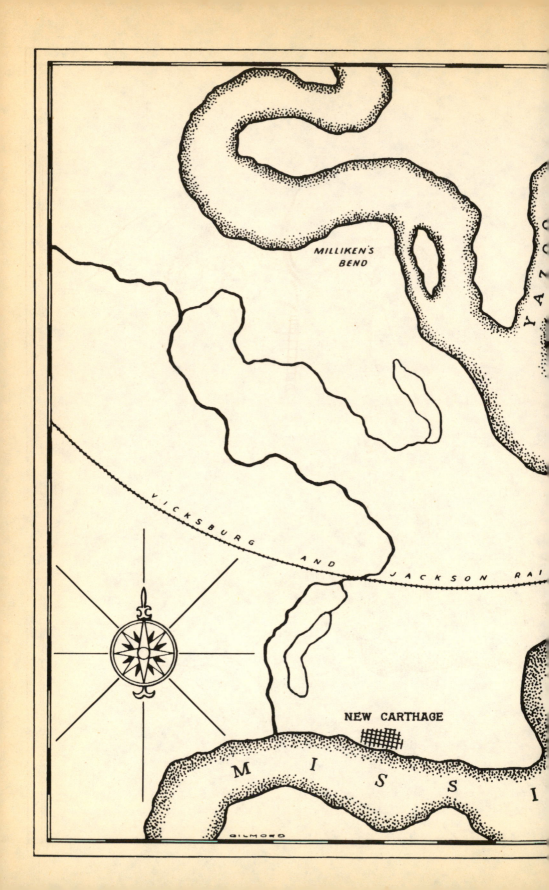

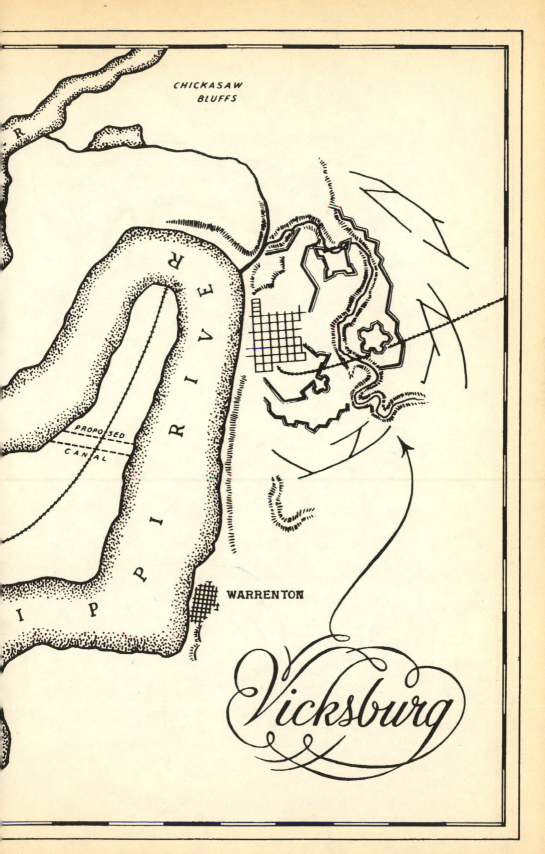

CHICKASAW
BLUFFS

PROPOSED
CANAL

WARRENTON

Vicksburg